INSIDE THE INNER CIRCLE

Get A Sneak Peak Inside The Doors Of 'THE INNER CIRCLE'
*And Hear Conversations From The Most Innovative And
Aggressive Marketers In The World!*

RUSSELL BRUNSON

JUSTIN BENTON

INNER CIRCLE MEMBERS

LEGAL DISCLAIMER AND TERMS OF USE

Get A Sneak Peak Inside The Closed Doors Of
'THE INNER CIRCLE'

And Hear Conversations From The Most Innovative And Aggressive Marketers In The World!

InnerCircleForLife.com

Russell Brunson, Justin Benton, Damon Burton, Tyler & Emily Watson, Dany Therrien, Erik Sorenson, Justin Wubben, Doug Boughton, Ryan Jaycox & Joe Wood, Eric Thayne, Junior Anthony, Stephanie Dove Blake, Sam Kwak, Anissa Holmes, Mark Stern, Bill Allen, Rich Forget, Lauren Golden, Allie Bjerk, Joshua Stephens, John Golat, Mike Schmidt & AJ Rivera, Jason Feltman & Craig Pretzinger, and Bart & Sunny Miller

CONTENTS

INTRODUCTION - RUSSELL BRUNSON

One of the first books I read when I started my journey into online marketing was the book *Think and Grow Rich*. In this book, Napoleon Hill talked about a concept that he called a "master mind." He explained it like this:

"The coordination of knowledge and effort between two or more people who work towards a definite purpose in a spirit of harmony...

No two minds ever come together without creating a third, invisible, intangible force, which may be likened to a third mind (the master mind)."

Napoleon Hill, *Think and Grow Rich*

While I loved this concept of a mastermind, I didn't know how to actually create one. At about the same time, while studying marketing, I kept hearing the name "Dan Kennedy" over and over again. If you don't know him, he is the godfather of the direct-response industry.

Dan was the first person I'd ever seen who had actually taken this almost ambiguous principle and turned it into a business model. I found out about it after buying one of his courses on eBay—it was called "$252,000 Platinum Meetings." It was a CD set from inside his Platinum group where they were discussing different marketing strategies and principles.

I had tried to listen to CDs a couple times before, but for some reason none of them ever really connected with me. But one day my yard had flooded and I had to spend about eight hours digging out some pipes in my front yard, so I thought it was a good time to start listening to the CD set. Now this was pre-podcasts, pre-Audible, so there weren't a lot of audio courses to listen to.

I started listening, and it was fascinating because all these people inside Dan's mastermind meeting were sharing ideas and strategies about how they were growing their companies—what they were doing and how they were scaling. I remember thinking, *Man, I have to figure out how to be in that room to listen to these conversations. I would grow as a human, I would grow as a business owner, and I'd grow as an entrepreneur*. I needed to figure out some way to get inside that room.

The next day, I messaged Dan Kennedy's office and said, "I need to join Dan's Platinum group!" They told me it was sold out. But because I'm a good entrepreneur who doesn't take no for an answer, I messaged him again the following day.

"Well, how do I get on the waiting list? Who are the people in the mastermind now? I want to see if I can buy one of their spots."

And I kept messaging them over and over, trying to figure out how I could get into that room, because I knew that was where things happened and I needed to be there. After five or six weeks, they finally gave in and sent me an application to join. At the time, entrance into this exclusive group was $25,000 a year, which is about $20,000 more than I'd made up to that point in my business. So I decided to put it on a credit card.

About a month later, I was in Baltimore, Maryland, in a small room with about 18 other business owners and Bill Glazer. Over the next six years, I would make that pilgrimage to Baltimore three times a year to sit in this mastermind group and have a chance to learn from the top people in fields like real estate, stock markets, investing, direct-response marketing, dentistry, and chiropractic—all sharing their marketing best practices. It was fascinating!

I was selling stuff online, but as I watched the real estate gurus talk about their live events, I realized that I needed to do those as well. And that's how Funnel Hacking LIVE was born.

I heard those who were running call centers talk about their business models. And I realized that I needed to build a call center, which is where all of our high-ticket trainings and courses came from.

While listening to Dan Kennedy and Bill Glazer talk about postcards and direct mail, I realized that I needed to be doing that too.

Every single mastermind meeting, I would go with an open mind and collect these ideas. Then I would take them back home and immediately implement them within my business. And I watched my business go from startup to six figures…then to seven, eight, and beyond in record time.

I tried every single one of those ideas. I had a lot of successes and a lot of failures, but I quickly learned what worked and what didn't.

I was in that mastermind for six years, but then Bill decided to sell the company. So I started looking for other similar groups I could plug into. The next year, I joined three or four, hoping to find a similar experience. But despite the fact that these were the biggest masterminds in the entrepreneur business communities, all of them left me wanting. I would leave every meeting wishing that I had gotten the same growth and expansion that I had from Bill and Dan's. I joined another group and another group, sometimes spending more than $100,000! Yet I never left any of those meetings fully satisfied. I felt like I was coming to a dinner table hungry, but no matter which group I joined, I never left feeling full.

After a couple years, I decided to start my own mastermind group, like Napoleon Hill had suggested and I'd seen Dan Kennedy do so successfully. That is when I launched my Inner Circle. It was a unique name at the time, but since then, it's been copied by hundreds of other marketers in many different industries.

I created the Inner Circle and then we started allowing people to sign up. By our first meeting, only eight people had joined. But as I sat in that room, it felt different because this time I was facilitating the group. It was the first time in almost a decade, since being at the feet of Dan and Bill, that I felt like I was growing again. Each person who joined this mastermind was from a different industry and background. Every single meeting brought new ideas and new strategies to the table, which I was able to implement as well as the other members, even though I was the one facilitating.

I got so much value out of the Inner Circle that I decided to double down: we grew it from 8 people to 20. But then I knew that group was at capacity, so I decided to open up a second group. Within days, I went from 20 members to 50! I wanted to run even more groups, but I had to cap it so everyone could still get value. I decided to allow only 100 people inside the Inner Circle.

I announced this new cap to my email list, and within three short weeks, we'd filled all 100 spots. Inner Circle was officially locked down for the very first time. At Funnel Hacking LIVE each year, I would talk about Inner Circle but never allowed people to sign up for it because it was full.

Also, every year we'd have a handful of people drop out, which was discouraging to me because I was getting value from them and I was watching their businesses grow. So I decided to implement a change, which was one of the keys to making this group successful.

First, I changed the name from "Inner Circle" to "Inner Circle For Life." I told my members, "Once you're in Inner Circle, we will love you and serve you. And if you want to leave at some point, that's completely fine. We'll still love and care about you!"

But this was not a program for people to jump in and out of. Inner Circle was about "Once you're in, you're in." So we made a rule where if someone left the Inner Circle, they couldn't get back in. And that completely changed the dynamic. Now people came in, joined the program, and invested in it fully knowing that this was their tribe. This was the people they were there to serve. And it changed everything very quickly.

The people who were upset by the rule change dropped out, and the right people got back in. The Inner Circle became much more than just some entrepreneurs who help each other. It has become literally like a family, where people come in and they stay for life. That's why we call it Inner Circle for Life.

As businesses grew and the mastermind members started having different challenges, the program evolved as well. The core "Inner Circle For Life" mastermind has openings for 100 entrepreneurs at $50K per seat. Then we opened a second group called the "Category

Kings." This is for people who want to be the best inside of their respective markets. The ticket for this group is $150,000 a year, and it sold out in less than 36 hours. A year later, we opened one more tier: the "Atlas" group for $250,000 a year. Over 90% of the people who had previously been in the Category Kings signed up for the Atlas group to lock in their spots for life. And the new Category Kings group filled up in one day.

That is the power of the Inner Circle. Open spots are limited, but these people have an amazing chance to be part of a family of entrepreneurs who are literally changing the world.

These are the best of the best.

These are the people in every market and every industry who are leading the way.

They are the innovators.

They are the market movers.

They are the category kings.

They are the people who are not here just to make money, but who are called to serve others.

And they serve at a level higher than any other entrepreneurs I've seen in the entire world.

This is a group I am proud to call my friends and my family. We meet multiple times a year—sometimes in Boise, other times in exotic locations—to figure out how we can serve our audiences better and how we can change their lives.

All of the innovation within the marketing world is happening inside this group. Others copy and clone what we do, but we're setting the trends, we are creating the new movements.

My guess is that if you see someone who is dramatically successful in your market, it's because either they or their teacher, the person they're learning from, are in the Inner Circle. We share ideas oftentimes months or years before the mass market even knows about it and have been quietly implementing them. That is the power of this Inner Circle.

Our Inner Circle members support each other. They help each other with their launches. They brainstorm together. They help each other with their challenges and their funnels. They give back. Every single month, members are serving each other. Even where they would normally charge maybe $25,000 a day for consulting, they're giving it freely to their Inner Circle mastermind members. Because they know that this is their family, this is their crew.

And every time that they give, they receive tenfold back. Inside this community, they know that if they share one idea, one tip, it will be amplified and it will change the world in other markets. That is why this is such a powerful group.

I want to thank all my Inner Circle members. It's been so rewarding to collaborate with them, to serve them, to grow with them—they are all changing the world in such unique and exciting ways.

Inside this book, you will read stories from dozens of people who had the chance to be a part of the Inner Circle. Each person heard about it, they wanted to get in, and when they finally did, they had a life-changing experience.

To see whether any coveted spots are open, go to InnerCircleForLife.com. You can fill out an application that will put you on a waiting list. Then when spots open up, you'll have a chance to grab one.

I hope you enjoy reading this book!

Thanks again,

Russell Brunson

P.S. Don't forget, you're just one funnel away…

JUSTIN BENTON

From Desperation to Inspiration: Justin Benton's Inspiring Miracle Plant Journey That Led to Writing This Book

Justin loves helping others, seeing them realize their potential & being a change for good. He discovered the power of this miracle plant in its Raw form when it brought his child back to him from the fog of a severe Autism diagnosis. So when his prayers were answered he committed his life's work to pay it forward by educating the world about his story and how the hemp/cannabis plant can help billions of people around the world with its seemingly endless healing capacity.

First, I'd like to thank Russell Brunson and his fantastic team at ClickFunnels, especially those who are so instrumental in running the Inner Circle, including Robbie Summers, Mandy Keene, Jenny Sage, Steve Bartetzko and Dave Lindenbaum.

I'm so excited that so many of my fellow Inner Circle family wanted to share their incredible journeys with you. I simply posted to our Inner Circle Facebook group, "Since so many of us have such incredible journeys to get inside the Inner Circle, would anybody want to submit a chapter and make a book to share with the world?"

The response was overwhelming, and the result is 23 incredible journeys for you to enjoy.

What you are about to read is filled with all the human emotions: joy, happiness, fear, doubt, and hope. I hope you find inspiration and pearls of wisdom to help you on your journey to serve those you were called to serve.

So let me start by saying how grateful I am. It is such an honor to get to share my family's miraculous journey that led us to discover Russell's world and his Inner Circle just when we needed it most.

Getting our miracle story out there is our way of paying it forward for what a misunderstood plant with so many names gave us.

This story started on October 5, 2012, when our second child was born. He came into this world with bright red hair. We had been kicking around some names, and since I'm a blend of Irish and Scottish, when he appeared with that beautiful red hair, Shea (short for Seamus) was destined to be his name. This is another reason we like to not only wait to find out if it's a boy or girl but also see their face to make sure we pick the right name.

(Now, my friends might think that because I'm a die-hard New York Mets fan and our old stadium was named Shea, that had something to do with it, and they wouldn't be entirely wrong.)

I remember life was good. Business was good. Our family was good—heck, who are we kidding?—we were great. Even my golf game was peaking.

We were living our dream life while running a successful direct marketing company, playing golf with the kids, and playing catch in the backyard with Shea, now two years old, and his older sister Zoe. Shea was learning new words, exploring the new world around him, and doing what two-year-olds do; he really liked to climb things which meant we found him in some startling places!

We had our boy and our girl, and life felt complete.

Shea was a happy, healthy kid and did all the usual kid stuff like play outside, go to the park, make messes around the house, and play on the jungle gym, just like his sister before him.

But then, after going in for a routine visit to the doctor's office, we noticed a change in his behavior.

He quit smiling, he quit talking, he stopped making eye contact, he quit engaging in our world, and he slipped into another world, isolating himself from the world around him.

He didn't seem to be with us, started throwing massive tantrums, and withdrew from the world around him.

Us dads tend to be like, "It's just a phase. He'll grow out of it. It's probably just a growth spurt or something."

But something was wrong with our healthy baby boy, but we just didn't know what.

My wife, Mollie, decided to get it checked out. She went in and had some tests run.

Then we got a phone call that changed our lives forever.

Shea was diagnosed with autism, on the severe side.

I barely knew what autism was.

These questions kept circling in my mind.

What happened to my boy?

How could we get our healthy son back?

What can we do?

Shea losing his health was the biggest gut punch in my life and would forever change our family.

Suddenly, our whole world stopped spinning, and we had to figure out how to get our son's health back.

I remember feeling deep sadness and periods of doubt, afraid my child may never be the person he was.

Is he ever going to live a normal life? (whatever that is)

Is he going to be able to live on his own?

Will he be able to go to regular school and have best friends and girlfriends?

We were told to just deal with it because there was no hope for recovery, just moderate improvement.

We definitely had our moments when the fear was winning.

But our faith was strong, and we knew he was healthy before, so we were going to do absolutely everything we could to get him healthy again.

When you see such a drastic regression from a healthy, happy, bouncy, talkative, playful child to someone who just basically sat in their own world not making eye contact, lost the ability to talk, and didn't want to play with anyone, making these repetitive motions like spinning wheels on a toy car, it tested our faith to the very limits and beyond.

But obviously, I'm his only dad, and my wife, Mollie, is his only mom, and we were gonna do everything we could to clear the fog and get his brain and body working again.

Fortunately, I was raised holistically and understood that food is our medicine and plant-based medicine is the best medicine. So I had a great foundation because of my mom, Janet.

She also was a school psychologist for over twenty-five years, working with children with special needs. So I had the upbringing and knew whom to call when we got the diagnosis.

My mom flew out to give her professional opinion, agreeing with the initial diagnosis.

When she told me she agreed there was a problem, I remember collapsing because then it became very real; we had a major problem.

The next day I picked myself up and decided we could focus on the problem or focus on the solution. I chose to focus on the solution and got to work.

My mom is a world-class expert in holistic healing, especially children, so she was going to be our guide. She moved out to California, and we went to work.

First things first, we had to clean up his diet. No junk food, sugar, processed foods, gluten, dairy, any of the other things that clog up our brains and bodies.

Then we got food and allergy tests to see what his body was allergic to and what his body was receptive to.

Then we sent out for a hair analysis to see if there were any pesticides or heavy metals in his system and the overall health of his body and organs.

When his test results came back, it was the scariest thing I've ever read to this day. His body was overwhelmed and failing. His body was unable to detoxify, so he was retaining 99 percent of the pesticides and heavy metals found in our nonorganic food and other external things like our medicine, sunscreen, soap, vaccines, deodorant, water, and even the air we breathe.

Fortunately, we were progressing with a great, clean, organic diet consisting of organic fruits and vegetables with supplements like probiotics to the point his body started to recover, and we even got his diagnosis to come down from severe autism to moderate after following this regimen for several months.

But he was nowhere close to being himself again and still behind where he was before his regression.

This meant I had to keep looking for solutions. I scoured the Internet. I met with world-class experts and doctors. We would get our hopes up when we discovered a new treatment, only to see little to no improvement trying it with Shea.

This led me to a diner in downtown Ventura, California, where we live, to meet one of my best friends, Todd, who wanted to meet for a serendipitous breakfast one morning to catch up.

We met at the Busy Bee Diner, one of those old-school '50s diners with the red vinyl booths and personal jukebox machines at the table that still serves the milkshakes in big metal cups.

We were sitting there having breakfast, and I asked him what was new. He said his friend Dr. Preston asked if he could help him make a CBD pen.

I was like, "What is a CBD pen?"

I was thinking, "Is it one of those cool pens like a Monte Blanc or one you can write upside down with, like the astronaut pen in the *Seinfeld* episode?"

He said, "It is a roll-on pen like deodorant that you roll on wherever there is pain."

I responded, "That sounds cool. What is CBD, and why is he asking for your help?"

Todd responded, "Well, since I'm a cannabis farmer and CBD comes from a strain of cannabis called hemp, he wanted to know if I would grow some for him to use."

I was like, "Wait a minute, you mean to tell me there is this thing called CBD that comes from hemp that a doctor wants to use to help his patients relieve pain? Why have I never heard of this until now?"

So when breakfast was over, I did what we all do, and I typed in CBD (short for cannabidiol) into the Google machine. I found out, sure enough, that it helps reduce pain and inflammation, but then I scrolled down, and I discovered CBD was also helping children with seizures.

I couldn't believe what I was reading. There was a plant helping children with seizures; I had never heard of it, even growing up in a holistic home.

Then a light bulb went off since my top priority was looking for a miracle for Shea: if this CBD was having such great success helping children with severe brain issues like epilepsy, maybe, by the grace of God, it could be the solution we were looking for.

I immediately called my wife, Mollie, and said, "You got to see this; CBD from hemp is helping kids with seizures. Maybe it will help Shea?"

At the time, I couldn't find any research on CBD and autism.

We immediately set up meetings with CBD experts around the world to best understand how it worked and make sure it would not get my son "high" because that was the last thing I wanted to do to his brain while he was recovering.

I started trying dozens of different products myself first to see how they worked.

Then we gave him the ones we liked the best.

But unfortunately, like before, with other treatments, there was little to no improvement.

But I wasn't going to give up, because it made too much sense. There had to be something we were missing.

So I kept studying the hemp plant and talking with experts like Dr. Rafael Mechoulam, who is the godfather of cannabinoids (like CBD).

Then I had the breakthrough I was looking for when I found research from Dr. William Courtney. His research showed how juicing raw hemp had tremendous results with people with late-stage cancer.

That was when the light bulb really went off. Being raised holistically, I understood the best way to consume a plant is in its whole plant raw form, just like eating it or juicing it.

When I found out Dr. Courtney was using this miracle plant in the raw, holistic whole plant form, as it was intended, I just knew in my soul this was the missing piece to unlock the full potential of this plant. This had to be the answer to our prayers we had spent years searching for to restore Shea's health.

As the universe works, hemp became legal to grow in the US again in 2014 (which should have always been legal since our Founding Fathers grew it for its over fifty thousand uses).

So I decided to grow some hemp plants in my backyard and make our own hemp juice and oil to clear the fog for my son.

One October morning, we packed up Shea and his older sister, Zoe, to head off to Underwood's Pumpkin Patch with the grandparents, aunt, and uncle to pick out pumpkins and go on a hayrack ride.

When we got there, Shea was overwhelmed by being out of his comfort zone and was screaming, covering his ears, hiding under a bench, and having an absolutely miserable time while the other kids played.

I reached into my pocket, got out a bottle of raw hemp oil we made that morning, gave it to Mollie, and said, "Let's see if this helps."

She squirted some in his mouth.

Then literally two minutes later, he looked up and snapped out of it. He got up, looked around, found his sister, and ran off to go play in the pumpkin fields.

Everyone with us saw the transformation and was like, what was that? What did you give him?

I told them it was some raw hemp oil we made.

Right then and there, I knew we had found what we were seeking. And after giving him what we affectionately call Shea's Oil consistently for a few short months, I'm so happy to report Shea no longer has the autism diagnosis!

He was a happy kid again, going to regular school with his sister, excelling academically, and becoming quite the baseball slugger.

Our prayers were answered!

As our way to pay it forward, we set up TheMiraclePlant.org to help educate other families affected by autism to give them hope and share our story and the same products that worked so well for us.

Once our story started to spread across Southern California, more and more people kept finding us for their own health concerns. In the beginning, the most common issue was pain.

Then people started asking if they could try some for stress and anxiety.

Then people started wanting to try some for sleep.

They would return after a few weeks and say it worked great and they wanted more!

Then people started tracking us down for complex things like rheumatoid arthritis, fibromyalgia, and neuropathy.

Each time they would come back and blow us away with their success stories!

I was absolutely stunned!

How could one plant help so many people with so many different health issues?

Then one day, this tall German lady in her seventies came in and said she would like to buy a bottle of our strongest oil for late-stage cancer that had returned.

She said she did all her research, and hemp oil helps reduce tumor growth, and we had the best product around, so she was going to use it versus doing radiation and chemo again, which she tried before, and she said she would rather die than go through that again.

At the time, I thought of cancer as this life sentence and the scariest thing ever.

So I was really taken aback.

So we gave her our compassionate discount and waited to hear from her.

A few weeks passed, and then she came back into our office with a glow about her (That is how I can best describe it.) and said she wanted to buy another bottle.

We asked her how she was doing, and she said she felt great and she was playing tennis multiple times a week.

A few more weeks passed by, and she returned, and I finally worked up the courage to ask her, so how is everything going with you now?

She said she got her blood work back and the cancer was in remission!

I was so blown away. I didn't know if I should cry, laugh, hug, or dance! So we both did them all!

I knew right then and there that this was what I was called to do for as long as there was air in my lungs!

We started opening more locations, working with international governments, and aligning with holistic healers like chiropractors.

Everything was going great; we could see a clear path to reach one billion people by 2025, which is our mission!

Business was great as we became known as the original raw hemp supplement company. We were opening new locations in California and the Rockies, with plans to open more locations in the Midwest, on the East Coast, and overseas in Europe and Latin America.

But something happened in March 2020 that none of us could have prepared for.

When the lockdowns started happening in California, things were really scary. Were we going to have to close our doors? At the time, we were told our business was nonessential and to shut down the office. But because we knew our clients needed our products to help with stress, pain, sleep, and severe health conditions now more than ever, we decided to fight back with our legal team and won an injunction to keep our doors open.

We were happy we won the ruling and never shut our doors, but people weren't coming out like they used to. Because of Covid, the way we shop changed forever.

Our clients were made up mostly of baby boomers aged fifty-five and up with health issues themselves or looking for healthier alternatives for their loved ones because they had had enough of taking pills with side effects.

Before Covid, according to one survey in 2019, 17 percent of Americans did the majority of their shopping online, including Amazon. Groceries, food delivery, and anything else they wanted, they went to the internet first.

Since then, that number has tripled to over 51 percent of US shoppers going to the internet first or asking Alexa or Siri to shop for them.

We are never going back to the way it was before 2020, and we knew if we wanted to complete our mission of reaching one billion people by 2025, we were going to have to become digital marketing and online experts. There is only one way to do that: choose the right mentor and learn from the best.

So that's exactly what I did. I started joining masterminds, starting with the very first one I joined with digital marketing guru Joe Soto, who ran it along with the King of Sales Jeffrey Gitomer. That's when my eyes were opened to what was out there and how much there was to learn about the online shopping world.

Joe had worked with Russell Brunson and the ClickFunnels international team and confirmed what I already knew, which was that

Russell's framework and funnel expertise, especially for growing our business online, was second to none. I decided it was time to go all in with Russell.

We quickly learned that the way we were going to complete our mission was in this exciting new world filled with upsells, autoresponders, and lead magnets, oh my. I knew I had to become an expert to ensure I knew the best strategies to deploy to my marketing team so they could carry out the mission.

We had to figure out how to attract our clients online, which is very difficult because powerful people and organizations within Big Pharma do not want their bottom line affected, so they have done everything they could to pressure the FDA and online advertisers like Facebook and Google to restrict our ability to share our story.

That's when Russell taught me about his Dream 100 concept of aligning with influencers that already had a relationship with our ideal clients. It was reconfirmed yet again that choosing Russell as our guide to navigate us through this treacherous path was clearly the right choice.

I remember signing up for the One Funnel Away Challenge and getting my first Shock and Awe package in the mail with all the goodies, including the *30 Days* book, which inspired me to do this book, *Inside the Inner Circle*.

I was absolutely blown away by the thirty-day training being given for a mere $100!

I learned about things like order form bumps. Are you kidding me? It's like getting a candy bar at the checkout to quiet your kids in the grocery store. Allow your clients to say "Yes!" to a great product and price, and they won't think twice about adding it to their cart.

I also loved the game-changing concept of Who, Not How. When you break down what your hourly rate is, then write down how many hours it would take for you to do something like editing a video (10 hours @ $420 an hour = $4,200). Why would you do something you're not an expert at when you can have someone else do it on Funnel Marketplace or Fiverr for $50?

I also loved learning from Russell by listening to the Marketing Secrets podcast and learning all the insights right before ClickFunnels started. I went back and started with the first iteration, "Marketing in Your Car," and listened to every episo

de, including all the intro music changes. Listening to those episodes with insights being shared from the very beginning to scaling ClickFunnels to nine figures is an education unlike any I got in college or anywhere else.

That's where I started hearing stories like Myron Golden's, attributing his massive success to joining the Inner Circle.

When you look at the names of people inside the Inner Circle, like Alex Hormozi, LadyBoss, Allison Prince, Stacey and Paul Martino, Annie Grace, Liz Benny, Jaime Cross, Nicholas Bayerle, and Peng Joon, to name a few that are a part of Russell's Inner Circle family, and the success the experience, it is undeniable.

When I started to follow the journeys of the members of the Inner Circle through all of the live presentations given onstage and online, I just knew I had to get into the "cool kids" club, whatever it took. Not to mention when you watch all the amazing presentations from Funnel Hacking Live, it's undeniable that being inside the Inner Circle is where I had to be if I was going to surround myself with the best of the best to complete my mission.

So when I first found out about the Inner Circle, it was closed. I applied for the Inner Circle, but it wasn't open because Russell shut it down to focus on scaling ClickFunnels.

I knew that if and when he ever opened it again, it was my ultimate goal to join the Inner Circle.

I remember getting psyched for Funnel Hacking Live 2021, which was delayed six months because of Covid; Russell started teasing that he might open up the Inner Circle after closing it down for a few years.

Russell was doing social media posts saying, "Look what am I working on, mua ha ha ha!" You could see Inner Circle application pages were being built, and I remember screenshotting the social media posts to zoom in to learn every little detail I could.

I remember it like it was yesterday, Funnel Hacking live 2021 in Orlando. Rumors were floating around that Russell was officially opening back up the Inner Circle, but I wasn't sure how to get in.

I was there with some friends, Jamie Greene and Alex Foote, and they were talking with Robbie Summers after they officially opened it back up at the end of a lunch meeting.

As soon as I heard the conversation was about joining Inner Circle, I was like, "Hey, Robbie, I want in!"

Let me take a minute to give a shoutout to the one and only Robbie Summers. First off, there's not enough good I can say about him.

Obviously, he's the most fired-up salesman on planet earth. There are just no two ways about it; Robbie is the man.

He reminds me so much of the DJ character Robin Williams yelling, "Good morning, Vietnam!"

The crazy thing is Robbie yells, "Good morning, ClickFunnels!" at the beginning of every daily meeting, I'm told.

I always kid him and call him the Energizer Bunny, because he's got that kind of energy. He keeps going and going and going!

Plus, he's always in a good mood, always super-high energy, and always ready to get the party started, especially when it comes to kicking off an event.

As I was saying, Robbie was there talking with Alex about joining the Inner Circle, and when I heard what they were talking about, I was like, "Dude, I am so in. Let's do this!"

Robbie said, "I love you guys, and I know you guys are gonna be a perfect fit. Go over there to the table in the back, fill out the application, put down your deposit and expect to hear from us in a couple weeks."

So I raced over to the table, filled out my application, handed it in, and got my Inner Circle sweatshirt with a grin from ear to ear, baby. I don't think I took the sweatshirt off or that smile for the remainder of FHL!

I felt so proud to wear it. My dream had come true. I was in the Inner Circle!

When Alex and I walked back to our hotel rooms afterward, we were walking on cloud nine; I bet our feet weren't even touching the ground. "Can you believe we are in the Inner Circle?" we both kept saying.

When you look back to all the Inner Circle success stories from all the names you've heard of, it's just so impressive.

It reminds me of the NFL Hall of Fame. In order to get in, you have to have at least ten thousand rushing or receiving yards or throw hundreds of touchdown passes or win Super Bowls to even be considered to get voted in.

You can't just decide to join the Hall of Fame; you have to spend your whole professional life earning it.

I felt like I was able to join the Hall of Fame when they opened the Inner Circle back up. They were allowing us to join the Hall of Fame to be with the greats of our time in business, sales, marketing, and making a real impact in the world.

I had to keep pinching myself. Because it really was a dream come true that I got to be a part of the best of the best mastermind.

It's been everything I could have hoped for and more since joining, truly a dream come true.

I remember our first Inner Circle meeting in October; we met at the Knitting Factory, which is this cool venue where they have concerts. I remember seeing the Inner Circle logo on a sign right outside the building and being so honored to be walking in and meeting my soon-to-be best friends and business partners whom I could share the ups and downs with and know they were going through the same things and that we were really going be able to help each other.

I was blown away that so many people were there when I walked in from the original Inner Circle 1.0, like Myron Golden. I remember walking up to him, shaking his hand, and thanking him for continuing to be a part of this amazing mastermind and giving back.

I know how important Inner Circle is to Myron's incredible success because he talks about it often. Since then, Myron and I have become golfing buddies; he has the best short game in the group, by the way.

Myron has gone on to have so much success and teach so many people how to have six- and seven-figure days. And here he is still showing up, still learning and still giving back.

That's one of the best things about the Inner Circle: it really is a community about giving, and that precedent was set by Russell, who showed us all how to give and give and give. #overdeliver

One of those standards is to give first, seeking nothing in return like Russell did for Tony Robbins for ten years when Tony was on top of Russell's Dream 100 list.

Another thing I love about the Inner Circle is our biweekly calls that Stephanie Dove Blake set up; we start out seeing if anyone has an "ask" or a "give." Nine times out of ten, people are there wanting to give because that's just who we are: big-hearted givers.

But you know what is crazy is when people have an "ask." They actually become more helpful for me because someone will ask how to hire the right integrator. And then everyone starts to weigh in with what they've seen work for their business or a company that does a great job of doing that particular thing that they've worked with.

Then it just turns into this conversation where you're writing notes as fast as you can because there is so much gold being dropped on how to really scale your business. Once again, it always comes down to Who, Not How.

Another great thing about Inner Circle is the private Facebook group and Slack channels.

You got a question? Multiple people have experience with what worked for them and want to help, and their answers are just minutes away!

We were all attracted to Russell's values, what he stands for, the work he has put in, and the standard he set.

I'll never forget the moment I absolutely knew I made the right choice for Russell to be my mentor was when he was sitting in between Tony Robbins and Dean Graziosi for a huge mastermind launch, and he talked about listening to that voice inside of you and stepping up and serving the people you were called to serve.

Because our mission was about healing the world and serving others, I knew right then and there Russell was the one who was going to help us reach one billion people by 2025.

And boy was I right.

So come join us if you ever get the opportunity to join the Inner Circle if and when it opens back up at an upcoming Funnel Hacking Live.

It was the smartest thing I ever did for our mission and for my organization to make sure that we were equipped to thrive in this new world, where people do the majority of their shopping online.

We're never going back to the way things were in 2019. Life always moves forward. So if you are getting that tug to see if the Inner Circle is just what your mission or business needs, head on over to www.innercircleforlife.com and apply. If you're lucky like me, you'll be hearing from Robbie.

#InnerCircle4Life

DAMON BURTON

and the $50K Bracelet

Over a decade ago, this husband and father of three beat a billion dollar company by outranking their website on Google. Since then, he knew he was onto something and went on to build an international search engine marketing company that's worked with NBA teams, and Inc 5000 & Shark Tank featured businesses.

How I joined Russell Brunson's Inner Circle is a story of unexpectedly spending $50,000. Here's how I've made that money back . . . and then some.

There I was, a first timer at Funnel Hacking Live. FHL veteran Josh Forti was kind enough to let me tag along and network with him.

In Brunson's world, Forti is a mini celebrity known for having vocal opinions on topics most of us shy away from: politics and religion. He introduced me to FHL alumni as we walked all over the venue together.

But there was one thing I couldn't do with him. I couldn't go beyond a magical sash because Josh's wristband was blue and mine was red.

There was nothing significant past the invisible line other than bagels and the opportunity to get early seats. But this invisible line meant I couldn't hang out with my friends on the other side, even if only for a few minutes before the next speaker, and that drove me crazy.

I asked the security person at the sash if I could upgrade wristbands. I didn't expect anything for free. In my mind, I was willing to pay the ridiculous amount of $1,000 to change my wristband from red to blue.

They said yes and to talk to Guest Services where they were handing out T-shirts. After walking over to Guest Services, they said otherwise: "No."

Early access was only for those that had won a Two Comma Club Award or were in their coaching program. I asked what coaching programs they had.

Enter Robbie Summers.

Robbie is the lead sales magician at ClickFunnels. The gatekeeper. Energetically, he walks up and puts his hand on my shoulder. "What's up, what's up, what's up?"

I told him that I was with friends that had early access, couldn't go past the line, and didn't want anything for free, and I asked if I could pay to upgrade.

He asked who my friends were, and I said, "I'm not going to name-drop."

To which he replied, "I don't know who you are. I need you to name-drop."

Fair enough.

I told him the names of a few friends, and he still confirmed that early access wouldn't happen unless I had won an award or was in their coaching program.

He asked if I was interested in coaching, which I wasn't. Then he asked, "What about a mastermind?"

"Maybe," I replied.

"Here's the deal . . . we're reopening Inner Circle at a luncheon in ninety minutes. You have to do at least a million in revenue; someone has to vouch for you . . . and it's $50,000 to buy in."

WTF? What is Inner Circle, and how did I go from an astronomical number in my head of $1K for a bracelet to $50K?

But time slowed at that moment. Knowing nothing about Inner Circle thirty seconds earlier, my inner monologue told me it might be what I had been looking for.

Right then, Josh Forti walked by. I hollered and asked if he could come over and do the vouching.

Robbie asked Josh if I was Inner Circle material. He told Josh that I had logged into my phone and proved income, then asked him with a wink, "But is he good for Inner Circle?"

He was trying to find the right balance of asking Josh if I was legit while also trying not to offend me. Understandable. Just as I didn't know who he was thirty seconds ago, he didn't know who I was. Was I legit? Was I wasting his time?

Now more than ever, I realize that $50,000 is a quality filter. At that large of an investment, you want to protect the integrity and professionalism of the group.

Josh replied, "I'd put my reputation on the line for Damon. He's good."

After that vouching, I bought in.

With an Inner Circle hoodie in hand, I returned to the hotel room and asked my wife to guess how much the new blue bracelet cost. She didn't think it was as funny as I did.

Ten months later, Inner Circle member of the month, up nearly double in revenue, and traveling the world for some fun events, my wife now appreciates the $50K investment.

Let's go back in time to see how I got here. What's the story behind how I made millions in the first place to be able to join Inner Circle?

I grew up lower-middle class. Not having a computer at home made me appreciate them. In my senior year of high school, they came out with an HTML class. Long before ClickFunnels, WordPress, or Shopify, you had to build websites by hand. Web design was still in its infancy, but the creative freedom of having a blank digital canvas to build websites with HTML was attractive to me.

That single high school HTML class was later followed by a communications class in college. The semester project for communications was to build a website following a list of criteria. I started thinking about how much time I would spend making a website, knowing that at the end of the semester, the school was going to wipe it off of their servers. I asked the professor if I could buy a domain and build my project as a live website instead. On January 27, 2001, I registered my first domain name, EliteRides.com, a website for car enthusiasts.

I still own the domain. However, I've since archived the content.

During its peak, Elite Rides grew to have several thousand active members, which is where my hobby started transitioning into a career.

As the website grew in popularity, I asked myself, "How do I improve this?" That inspired me to learn and be more intentional about web design.

Next, I asked, "How do I monetize this?" That's what exposed me to online marketing.

In June 2001, there was a wild card, a movie that blew up out of nowhere. It was called *Fast and Furious*, and it amplified the world of automotive enthusiasts forever, drawing more members to Elite Rides.

Marrying my hobbies and passions with online communities continued with other successes. Still in college, I took an elective credit interning for a radio station. Through great timing and good fortune, I found myself on air after just three months of interning. I took advantage of idle time between talking on air and would work on Elite Rides. I also took advantage of access to radio concerts and nightlife to start another online community called VIPnights.com.

Another success was SEMAgallery.com. SEMA Gallery was a website dedicated to the huge automotive convention in Las Vegas, Specialty Equipment Market Association. SEMA takes up the entire Las Vegas convention center, something like a million square feet, and lasts four days. Despite how large the convention is, it's not open to the public. By invite or application only, SEMA is accessible only to those in the automotive industry. Hello, Elite Rides.

Leveraging Elite Rides to access SEMA, I was overwhelmed by the endless rows of aftermarket products and new concept cars. After my first year at the show, I wanted to see more. Upon returning home from Vegas, I found surprisingly little about this event online. How could there be days of eye candy and so little of it shared online?

"Why don't I solve my own problem?" I asked. "Why don't I become the go-to website for this event?"

I loaded the few dozen pictures I had taken that year and started SEMA Gallery. The following year I took several thousand photos, optimized the website, and outranked the convention's own website.

I started to notice a trend of opportunities . . . identify a gap in a market and make a website for it. But the next website I applied this concept to wasn't based on passion. This was purely a marketing play, and I was eager to see if it would work. It did—becoming the first time I outranked a billion-dollar company.

In 2007, my wife was watching *The Bachelor* and asked me to sit with her for the season finale. I remembered from past season finales with her that they'd leave a cliffhanger. They wouldn't announce who the next bachelor was, but this year they did. His name was Andy Baldwin.

The marketer in me started thinking, "Why did they announce the bachelor's name this year and not years prior?" It was clearly intentional, but why? I started looking him up online, and queue déjà vu.

Much like content for SEMA, I could find very little about Mr. Baldwin. I started thinking, "If I'm spending this much time looking this guy up and I don't even watch the show, imagine how many other people are digging deep and can't find anything."

That night, I built a website. I took what public information I could find about the guy, cataloged his bio and pics, and applied what I had learned about SEO. Within a week, I was outranking a billion-dollar company, ABC, for their own *The Bachelor* brand.

I passively made thousands of dollars per month on these community websites and was sold on the concept of SEO.

Over the years that followed, I started building up a few design clients on the side while maintaining a nine-to-five job. What ended up being my last day job before starting SEOnational.com was designing affiliate marketing landing pages for a company in Las Vegas.

It was a new but aggressive affiliate company. They were looking for designers that could do landing pages and ad creatives that converted. The owner asked around and kept hearing my name. As timing would have it, I had just quit doing landing pages for a toxic employer. The new guy caught word, called me, having never talked before, and offered me a job on the spot, allowing me to work remotely from Utah.

At the time, my wife worked at a hospital. She'd get up at 3:00 a.m. to get ready for work. I thought, "Why not wake up early and use my new work-from-home arrangement to invest time toward creating my own opportunities?"

I started waking up with my wife and would work on my day-job duties from three or four in the morning until about 8:00 a.m. By the time Vegas was up and at it, I had already knocked out my responsibilities for them for the day. I used the rest of the day to work on my own thing, continuing to build up a portfolio of clients on the side.

Over time, my side hustle made about 40 percent of my income but took only 20 percent of my time. My day job made 60 percent of my income but consumed 80 percent of my time.

And then came an interesting crossroads.

Before Slack, AOL Instant Messenger was a go-to form of online communication. I was trying to message the Las Vegas team and couldn't get ahold of anybody. I also tried calling the office phone number. Nothing.

Then I received a message from one of the other designers. "Did you hear what happened?"

The Las Vegas company owner had gotten into some legal trouble years prior for his previous business. He had a civil suit for fraud that he lost for several million dollars, but no criminal case . . . until now.

I couldn't contact anyone that morning because the FTC raided the company and shut it down.

I finally got a hold of somebody later in the day. They confirmed it was true; the company was raided. But everything was "fine," and I'd get my paycheck that Friday.

I had three choices at that moment:

1. Wait to see if I still had a job and received the next paycheck

2. Assume the business was gone for good and look for a new day job

3. Take the leap of faith and start my own business

If I chose #3, I would take a hit to my income. But I had a few clients on the side, and my wife had a job. I did the math, and under a worst-case scenario, we would be house poor but could still pay our bills. That seemed about as calculated of a risk as I could imagine.

I chose option three and bet on myself. Good thing because I never received that paycheck or heard a single word from anyone at that company ever again.

That ended up being one of the best decisions I ever made. By freeing up 80 percent of my time, I was able to make up that lost income in just two or three months. Fifteen years later, I often make more in a day than I used to make in a year.

There were a lot of important evolutions to my career after that decision. I like to tell other entrepreneurs to "date" phases of life.

Maybe you're stuck in entrepreneurship. Or maybe you haven't even taken the leap of faith yet. Perhaps you're in a nine-to-five and you don't enjoy your job. What I mean by "date the phases" is to avoid focusing on the negative. Instead, focus on the positives and what you can learn from your current situation.

Just like when you're dating somebody, you're continually weighing what you like and don't like in that relationship. As one relationship ends, you learn from it and level up the next relationship. Do the same thing with your career.

You have to continue dating those phases, identifying what you don't like so that you can appreciate what you do like, until you find an opportunity to "marry."

As I dated the phases in my new self-employed role, I was never in a rush to grow my company because I didn't want to screw it up.

The first year was cool just to be self-employed.

In the second year, I hired my first team member. This is also where I started to transition from web design to search engine optimization.

One of my design clients asked, "What do you know about Google?"

I told them that I knew enough that I was confident that I could help them. However, I didn't know enough that I felt comfortable charging them. Understandably, I didn't want to work for free either. I made them an offer.

"How about we agree on goals? Until I hit those goals, you pay me nothing. But if I do, you owe me retroactively, *and* we start a monthly retainer moving forward?"

That way, they had nothing to lose, but I was incentivized to win.

A few months later, we crushed those goals, they paid me retroactively, and we started a retainer for my first SEO client.

I enjoyed the process and made the same offer to another design client. This second client had been referred by the first, so the opportunity was easier to explain to them. They bought in and also succeeded, and fifteen years later, both of those businesses are still clients today.

A few years into focusing on SEO, I was listening to two books around the same time; *The 4-Hour Workweek* by Tim Ferriss and *E-Myth Revisited* by Michael Gerber.

If you're familiar with *The 4-Hour Workweek*, it tells you how to find shorter paths to success in business and life. *E-Myth Revisited* illustrates the importance of building a company based on processes.

If you don't build a business focused on processes, as you hire and fire talent, the skills of those people come and go, and the company's output is inconsistent. But if you document processes, you can scale fulfillment while maintaining quality control, regardless of the talent you put in that role.

After those books, I asked myself, "Why do I have only two or three team members instead of ten or twenty? Why don't I delegate more so I can get out of production and focus on growing the company?"

Shortly after, I went from two or three team members to about a dozen. Having that many team members was new territory for me. I took the responsibility of supporting that many people seriously and dated that phase for a while.

After dating and ascending phases for years, I kept reflecting on how much I had accomplished, yet how much more I knew I could do. I got to the point where there were no more foreseeable insecurities with the idea of scaling and asked myself, "Why not shoot for the moon?" If I had accomplished this much without marketing, ironically while owning a marketing company, imagine how much more I could achieve if I layered in some intentional lead generation.

When I was in the middle of my SEO book, *Outrank*, I was looking to leverage it to grow an audience. That's when I bought Russell Brunson's *Dotcom Secrets* and *Expert Secrets* books. I purchased his black box combo that came with an MP3 player.

At the time, I was building a cabin at Bear Lake. If you're unfamiliar, Bear Lake is a crystal-blue lake on the border of Utah and Idaho. The MP3 player allowed me to listen while working on the property. Coincidentally, Russell talks about a lake he loved growing up with and now takes his kids to. He was talking about Bear Lake . . . in his marketing book . . . that I was listening to while at Bear Lake . . . in the middle of writing my marketing book. I can now look back and appreciate how that moment would come full circle.

I finished writing and publishing my book, which became an Amazon bestseller. It's opened many doors and closed many deals. But what's proven most effective in monetizing *Outrank* is giving the book away for free.

- I give away free downloads in a funnel at <u>FreeSEObook.com</u>.

- I mail physical copies to leads.

- I send copies in new-client welcome kits, to people that message me online, and to anyone who asks (including you, the reader).

I've spent around $30,000 on writing, publishing, printing, and giving away free book copies. Outrank has since grown my reputation, made and solidified relationships, and generated six figures from a five-figure investment.

Here's where we come full circle to joining Inner Circle.

Looking back, I started my business in 2007, before the '08 recession. Relatively speaking, one of my most significant growth spurts was during that recession. I wasn't making a ton back then. But that was when I saw the potential in this business and hit my first six-figure year shortly after.

Fast-forward to today's world shutdowns, crazy inflation, and fears of recession, and my agency, SEO National, is growing at a record pace again.

During the first year of the pandemic, I grew from fifteen team members to fifty. The year after, our revenue doubled. The following year nearly doubled the previous double.

What's fueled the growth? Staying in my lane, focusing on a single SEO product, and continuing to be intentional about relationships and giving without expecting in return.

Inner Circle has been an amazing opportunity to learn and teach simultaneously.

The seed that blossomed into being recognized as Inner Circle Member of the Month came from a presentation I shared with the team in Boise,

Idaho. It was a strategy of applying SEO concepts to lower PPC cost per click. The faster a landing page loads, the better the user experience. The better the user experience, the lower your cost per click. Lower cost per click = lower cost per lead or acquisition, increased conversions, and increased sales.

A few days after my fifteen-minute presentation, the first Inner Circle member to embrace my recommendations came forward. My advice took them only twenty minutes to implement, and it lowered their cost per lead from $9 to $3.80. They sent me a heartfelt video of gratitude.

"I literally cannot believe this," they said.

Before this, they had tried conversion rate optimization to lower their CPC. They had wasted thousands of dollars changing copywriting, colors, and images. Nothing worked until a minor tweak to improve page speed cut their CPL in half.

A few days later, a second Inner Circle member messaged me. They also implemented what I shared in the presentation, which increased their conversion rate by 27 percent.

Inspiring them has equally inspired me. I'm working on my next funnel, www.FunnelsSEO.com, where I will share with you what I've shared with Inner Circle.

The events put on by Inner Circle and ClickFunnels have motivated not only me but also my wife and mother-in-law and inspired my two young boys to start their own businesses. They're only seven and eleven and have already sold nearly $2,500 worth of stickers just two months after being inspired at Russell Brunson's Unlock the Secrets event.

I often get asked, "What advice would you give other entrepreneurs?" It's simple. Two things.

1. Start.

2. Don't stop.

The book you are holding is a wealth of opportunity. Your potential is unlimited if you trust in yourself.

Thank you for being a part of my journey, and I wish you continued success.

TYLER AND EMILY WATSON

How I switched From Flint to Flamethrower To Ignite My Success Path Into The Inner Circle

Tyler J. Watson is an Elite Performance coach and creator of Cellular Alignment Technique, the fastest duplicatable system for lasting personal change. Because of his unique approach to achieving real results in record time, he has been called "A mix between Tony Robbins and Houdini." With decades of experience in personal development and mastery in hundreds of processes, Tyler helps high achievers, entrepreneurs, and athletes live a legendary life without limitations. Most importantly, he is a passionate father and husband who loves to see people find true freedom while having fun.

"When are you going to start the Inner Circle again?"

That was the question I asked.

We were on a cruise ship in the middle of the Caribbean, having just finished a spectacular dinner, and now we were standing around chatting before we returned to our staterooms.

I was standing right in front of the one and only Russell Brunson.

And that was the one question I wanted answered.

Somehow, I think I must have known that Tyler and I were destined to be part of this incredible group of elite entrepreneurs and all-around amazing human beings, and somehow I must have sensed just how much it would impact our lives, even many months before we found ourselves actually in the room for our first Inner Circle meeting.

This is the story of where we came from, how we made it in that room, and the insanely cool and challenging experiences we've had in the Inner Circle so far, as well as a few of the lessons we learned along the way.

I hope that by sharing what we learned, you will be inspired to realize that you are able to create anything you want in your own life with a little bit of skill, a lot of courage, and the right "circle" around you.

Let's go.

So first, a wee little bit about us.

The first thing you need to know is that we are perfectly ordinary people. (Well, at least I am. Tyler maybe not, lol.)

I (Emily) was born into a very standard middle-class family. My dad went to work every day. My mom stayed home with the kids. We had enough money to have everything we needed, but very little that we wanted. "We can't afford it" was a very common phrase in our home.

Tyler grew up going to thrift stores for clothes and occasionally having to receive charity in order to eat. When he was twelve years old his parents divorced, and he lived through four more divorces on his mom's side and another one on his dad's.

We met and got married in Branson, Missouri, close to where Tyler grew up. That first year, we were very poor. We lived off of less than $1,000 per month combined income.

Then, almost a year into our marriage, Tyler invested in his education and learned how to sell. He started a coaching business teaching others what he'd learned. And our life changed dramatically. Our second year of marriage, we made six figures. And we thought we had it all figured out. (Cue laughter from anyone who has ever grown a business . . .)

The next few years were a roller coaster of ups and downs as we had babies (leaving me flat on my back sick for nine months each time) and Tyler traveled all over the country learning from many different gurus and sharing his message with them.

We made our first million dollars solely from Tyler's ability to network and our live events. We knew the online game existed, and we'd even heard about this software called ClickFunnels, but we were too busy bringing in the bacon each month (and taking care of kiddos) to do much about it.

At this point, we had a decent lifestyle and income, but we both knew we were made for something more. I was tired of Tyler always traveling, and he wanted to reach more people without having to be physically there every time.

And then we found a book put together by Russell Brunson.

And, no, it wasn't one of the "Secrets" books.

It was a book titled *30 days* about a bunch of top entrepreneurs who each shared what they would do to save themselves if they suddenly lost everything. I was amazed by their incredible stories and ideas, plus the fact that they had made millions of dollars online—something that still seemed pretty mysterious to me.

And, oh yeah, most of them were also part of this group called the Inner Circle.

Although I didn't know it at the time, the dream was born.

A few months later, Tyler and I attended our first Funnel Hacking Live.

We walked into the Gaylord Hotel in Nashville and saw Russell's face everywhere—on our room key, above the escalators, even on the gondola in the little indoor river. We heard from many speakers, including Lindsey Stirling, someone I'd been following for years. We laughed, we cried, and our perspective changed. And we met in person so many of the Inner Circle members I'd read about and who I'd thought must somehow be superhuman because of the impact they were having and the money they were making.

Funnel Hacking Live Blew. Us. Away.

It gave us the courage to go online and start selling a course about this little process Tyler developed that helps people change almost anything in their life in record time by shifting their cellular memory.

Little did we know that the Cellular Abundance Alignment Technique and those funnels would be the catalyst to a work and an impact far greater than Tyler had ever imagined.

Including landing us in the Inner Circle.

At that first Funnel Hacking Live, Tyler and I decided to go all in online.

We also took the plunge and joined Russell's Two Comma Club X coaching program, which was the only higher-level program he offered at the time, since the Inner Circle had been discontinued for a little while.

This is why, almost exactly one year later, we were on a cruise ship with Russell Brunson and a bunch of other 2CCX members, enjoying the view (and the food!).

We'd seen Russell around the ship and excursions, but we never got close enough to actually talk to him. (And to be perfectly honest, I was really nervous about doing so.)

Then, on the final night of the cruise, Russell joined a group of us in the dining room for dinner. Now was our chance.

We stood around after dinner chatting, and Tyler and I got to talk to Russell and Collette Brunson face-to-face.

It was one of the most impactful conversations of my life to that point. Russell and Collette were so kind and genuine, and I felt how caring they are as well as the power of the mission and purpose they are sharing with the world. Tyler had a great chat and shared a lot of things, and Russell even offered to connect me with someone he knew who could help me with an important project.

But there were just two things I really wanted to say.

First, I wanted Collette to know how much I admired her for raising a family and staying true to her faith while she and Russell changed so many lives. (Still true today!)

Second, I wanted to know when the Inner Circle would be happening again, because I knew in my core that is where I was meant to be.

I was thrilled when Russell said it would be reopening sometime, hopefully soon.

Now, all Tyler and I had to do was earn our Two Comma Club award for earning a million dollars through a funnel before then.

This brings me to the first lesson I want to share with you on your journey toward your own "Inner Circle"–like goal.

It's this: define and redefine your goals.

I'm sure you've heard it a million times . . . "Write down your goal, and you will get it faster."

This is different.

Oh so different.

Let me show you why.

To do so, I'll return to my story.

Tyler and I left the 2CCX cruise with one goal in mind: get our award before the next Funnel Hacking Live. ("So we can join Inner Circle," I added in my mind.)

We worked and worked on it and made some good progress, but the final push always seemed out of reach.

Finally, just a few months before the deadline, Tyler and I sat down to redefine what the Two Comma Club Award meant to us.

We talk about this process more in Tyler's book *The Alignment Effect*, at Alignmenteffect.com. I'll quote some of it here:

To further illustrate the power of definitions, especially in relationships, consider this story. When my wife and I were working toward our first Two Comma Club Award from ClickFunnels . . . we reached a point where we were almost there, but things seemed to be stagnant. To receive the award, you have to do over a million dollars with one funnel or product online.

We had made seven figures offline before, and we were excited to join the "club" online as well. But like I said, we'd been working really hard and were getting ready to finish the $1 million and apply for it, but for some reason I just kept dragging my feet. I just didn't seem to have the drive to get over the last little hump and actually receive the award. My wife, on the other hand, was super driven. She kept saying, "We need to finish the award!" and I'm like "Screw the award. I hate awards!"

It was actually beginning to cause a little friction in our relationship, so we did what we always do, which is align.

The first part of aligning is redefining, so we mapped out what the Two Comma Club Award represented to each of us.

And, of course, come to find out, part of the interpretation of awards in my body was definitely not serving me. I wrote down things like, "Awards are for the weak. Awards are ways that people who don't know you invalidate all the hard work that you put in because they don't care about you as a person. They don't understand you and what you've been through, and instead they give you a little plaque to represent all the pain they don't care to understand."

Pretty unhelpful definition, right? You'll notice, though, that none of this made sense at the moment. Logically, I wanted the award, and I certainly didn't believe that ClickFunnels was trying to invalidate me. However, even though my mind didn't believe them, these interpretations in my body were actually preventing me from receiving the award.

Behind these feelings were interpretations linked back to when I was a kid and didn't feel loved or understood. I felt frustrated with people saying things, doing things, or giving me things to try to ignore the truth that was deep inside. It was almost as if they were trying to use the award as a replacement for love. For years I had avoided getting awards. In fact, when I graduated from college, I literally skipped the graduation ceremony because it represented an award. I had dyslexia back then, and for me, college was so hard. I wasn't very good at memorizing, and I had difficulty with tests. I had a lot of these symptoms that I didn't realize were allergies and addictions that made it so I was the one who always had to study more and yet really struggled. And the "award" of graduation just seemed to negate all of the hard work I had actually put into my study. In a way, it felt like a slap in the face.

To my wife, however, awards represented validation. They represented a feeling of excitement, love, and like she was good enough. Growing up, she received praise when she got awards. It made her feel like she deserved it, she earned it, she was credible and real. Awards meant that she belonged with all the other people.

My wife and I had opposite definitions, and even though my wife's definitions seem to be more "positive" than mine, they weren't really serving either of us. More on that in a minute. With these opposing interpretations of the Two Comma Club Award, we had constant tension toward each other in going for this goal. I would procrastinate. She would push harder. I would go do something else; then she would try to force it. It was like we were fighting each other while we were supposed to be working for the same thing, and we were getting nowhere.

Then, once we redefined, we gained a deep understanding of why I had felt this way and why she felt that way. No wonder it was taking us so long to get the award! Redefining changed how we saw each other and ourselves. Then we aligned, and within a couple of weeks, we finished the application and received the email that we had qualified for the award. Aligning is so amazing. It can work in so many different ways, and it all starts with the definitions or our body's interpretations of what's actually going on.

To recap, as you move forward toward your own goals, be sure to write them down and "define" them, but also redefine them to make sure they are not attached to any negative stuff that is actually pushing them further away, OK?

At the 2021 Funnel Hacking Live, we went to a special lunch for Two Comma Club award winners, and you guessed it! We were given the opportunity to join the Inner Circle. What a thrill!

And also, how terrifying!

I don't know about you, but sometimes the reality of achieving one goal is accompanied by the fear that it is actually real. Imposter syndrome, anyone?

Tyler and I took the leap.

At the first meeting after Russell reopened the Inner Circle, we were so excited to be in the room with so many amazing people.

And then our doubts kept coming up.

Did we really fit in?

Were we really good enough?

Everyone in that room was so incredible . . . could we contribute?

Thankfully, we had an amazing chat with some of the wonderful coaches in the Inner Circle who assured us that this was exactly where we needed to be.

Plus, we applied what we teach and aligned every cell in our body with what we wanted to happen. We continued making changes inside of ourselves until the voices went away and were replaced with a sense of belonging and desire to serve.

And our experience certainly has paid off.

Tyler describes some of the amazing experiences he's had . . .

It has now been almost a year since being in the Inner Circle, and since joining, I have had several of my dreams turn into a reality.

One dream of mine was to be able to work with the most influential leaders in the world. I believe that if the leaders of the world can use the power of alignment and get into full connection with every part of their being, the already massive influence they have will make an even bigger and more profound impact on their own families and millions of lives for good. I believe a ripple effect of transformation will happen.

Ever since I developed the Cellular Abundance Alignment Technique, which I describe as "the fastest duplicatable system for lasting personal change," I've wanted to share it with Russell Brunson. At the very first Inner Circle meeting, I was able to give him a small sample, and then revisit it again with him several times.

I've been able to help so many leaders in the Inner Circle drop unwanted limitations, habits, and fears in minutes by shifting their cellular memory.

I was personally invited to spend time with the Category Kings, Russell's top-level mastermind, and got the opportunity to speak to and help transform their lives.

Another highlight of mine was having a room of a bunch of Inner Circle members all aligning to hit their next $10 million as fast as possible. I heard back from a number of them afterward as they shared their incredible results, such as being tuned to their true passion or landing an unexpected $125,000 deal within hours of my session with them.

I am a believer that the only reason we don't get a goal is if some part of us is allergic to the idea and addicted to what is normal or familiar.

So I continued to work on myself, and the opportunities continued to flow my way to serve in bigger capacities.

Our bodies and minds are capable of sooooo much more than we think.

Now my goal is to continue to serve and spread the message of transformation to all who are ready and hungry for change.

I absolutely love seeing people change as quickly as possible and not allowing anything to stop them.

As you read this, I want you to ask yourself this question: "How would I show up if I was in the Inner Circle?" Start being and doing what comes as the answer, and move through any resistance. You were born to be here. See you soon,

Emily and Tyler Watson

DANY THERRIEN

I Already Lost, So That's Why I WIN

After seeing Russell's 10X presentation at 10X Growth Con 2018 and seeing what closing 3M in 90 minutes looks like, Dany went back home a changed man with only one desire: Master the art of One-To-Many. I instantly bought Russell's book Expert Secrets and got to work, writing my first webinar in 9 days.

Having achieved so much success in many markets Dany barned a Two-Comma-Club Award and now is called The Webinar Whisperer among elite marketers. Dany is ready to share his story with you in hopes to inspire and motivate you to bet on yourself at every time, no matter what.

How I wrote this story:

I wanted to share with you the story of how a French guy with nothing but ambitions made it to the 2CC and the Inner Circle, but most importantly, I want to share with you the most important principles I've learned along the way.

I've divided this chapter into five phases, each one representing the biggest shifts in my career, and I also wanted to give away the top three lessons I've learned during each phase.

As I've heard Stephen Larsen hammer since 2019, in order to go faster, you must "learn just in time."

I strongly believe that the best thing you can do in order to grow your life faster is to realize that no matter where you are right now, you are one "aha" away from a completely different life.

And since I'm the most normal human on planet earth, I'm pretty sure a lot of people might recognize themselves in one of those phases, so it's an honor for me to share my journey in hopes of helping you level up yours.

I hope you like you reading it just as much as I loved writing it!

Phase 1: The Fall

"That's it. It's over for me, man," I told my sales manager at the time.

That was in 2016.

I had just gone ALL IN.

Over the last year, I had saved $10K and was ready to launch my business. Like many others, I've always dreamed of owning my own business, but really, had no clue which product or service I wanted to sell.

I was ready to fly on my own, and I wanted to sell my expertise: selling.

I was a top salesperson in the automotive Industry, and I wanted to teach others how to sell . . .

As I was in the car industry, I was used to having walk-ins coming by without me having to prospect.

So I approached the business game the same way:

"What can I do in order to generate leads?"

So I did what is taught . . .

Invested six weeks into building a website on wix.com . . . I suck at tech, so that's why it took me this long . . .

Then I invested some money for a professional video shoot with a perfectly tailored custom suit, as I thought it was really important.

I also invested time and money to get a perfect logo, with the right color, tone, and expression . . . (What does this mean? I don't even know now, lol, but I thought it was important, so here we go . . .)

And you know what?

Over the course of the next six months, I sold zero of my sales-training service!

0!!!!

AS A SALES TRAINER!

Because I didn't know how to generate leads effectively, I had nobody to sell to, and let's be honest, cold prospecting nowadays just sucks bad.

So again, I went from taking a year to saving $10K just to be $20K in debt six months later because I didn't want anybody to know that I would have to lower my lifestyle or anything . . .

I'm an entrepreneur. Everybody needs to know I win big, right? (See **BIG** irony here.)

And I had to go back to the same exact dealership I used to work and ask for a job . . .

There are just absolutely no words in the world that can describe the pain you feel in your chest and how heavy your legs are when you are about to open the door of the dealership you left . . .

In order to ask for a job . . .

Because you failed . . .

Knowing they told you it would happen . . .

—- Top 3 Principles I learned from failing HARD:

1. Don't just ask if you are good at something; ask if you are good at selling it.

2. No matter how hard you fall, it's 100 percent about what you learn from it. **Losing is only losing if you quit.** It's not because a business goes bad that your entrepreneurial journey is done. Those are two completely different things. Every journey is preparing you for the next one.

3. NEVER start a business with a black belt mentality. I've learned over time that a white belt mentality is the way to go. You want to

approach every day with a "What can I learn?" or "How can I get better?" mentality.

GO SEEK FOR HELP. YOU WON'T DO IT ALONE !

Phase 2: When the Universe sends help, say YES

I was lucky they gave me back my job.

Deep inside, I was destroyed. It never felt so hard to wake up in the morning.

Going to work at a dealership I hated, to a job I hated, with a schedule I hated, was making me hate my life.

One day, as I was scrolling Facebook, I came across an ad from Lewis Howes that said:

"If you want to be a millionaire, learn sales **AND MARKETING**.

(Since I'm a French Canadian, we almost NEVER get targeted by English marketing ads, and back then it was literally zero targeting toward us.)

So I clicked the ads and was sold.

"I need to learn marketing, NOW."

As I had already spent years acquiring real sales skills, I knew how to learn a skill at a deep level.

So I invested time, energy, and money and immersed myself in marketing.

That's where I found out about **Russell Brunson**.

I bought a ClickFunnels account and started understanding funnels.

I also joined his Facebook group, ClickFunnels, at a time when he had forty thousand members.

And I asked for help.

Alex convinced me he would help me generate leads fast without any cost for my business, so I said yes immediately.

"If it works, I'll have the life I want. If it doesn't, I'll be $2K short. Seems like a no-brainer to me," I told him.

He laughed.

The only problem was that I just went back to the $0 mark, which meant I paid my $20K debt but had absolutely nothing left.

So I went to ask for loans.

Yes, $1,500 loans; that's how broke I was, but also how determined I was.

"I'm sorry, Mr. Therrien, there's no way we can lend to you," said two bankers.

The third one, from TD bank, said yes. They got me the money in my bank account, and I paid Alex.

Then I started the coaching: a four-week program, one hour weekly, one-on-one training for four weeks in a row.

At the beginning of the first week, I can remember how he told me that we had a four-week program, telling me that after the third week, I could start trying to sell my offer.

I didn't have time for that.

After our first session, without knowing what I would do, my niche or anything . . . I started hustling and creating connections.

No time to lose.

Then, by the end of the third week, even if we hadn't finished the program, I left my job again and started using the skills I learned from my new guide to sell like crazy.

I left my job around 11:00 a.m.

I got my first customer (Catherine) at around 2:00 p.m.

The second one, Dimitri, at 4:00 p.m.

My first day of business (with a MENTOR), I did more than on a typical day at my job . . .

And more than I did the past six months of business with no help.

And then it just kept on booming since then.

And this year, for the first time in my life, I made over $100K.

I was hustling like I'd never seen anyone in my life.

I remember sitting in traffic morning and evening and inviting three hundred to five hundred people on LinkedIn.

I would be back home at night with hundreds of new connections that I could not wait to start talking to.

For the first time in my life, I was playing "entrepreneur."

Created my offer, sold it. Rinse and repeat.

(BTW, I called it an offer back then, but it was more of a 100 percent custom on every customer that was absolutely zero percent scalable.)

But who cares? In my mind, I was on top of the world, right?

What a feeling it was!

I was on top of the world!

Ready to rock and roll every challenge that would come my way.

——**Top 2** principles from failing hard to having the most successful year in my entire life:

1. Find a guide and go ALL IN! . . . <u>EVEN WHEN YOU THINK IT WON'T WORK FOR YOU, YOUR MARKET, YOUR COUNTRY, YOUR CULTURE, OR ANY OTHER EXCUSES!</u>

2. Don't be paralyzed by the fear of failing. FEAR HARD, being at the same place one year from now.

80 percent of people are motivated by avoiding pain, and I'm one of them. The motivation of NEVER FAILING AGAIN IN MY DAMN FREAKING LIFE was a hundred thousand times more powerful and drove me way harder than the motivation of achieving $10K months like I wanted to with my first online business.

Phase 3: The Expansion

It was 2018 and life was awesome.

For the first time in my life, I had money to go to a restaurant anytime I wanted, buy great clothes, and have a nice apartment.

Back then, I was a big fan of Grant Cardone, and I'm still one!

I had read his book, *The 10X Rule* a week prior to quitting my job.

(I remember being in the car lot one day, walking around SUVs in the back of the lot, listening to the *10X* audiobook and just being so primed, it was like I was about to explode. This book changed my life, BTW, big recommendation!)

I was sitting on my couch with my laptop on my thighs when I saw an ad of Grant where he was selling tickets for his 10X Growth Con 2018.

Believe it or not, it was $97.

I had never traveled out of Quebec, not even once in my life. I thought it was a sign!

So I bought my ticket, bought my plane ticket, and scheduled my hotel trip in less than thirty minutes.

Air Canada, Luxor Tower, and 10X Growth Con—what else could you ask for, right?

When I arrived in Vegas, I was sitting in the Uber, and I remember seeing palm trees for the first time in my life. At the time, I was so grateful I cried. The Uber driver had to ask me if everything was okay.

(She told me it was her first time seeing someone crying of happiness in her whole life, ha ha.)

I remember how everything was SOOO big and impressive. It made me see a part of the world I hadn't seen with my own eyes before.

Since my goal by going to the event was to learn about sales and mindset, half the job was done.

It got me thinking big.

It got me dreaming like a kid again.

And there comes the conference.

Grant Cardone, Ed Mylett, Andy Frisella, Brad Lea, Tim Grover, Tai Lopez . . .

"Do More, Get Better . . ."

"I own this . . ."

All those perfect sentences from perfect keynotes from perfect speakers. They are life changing for real. They have an impact.

They are powerful.

My brain was about to explode with ambitions, energy, and drive for the future.

And here comes the master himself, Russell Brunson.

I remember seeing him arrive on stage and being a totally different experience from the others. He was the first one to make you feel like a friend from the very first second.

Something about him was really magnetic.

He delivered his ninety-minute presentation, which was basically a perfect webinar, and closed a $3K program at the end of the presentation . . .

And believe it or not, he sold three million in only ninety minutes!!!

It was CRAZY!

We were at MGM Grand Arena in Las Vegas. The arena was oval shaped.

At each one of the four "corners" were stands where you could buy the products that the speakers pitched.

Since I've already bought a couple before (Yes, I know, I am a hyperactive buyer ha ha, but I strongly believe that success requires naivety), I could compare the line.

The lines were literally fifteen time what any other speakers had done.

The arena was filled up with four lines of buyers, including me. The line from the first stand was 100 percent filled until the second stand. The second stand line was filled to the third stand, and this continued until the arena was completely filled with buyers.

I knew I'd just participated in something amazing.

For the first time in my life, I could see what closing millions of dollars at once looked like.

It expanded my mind. For the first time in my life, I'd seen that it was possible.

This presentation made me dream of selling my own product to the masses, so one day, I could make some million-dollar days too!

But the only problem was I had no idea where to begin.

At the time I did not even know this was called a webinar, so I didn't even know what to look for.

All I knew was that one day I would be the best at doing this.

This was my introduction to Russell's world and the Funnel Hacker community.

And this introduction made me want to dive deep into this universe!

Although I planned to learn about sales presentations to sell to the masses, coming back home, I did what I did best and what 10X also makes you want to:

Over the next year, I bought the books, bought Russell's program, and dove deep into the funnel world.

In 2019, I went to my first Funnel Hacking Live in Nashville. It was awesome.

I'm a BIG country music fan, and for me to go there to learn my favorite subject from the best in the world at this game in a legendary country was a no-brainer.

At the event, he had this part where he taught us about the perfect webinar script and gave us a clear framework on how to create the stories, how to create the secrets, and how to stack your offer.

I was so happy that for the first time ever, it clicked. I felt like I understood how to create a webinar, but the only problem was I had never created any.

And to be honest, theory-wise, it looked easy to do. Basically, you get their attention, make them connect with you, and sell them on the new opportunity, why they can and why nothing in the world can stop them.

I understood the concept but didn't know where to begin.

But who cares? I wanted to make it happen, so I knew I'd do it for sure.

Coming back home, I wrote on messenger to my mentor, Alex Schlinsky, asking if his webinar followed the perfect webinar script, and he said, "Yes." I asked if I could use his webinar as a template for mine, and he said, "As long as you don't copy, it's perfectly fine."

So I started going slide by slide.

If his slide #2 was "The Goal," my slide #2 was "The Goal."

If at slide 120 he had two testimonials, guess what I had at slide 120?

Bingo! Two testimonials!

The offer I sold was about prospecting and selling B2B services with LinkedIn Automation (which had 100X fewer rules back then).

By using this strategy I call *webinar hacking*, believe it or not, my first webinar was ready, as you can see in the picture above, in only nine days, which is crazy considering most people take years to create their first one once they make the decision that they need one and will have one.

At that time, I had a very, very small list which consisted of my Facebook profile friends (about 1,000-1,100 people.) This is what I used to launch the webinar along with $500 of ads.

The day of the webinar came, and it was a crazy day for me. I was so impatient to do it, it's hard to explain. I felt like a kid on Christmas Eve wanting to get out of bed to open his gifts in advance.

My heart was beating so hard that day, almost all day long, just because of how much I anticipated it!

The webinar started at 11:00. It was 10:45, and I was sweating badly. Like really, really badly. The stress had gotten the best of me: 1-0 anxiety.

I live in Canada, and it was a pretty cool day outside. The webinar was coming fast, so I jogged all around the apartment to open every window and the patio door.

I was almost completely undressed, having taken everything off but my underwear. I thought I was having a panic attack.

You can bet there was no camera turned on at this webinar, ha ha.

10:55 came, and I started the webinar.

As a trained salesman, I was able to keep composure even with all this stress, and I delivered one hell of a presentation, with all the energy in the world.

I had my 2017 MacBook air in my hands and was walking back and forth between the kitchen and the living room, still sweating like crazy, while talking and delivering the webinar.

In the end, I remember I didn't want to look at sales.

I was so stressed that it failed, I thought.

After all, why would anybody buy something from me? I'm a nobody trying to sell a skill they can learn on their own on YouTube . . .

Since I had sweated so much, I decided to go eat an ice cream nearby.

I went with no phone, and I took time to breathe and relax.

I took time to think. I accepted the worst-case scenario (a habit I love to do before a big decision or after a big event.)

Everything was good, and life was still going pretty great. Even if I failed, I'd still eat next week. I'm pretty lucky when you look at it from that perspective.

I can try new things, fail at them, and fall asleep in warmth with my belly filled with whatever I want.

So I came back home sprinting. At that moment, I now REALLY wanted to know how much I had sold.

And I had sold 52 x $497 programs for a total of $25,844!!!

Never in my life had I had a $10K day . . .

Now I just had a $25K day!!!

And the best part?

Since I'd only invested $500, it gave me an INSANE ROI of 5,168.80 percent!

At that time, I was reading investment books teaching me how to double money in seven years.

And I'd just multiplied my money by fifty in ten days.

Life was good.

I remember my wife and I lay in our basement bed. (We have a bed in the basement so we can look at the TV while lying down, ha ha.)

And we were filled with joy, filled with vision, and filled with confidence.

I do not fear the man who practiced ten thousand kicks one time. I fear the man who practiced one kick ten thousand times.
—Bruce Lee

At that time, I still had an agency, and that was my main cash cow.

But I wanted to practice with webinars so much that I did not become good, I became legendary.

I really wanted to become the best at that, since it was a business model that clicked so much with who I was, and the benefits of it were clear as crystal water to me.

So my first webinar customer was Jacques Dionne, a guy I worked with in the real estate investment niche.

We created his first webinar, promoted it on his social media, and did a launch with his $15K people email list.

We created an offer to help real estate investors expand fast via buying houses of people about to lose them and renting them to them for three to five years.

On the first webinar, we sold $168K.

But do you know what is ten times better than selling $168K?

Doing it without even starting the slides

The presenter never realized he did not have his slides turned on and delivered his presentation on a white screen, without looking at the commentaries.

He just did his thing, and it was such a good presentation. (He was very good as an attractive character.) He sold $168K with no slides!!!

My second customer was Jacob Hamel, a coach for online bodybuilding training, who wanted to sell his knowledge to help bodybuilding coaches get better at their craft.

Over the first month, we sold $100K, with absolutely zero ads at all, only promoting on social media.

Our third customer was Jocelyn Grégoire, another real estate investor, with whom we launched a 100 percent online program to help employees with no money who wanted to start investing in real estate via private loaning.

Over four webinars, we sold $116K with less than $10K in ads.

I was hooked.

Webinar was THE THING.

It's the ONE THING that was about to change my life forever.

And I was willing to do whatever it took in order to make it work!

—**Top 3** principles from scaling from $100K to $1M year:

1. Find a TACTIC and go ALL IN ! . . . You must find ONE WAY to make good money and stay FAR AWAY from the shiny object syndrome.

2. Thinking you can do it all alone is just plain stupid. I was stupid. When we scaled from me alone to me and my partner, we 10X'd what we could do.

3. **Move fast.** I wanted to do webinars, and the reason I became good at them is because I sold four at a time, before even knowing how good I really was. See it as practice, and make people pay you to practice.

Phase 4: The Partnerships

My girlfriend and I were at a spa in Quebec City because we were looking for ways to increase our cash flow without always being dependent on the next agency sales.

Since I had such results with webinars, I was looking for a way to multiply my impact and create multiple streams of income.

While looking at the river in an almost meditative state, it clicked.

"I will create everything from scratch for a customer, generate traffic for him, and teach him how to sell, and we will partner 50/50 with experts."

My heart was pounding like never before.

This is it.

I knew I could make this work bad.

I just had to find someone who wanted to partner up with me and split his business in half in order to make ten time more money than he ever made.

In late 2019, I had a public speaking engagement in front of five hundred people, in which I delivered a presentation on how to become liked online.

Since it was not an infopreneur conference, I didn't want to do a presentation on webinars. I was thinking I didn't have the skills to make it work for every business.

So I decided to teach the entrepreneurs in the room how to become great attractive characters and how to sell via social media.

Not long after the seminar, a guy who was selling cars at the time came to me and told me how great of an attractive character he would be, already generating hundreds of thousands of views but having absolutely no idea how he could monetize his knowledge.

So we started creating a strategy to help young adults create indestructible self-confidence so they can act on their dreams, without having to fear failure or the judgment of others.

At the time, I remember really wanting to sell the 50/50, but also wanted it to look like a savior instead of a big decision, so knowing really well he still had a $70K-a-year job, I said:

"It's your choice now. Either it's $100K or we create it and split everything 50/50."

And we decided to go 50/50.

Which was an awesome decision.

Over the next six months, we did half a million dollar in sales with $99K in ad spend, and he was able to leave his job, make more money than he ever did before. He is now the #1 French worldwide expert on personal development and self-confidence development.

He went from a car salesman to a superstar that speaks at the biggest French events in the world, is always interviewed on TV, and makes high six figures per month.

Starting with a webinar.

Life was so good, I decided to replicate the process again.

After all, why not? It is so easy to manage once everything is already settled.

At the time, I had a friend with whom I did MMA when we were younger coming over to eat after nearly three years without seeing each other. He was also going to introduce me to his new girlfriend, who, at the time, was pregnant.

So as we were talking, she told me about how she is already working online as a naturopath and has a filled calendar, but absolutely no more time left because she's exchanging her time and presence for money.

I talked to her about what we did with the personal development expert and how I'm sure it would be possible to do the same with her, and she immediately accepted the conditions.

I was stoked.

Weight loss for women already was the next niche I wanted to attack with a 50/50 webinar, and here was my chance, coming out of nowhere.

So I went all in.

We did $22K in sales our first week together with less than $2,000 in ads and a couple stories.

I was so happy.

So we continued to scale it to the best of our ability, and it was profitable.

In these times, my ex-partner and I decided to expand.

We hired a funnel builder that was awesome at funnel design, and we hired a "geek machine" that knew how to do almost everything and that was AWESOME at finding solutions to every problem. They were and still are awesome people.

I sucked BAD at creating funnels and webinars that looked great.

Everything I did up to that time was really ugly, but it sold because of the sales psychology I always relied on in order to sell anything to anybody, in any format.

I also suck at tech. I'm a salesperson, right? I'm not good with computers.

Every little problem we had took me an hour to correct.

For the new geek machine of the team, it took him minutes.

So it was a BIG relief to know that our weak links, design and tech, were now taken on by real professionals.

In the meantime, the self-confidence expert with whom we sold a half a million dollars referred me to one of his friends, who is a TV star here in Quebec.

He was called "Le Naturopathe des Stars" which means "The Naturopath of the Stars" in the sense that he helps people that are big names get in shape.

The team and I continued to work hard on our systems, knowing that the beginning of the year is always a great moment for the weight loss industry.

Over the course of the next few months we prepared, and we launched our new 50/50 partner in November 2020.

So we were now with three experts, two of those in the weight loss industry, which is wildly profitable.

Then came January 2020 for Funnel Hacking Live.

As usual, the event was so awesome, so impressive.

The networking is really great, and I was enjoying being around some awesome people in an awesome community.

But one thing that we did after Tony Robbins's speech was awesome.

We had to fill a paper sheet with our goals and dreams that we had to accomplish before the next Funnel Hacking Live.

I remember, I wrote that next year, we would be on stage claiming our first 2CC award with the team.

It was something the team and I were willing to pursue hard.

And we were ready to do anything in order to make it happen.

We came back and did so many adjustments to the webinar funnels we already had.

We went all in and implemented all of our skill set to make it work.

And over the course of Q1 2020, we sold $1.5M.

We were so happy!

I remember my girlfriend and I going to eat for breakfast on Sunday morning (all of our webinars were Sunday 10:00 a.m.).

We would arrive around 10:30, and our lunch would arrive around 11:00 a.m.

The close of our webinars starting at 10:00 a.m. were all around 11:00 a.m.

So when we received our plates, our stripe accounts just went "ding ding ding ding'" non-freaking-stop for ten to fifteen minutes. We were in the low ticket space, selling $200–$300 products, so to sell over $150-160K a week, we sold a LOT of programs.

I remember I was always saying the same joke to my girlfriend that I never got tired of :

"Let's say we have $50K profit left after every expense, employee and 50/50 share, and our lunch costs $100 with tips; it still leaves us with $49,900 profit. It leaves us enough money for the mortgage. We're good."

We were so happy, I remember wanting to cry with joy multiple times during these moments.

I was filled with gratitude.

The dream I had when I went to 10X Growth Con 2018 was finally starting to take shape.

I was able to sell to the masses, without even having to be present, changing thousands of lives per year in the process. (In this case, by helping people achieve better health, a healthy weight, better self-confidence, and unconditional self-love.)

—**Top 3** principles going from nobody to making $50K–$75K profit weekly:

1. If possible in your market, become REALLY GOOD at what you do and then take a percentage of the sales.

2. People are willing to pay you an insane amount of money as long as they make an insane amount of money in return.

3. Have a clear goal in mind and share it with your team. Make it a must. Build KPIs, make monthly teams, repeat again and again, cast and reinforce your vision often if you want people to get in your boat.

Phase 5: The Inner Circle Door Opening

In March of 2021, we achieved it: our first 2CC award.

Ten months after the launch of our first weight loss product, we achieved our first million dollars in sales with a 50/50 partner, and we did it in a very profitable way.

I remember I was shopping for new skates for our nephew's birthday gift at Canadian Tires, and while I was waiting for him to select the candies he wanted to bring home, I received a notification, checked, and it was the 2CC approval email!

I jumped in front of everybody, I was so happy!

I immediately called my girlfriend and said, *WE DID IT*!

We were so happy, and everything was going so well!

We continued to develop our skills and systems, trying to scale our partners to the best of our abilities, all until September.

September 2021, here came Funnel Hacking Live.

It was a CRAZY cool experience!

You've probably read about it already in the book so far, but here I arrived in Orlando, and we were invited to a private dinner for the 2CCX mentees, IC members, and 2CC winners.

The dinner was awesome, the food was unbelievable, and the ambiance was perfect.

After eating, we had a surprise waiting for us.

Some bus would take us somewhere, but we didn't know where.

In fact, Russell rented the Harry Potter Universal studio for us alone, the Funnel Hacker Community.

It was a magical night; everything was so finely tuned.

"Russell is really the man. What he puts in place with his businesses for everyday people who became Funnel Hackers because of him is just amazing," I thought. "If only I could find a way to get closer to him and help him and his community, it would be awesome."

And here came the dinner for all the 2CC winners.

Again, it was magical.

The food was floating in the air on platters that were turning around nonstop.

And Russell did his pitch, a five-minute pitch on how he built a new library.

To be honest, that was almost it, and if we wanted to get closer to him and be part of a wonderful community, it would be $50K USD ($75K for us poor Canadians ha ha).

I hesitated.

A lot.

$75K CAD sounded like a lot of money, but here came Sarah Petty and Erin Lagemann, and we talked about my hesitations.

They were so nice . . . You know those kinds of people you see and you know will be friendly from a mile away, and as they approach, they look so optimistic that it can only make you feel trust and happiness.

We talked for five to ten minutes, and only with them talking to me about how awesome the community was, how much it was a great decision for them, and how it was a NO-BRAINER for them to sign again every year, I was sold.

A month later, the first Inner Circle meeting was in Boise, Idaho, at the knitting factory.

It was so awesome. Everybody was so crazy cool and likable.

I remember how everyone was smiling and how I've never felt surrounded by that quantity of quality people in the same place.

I knew I was in for a treat and that joining the IC was the right decision to make.

Over the next ten months (we are in August 2022 as I write this), everything shifted for the better.

I became a better man, thanks to the IC community.

I became a better entrepreneur, thanks to the IC community.

I became a better marketer, thanks to the IC community.

I became a better visionary, thanks to the IC community.

I found a business partner who was exactly what I needed.

We launched The Webinar Guys, a company that can scale multiple webinars at a time with great profitability for our customers and great profitability for ourselves.

We are having ten times year, on target to finish the year with 400 percent better monthly revenue than that same date last year.

To be completely honest, it just helped me level up in every aspect of my life and business in every possible way.

There's just no way you can make this progress in a year without an environment like this (at least for me).

The Beginning of the End

Right now, this chapter is about to end, but I sincerely hope that this chapter will also inspire you to create a new chapter in your life.

And I want to end this with a little bit of my personal philosophy, something I've never seen, heard or read about before, and it's about to hit hard.

What's the biggest bottleneck to success?

The little voice, right?

The little voice that is about to tell you that it might fail . . .

That it's probably too good to be true . . .

That only happens for the "selected few" . . .

It might sound rough, but if there's one thing that I want you to remember from this chapter:

You already lost, and THAT should be your biggest ally to conquer fear and also your biggest motivator in taking action to achieve the final outcome.

Let's picture me five years ago. I was losing. Losing bad.

I already did not have that business.

I already didn't have the 2CC award.

I was already not part of any high-level community.

I already did not have a team.

I. HAD. NOTHING.

All that could happen to me, even if it went ALL WRONG, was still:

-Having no business

-Never achieving 2CC

-Not being part of any community

-Being solo and working my ass off

I WAS ALREADY THERE!

So what did I have to lose?

Time?

It's going to pass by anyway, so aren't we better off trying to achieve something awesome with it?

Energy?

I'll go to sleep, and it'll recharge. If I'm VERYYYY tired, I'll take a week off.

Money?

I would probably have spent it otherwise anyway, as I have a hard time being disciplined with building my financial freedom month after month.

I already had NO SUCCESS.

So the WORST-CASE SCENARIO was staying there.

I can pretty much handle that, right?

NOW!

What is there to win?

What would be the best possible scenario?

What if you gave it your ALL and you tried for enough time?

What if you took action on your dreams instead of procrastinating?

What if it's a homerun success and it sets you and your family up for life?

You see how empowering it is?

Knowing that you CAN'T LOSE and all you can do is WIN, no matter how small that win might be?

Because even a 1 percent better life is 1 percent compared to what you already have now.

And nobody ever lost anything (other than money) trying to launch a business.

And the way Funnel Hackers launch businesses requires zero to almost zero money down.

So go get that 1 percent today. Get it tomorrow.

Because the person you are now doesn't have the things you want in the future.

Stay the same and you lose.

Get 1 percent closer every day, and you'll reach your goals.

I hope I inspired you to take action and take absolute ownership of where you are now and the destination of your life.

Thanks for reading about my story,

Dany

ERIK SORENSON

Unleashing Your Inner Fire: The Entrepreneurs Guide To Empowerment

Entrepreneur, podcaster, author, public speaker, and marketer, Erik is an eighteen-year ad agency owner starting his first agency with no money and no experience. He then grew it to an eight-figure business working with Fortune 500 and 1,000 companies, including Walt Disney, TDS Telecom, Gold's Gym, the FBI, the US Air Force, USA Communications, Zion National Park, Bryce Canyon, and Moab, to name a few. Since then, he has created nine companies, including three 8-figure businesses.

Erik sold his ad agency in 2017 and created a strategic growth company including, marketing, automation, and professional development. He then launched a transformational leadership and coaching program speaking to thousands of business leaders across the country to help them extract their potential, accelerate achievement, and RISE to their potential.

In August of 2022, Erik's latest effort made the Inc. 5000 list of fastest growing companies in America, and Erik was announced as a top 3 finalist of the Bootstrapped Entrepreneur of the Year for 2022 to be announced September in Orlando, Florida.

Erik has ten children and is a serial entrepreneur, a marathon runner, an Ironman triathlete, and an instrument-rated pilot.

Ignite Your Fire Podcast: https://anchor.fm/erik-sorenson

Website: ErikSorenson.com

—

My story isn't the typical story that you hear on stage at Funnel Hacking Live. No, I didn't go bankrupt, I was never homeless, I wasn't on my last dime, I never had problems with drugs or alcohol, and my parents weren't abusive. I loved every one of those comeback stories I heard on stage, but I didn't have one. In many respects, I envied those who had experienced major events during their life that resulted in inflection points that led them to become great!

Ultimately, I always feared that because I didn't have some major traumatic event occur in my life that pushed me to rock bottom, I wouldn't have a compelling enough *why* to push me to the significant heights that I wanted to reach in business. It wasn't until three years ago—after enjoying a successful fifteen-year career in the ad agency space—that everything changed.

Be careful what you wish for.

During my first fifteen years in business, I managed a successful ad agency working with high-profile clients across the country. This entailed running a variety of campaigns ranging from traditional marketing and digital marketing to social media. The truth is, I didn't have many talents and abilities like countless others, but I did have one thing going for me: I was a hustler. In fact, I could hustle and provide more value than anyone else was willing to provide at the time because I was hungry. Coupled with the reality that I was laser focused on getting my client's results, this led to significant long-term growth.

As a small ad agency, we were going up against much larger ad agencies to win contracts with clients. Thus, we recognized that we had to provide more than any other agency was willing to in hopes that this would overshadow our lack of experience and high-profile case studies. It worked. I developed this little agency from $0 to over $50 million in revenue over just several years. It was an awesome run that ended when I was approached by a buyer interested in purchasing the agency. In essence, there were some challenges and shifts occurring in my life at the time that led me to finally agree to the sale when I probably otherwise wouldn't have.

I also viewed this as my opportunity to reap some rewards that I had spent years of time, blood, sweat, and tears to build. In my view, selling was the pinnacle of a successful career as an entrepreneur.

So many entrepreneurs tie their identities to the success or failure of their businesses. If the business fails, you are a failure. If the business succeeds, you are a success. The truth is, I felt the same way. I now see how misplaced that belief was; however, at the time, the business was me and I was the business. It was my identity.

The sale went through, and I had more money in the bank than ever before. This was the moment when I conceivably should have been dancing in the streets, smiling from ear to ear, buying the fancy car, living large, and sailing off into the sunset. It was awesome—that is, for about eight days.

I've spoken with many entrepreneurs who built up and sold their businesses, only to find that although it seemed nice to have that much money, the excitement of it all only lasted several days or weeks at most. This was the case for me. The money was there, but a feeling of emptiness was as well. I didn't realize it at that time, but when I sold the business, I sold my identity.

From one day to the next, I had no job or purpose. I had no employees or clients. Something that I loved and cherished was gone, and I didn't have any business success to look forward to in the future. In a matter of a few short weeks, I went downhill; my life turned for the worse during what should have been a moment of celebration. For me, the opposite was true. Thus, I began spinning my wheels trying to figure out what to do. Should I start another ad agency? Should I look at a different industry? Should I launch a new product? Should I create something I've never created before? It was almost as if I was back in college starting all over again.

On the one hand, my life was just beginning. On the other hand, I had no idea what to do. Things did not improve. Several opportunities soon came knocking, and I ended up starting a small agency with some partners, which ended up being a very bad decision. The partners with whom I had gotten involved did not have the same value, vision, and goals that I personally had in my life, and it was a struggle that set me back two-and-a-half years. Throughout my entire life, I had been a very positive and optimistic person, so it was strange to find myself heading to a dark place. Notably, everyone who knew me was aware of this optimism and noted that it was one of my greatest strengths. However, that strength quickly turned into a weakness. When you know that you were born for more, and you're not living up to it—or if you feel like you've lost your purpose—then it is easy to slip away into the darkness.

Months later, Garrett J. White taught me that darkness is divine. It's easy to believe that when life is good, but at the time, I didn't see anything divine about the darkness. I just knew that I was lost. After all, I had no direction or purpose, and I had lost all of my momentum.

I learned a lot about momentum years earlier as a marathon and Ironman competitor. It was extremely difficult and time-consuming to train for such events, but much easier to maintain the momentum once you were in peak racing condition. Accordingly, I learned to register for the next race *before* finishing the current race to avoid easing up after race day and losing momentum.

Unfortunately, when I sold the business, I hadn't considered this strategy, and the momentum ultimately faded away.

It was during this period of struggle when a friend asked me a simple question. It was a question that I had heard on many occasions, but which, for some reason, hit me with a tremendous amount of force. It was a question that changed everything for me.

"Erik, what do you want?"

Although this may sound like a really simple question, I had spent my life serving clients and creating campaigns trying to help their businesses grow, while always putting myself and my wants second. After being asked this question, I had no answer; I had no idea what I wanted, nor did I know why I was spiraling. I had to think long and hard about what I actually wanted.

The simple answer to this question was easy. We want to be happy, have a good family, be healthy, make money and earn a good living, be physically fit, and have a good relationship with our spouse and children. The deeper and more specific answer to the question is much harder to answer. The truth is, most people don't know what they truly want, and I was no different.

When asked this question, I was not thinking about anybody but myself. I wasn't serving anyone; instead, I was grasping at anything to help me regain momentum and purpose. I also started experiencing difficulties in my family and other relationships. Two of our children totaled two of our cars, we had several emergencies hit our families, and my relationships were deteriorating. It seemed like all hell was breaking loose in my life, and I was totally disappointed with myself and where I was in life.

I wish that I had known at the time that disappointments are a gift. They are telling you something critically important: that your current life conditions aren't matching who you are and the potential that you have, and that you aren't living up to and *rising* to your calling and who you were born to be. That gap beautifully creates an opportunity to choose to let it either destroy you or define you. It's a gift that can allow you to turn disappointment into fuel by saying, "I've had enough." Moreover, it's an opportunity to draw a line in the sand, say "no more," and use that fuel to turn a spark into an unquenchable fire.

Granted, I didn't know this at the time, for I was too caught up in my limitations and my head. It was at that difficult point that I read a quote that forever changed my life. I'm not certain who wrote the quote or where it came from, but the quote states, "The scariest day of your life is the day you die, when the person you are meets the person you could have become." That quote freaked me out and woke me up because I was not anywhere near the person that I knew I could become, and yet I had felt that I was called to do something great.

Mark Twain once stated, "The two greatest days of your life are the day you were born and the day you find out why." I knew that I was born to be more and make a bigger impact in the world.

Russell Brunson often talks about the fact that business is a calling and that you are called to serve people as an entrepreneur. That was the case with me. I felt as though I was being called to take my life and business in a very different direction. I felt pulled more than any other time in my life to become involved in an effort to make an impact in the world.

I falsely believed that I did not have the skills or abilities that would be required for me to rise up to my calling. Thus, just as most do when they are called, I refused to rise. The more I would refuse, the harder life became. After all, who am I? Who am I to do this great thing? Who am I to raise my voice and change another life? Who am I to impact the lives of hundreds if not thousands of people like some of the greats? Who am I?

If you find yourself asking these same questions, ask yourself, "Who am I not to? If not me, then who? If not now, then when?" There are no two people who are exactly the same. You have talents, skills, abilities, and gifts that no one else on earth has. There are people uniquely fitted for you and the message that only you can offer. With billions of people on earth, there are those who you were meant to serve. What a tragedy it would be if you allowed yourself to get in your own way and lose out on future opportunities to change lives!

After I struggled with this for months, my life didn't get any better. I knew that I needed to figure out a way to get out. Fortunately, reading this quote changed my trajectory, and there was enough pain in my life that it finally moved me to do something about it. I decided that I finally needed to reach up as high as I possibly could.

Now, it's important that you know something about me. Since college, and up until this point in my life, I had only read one or two books. I hated seminars, conferences, and virtual events. I didn't like to do anything of the kind. It's not that I didn't feel like I didn't have enough knowledge; rather, I just thought that it was a waste of time. If I wasn't moving, I was going backward, and because hustle was my biggest strength, I didn't actually take the time to sharpen my skills in any way, shape, or form.

Thereafter, I immediately changed my attitude about learning, humbled myself, and started by reading a new book every week. Each book opened my eyes to something new and offered me understanding. Each book also referenced other authors whose works I then sought out. I then began to read their books and attend events. In fact, I attended seven Tony Robbins events in one year, and I signed up for every mastermind, course, inner circle program, and virtual event that came my way. I started learning from some of the greatest transformational minds in the world.

Exposure to these and many other successful people changed me over time. Reaching up began to change the way I thought and pushed me to try different things. I started to get a clearer vision of who I was and what I was meant to do. I launched a program, and it failed. I launched another, and it failed. But even with the failures, I was gaining momentum, my psychology was changing, and I was headed in the right direction. I could feel it!

It was around that time (2019) that I heard of a man named Russell Brunson and Funnel Hacking Live. I didn't know exactly what it was, but I attended my first Funnel Hacking Live in 2020. If you've ever been to Funnel Hacking Live before, you can quickly discover whether or not it's for you. For me, I knew almost immediately that this was where I needed to be because I was around other like-minded entrepreneurs who also wanted to make an impact in the world and simultaneously make an income.

That first Funnel Hacking Live in 2020 was a life-changing experience. The speakers were incredible, and I met so many incredible people in the process. As it happens every year, I sat through the award ceremony and said to myself, "I'm going to be up there next year on the stage at Funnel Hacking Live 2021 with my first Two Comma Club Award."

Because of my past experience, hitting a million dollars didn't seem difficult to me, but hitting a million dollars through one funnel seemed impossible.

I didn't know much about funnels at the time, even with all of my years of experience as an ad agency owner. Much of this information was new and eye-opening to me. Often, I reflected on how much I wished I had acquired this information years before.

What happened next? You guessed it. I was on stage receiving my first Two Comma Club Award the very next year. The following year (2022), my company was named one of the fastest-growing companies in America by *Inc.* magazine. Today we are just about to hit the eight-figure mark.

While the excitement associated with my first Two Comma Club Award was exhilarating, what happened next changed my life forever. When you earn a Two Comma Club Award, you are invited to attend a meeting with Russell Brunson to discuss being a part of his Inner Circle. At the time, Russell had closed down the Inner Circle during the previous year and had just relaunched it at Funnel Hacking Live 2021. This presented an opportunity for many entrepreneurs to join since there was no previous class renewing their membership in the program.

I attended the meeting, saw the cost, and immediately dismissed the thought of joining the program. The truth was, I had never spent that much money on any training or coaching program in my entire life. I continued to listen to the presentation and then returned to my room. As I was walking back to my room, a feeling immediately hit me and kept hitting me over and over again. I knew I needed to join. At first, I dismissed the feeling, knowing that I had never spent that much money on anything like this before, but it kept eating at me.

I called my wife and said, "Hey, do you mind if I spend $50,000 on a coaching program? I feel like I need to do this." This is when you know that you're married to a rock star. She truly is a superhero. After a brief conversation, I knew that she had complete trust in me and said, "If you feel like you need to do it, then I 100 percent support it."

At this point, I was already back in my hotel room and wasn't certain if the slots had been filled. I immediately ran back to the room to sign up, and the room was empty. I thought I had missed my chance. I then ran back into the main event room and approached the tables in the back. I asked somebody if I could still sign up for Inner Circle and was informed that I could sign up. I filled out the form and paid.

As I walked out of the room and back to my hotel room, I thought, "What in the world have I done?" Then almost immediately, a thought came into my mind. "What if I can't generate a positive ROI from this investment? What if I can't actually rise to the level of impact and income that I want to have?" The fears kept hitting me over and over again, but as I returned to my hotel, the fears immediately dissipated. Interestingly, I felt an immense amount of peace regarding my decision.

Thereafter, another thought entered my mind. "What if I *can* quickly and immediately generate a positive ROI on this investment before I even start the program?" I've heard other people discuss the fact that the transformation is in the transaction. When you make a large investment in something like this, it almost unlocks a piece of you that was already inside, changing and shifting the way that you think. It's comparable to fully committing to something and burning the boats behind you.

A shift happened within me that night, and an idea came to my mind. I then spent the next two hours creating a program that could not only help a business grow but also that would impact lives and be a life-changing experience for anyone involved. I realized that I had a speaking engagement at a live event two weeks later, and I decided to launch the program at that event.

I called Robbie Summers from ClickFunnels, who helped me change my talk to the perfect webinar format and restructure it for this new offer. His counsel was invaluable, and he helped open my eyes further regarding the potential of this program. Then, I called my team and told them about the program. For some reason, I had a crazy amount of confidence in what I had created and told my team that we would generate $250,000 in one day off of this effort.

Not only did we hit that goal, but also we exceeded it by over $150,000, totaling $406,000 in revenue, all because of an idea I had by joining Inner Circle! Interestingly, I found out several months later that my team didn't believe that we could generate this much revenue in one day for a high-ticket transformational coaching and training program. In fact, they thought I was crazy.

Of course, creating an offer is one thing, but administering what I expected to be a powerful life-changing program is another, so we went to work and spent the next month or two creating it.

Here I am, almost one year after the program launch, now able to look back on the incredible experiences we had and the lives that were changed. We are about to launch year two of the program and have a goal to generate $1M in revenue at the same event.

By this point, many of you are probably asking, "How did you get into the Two Comma Club in one year?" I wish that I could tell you that there was some super-secret magical strategy that finally fell into my lap and helped me reach $1M in funnel sales, but I can't. I want to tell you that there was a specific framework that led to success, but there wasn't. Yes, I was exposing myself to brilliant people that had marched the path I was taking and gained a lot of knowledge doing so, but it wasn't the *how* that allowed me to break through. After all, it's easy to find the *how*, just read *DotCom Secrets*, *Expert Secrets*, and *Traffic Secrets*, and you'll have all the *how* you need.

When we know that we are called to do more, the first question we usually ask is "How?" We spend 80 percent to 90 percent of our time seeking out tactics, strategies, tools, and ways to leverage it all to achieve our dream outcome. The result creates a massive gap between those who are very successful and those who constantly struggle to get there. Reading this now, you are either thriving or surviving.

Why?

There are those who are successful with webinars and those who are not, those who are crushing it with challenges and those who are not, those who fill rooms at live events and those who do not. Is the tactic the difference, or is it something else?

Tony Robbins often discusses how 80 percent of your results involve psychology (i.e., the way you think), and 20 percent involve mechanics (i.e., the strategy and tactics you use). Yet most spend 80 percent of their time figuring out how someone else did it and what mechanics were at play.

When we are not achieving our desired results, our solution tends to be more hustle involving the "how."

Dr. Shannon Irvine, another Inner Circle member, explained that you cannot outhustle your subconscious mind, in other words, the psychology that accounts for 80 percent of your results. She likened it to putting on the gas and the brakes at the same time. It doesn't work.

If you don't believe you can be the success you want to be in your subconscious mind, you'll never become it. You might believe it on the surface and hustle yourself to death only to find that you were also putting on the breaks and getting nowhere. Your subconscious mind must also believe it. In other words, you must believe it with your entire self even when you can't see any evidence around you that it's true.

It took me years to understand this, and that is when everything changed. When I finally "broke the habit of being myself," listened to my future self, and stepped into the authentic me, everything started to change. It wasn't about the *how*; it was about the *who*. Once you know who you are, the how presents itself.

You must become your true self, and the world will open up to you!

Before you try to fix your funnel a thousand times and over hustle, discover who you are and who you were meant to serve. Discover how to align yourself with your true calling in order to attract the people who you were always meant to serve. This alignment will create a confidence in you that will start to change your negative and limiting subconscious beliefs and allow you to *rise* to the level of influence, impact, and income you desire.

Discover your true authentic self and stop trying to be someone else. That job is already taken. The only job that is not taken by anyone is being you. The greatest strategy you can deploy is to know who the authentic you is and be it to anyone and everyone, all day . . . every day. You must not care about what anyone else thinks, because you know who you are, and not be afraid to share it and shout it from the rooftops.

There is something magical when you finally step into and start being your authentic self. Your identity becomes clear, your message becomes meaningful, and those you were meant to serve are attracted to you! It's not, "If you build it, they will come." It is, "If you build you, they will come."

We are only born with two fears: the fear of falling and the fear of loud noises. Every other fear and limiting belief was learned from the time you were a child until now. So whatever fears you have about being authentic, you must be destroyed so you can step into the real life that has been waiting for you.

The best parts of life and the results that you desire in your business are on the other side of fear, but until you can understand that and change the subconscious beliefs that are keeping you small, you'll keep spinning.

After over three years of struggling to understand and accept my calling, every action removed the fog of the unknown and unlocked another chapter in my journey. Each effort brought me closer and closer to the alignment and fulfillment of that calling.

The result was a clear purpose and a feeling of fulfillment and happiness, knowing that I was becoming the person that I was meant to become. What followed was a massive acceleration in my business.

First, become you. That is the secret!

Being around dozens of other successful entrepreneurs over the last year in Inner Circle has created most of the powerful insights and realizations that have exploded my results over the last year. It was the best decision I have made to date for my business and life, second only to discovering the real me. It has allowed me to level up even more and be around others that know themselves and are achieving incredible things.

Always remember that being a successful entrepreneur is not about doing. Rather, it is about *becoming*. There is no one on earth who can become who you can become. Knowing this, you cannot fail.

It is not the tool, the tactic, or the strategy that is the difference—it is *you*!

If you build you, they will come.

JUSTIN WUBBEN

How I Grew My Brick & Mortar Business 800% When The World Shut Down

Dr. Justin Wubben has been in clinical practice in Sioux Falls, South Dakota, since 2010. He was awarded the Rising Star Award by the South Dakota Chiropractors Association in his first year in practice and has been lecturing across the nation to chiropractors and at medical facilities about complex patient cases ever since. He served four years as the president of the Sioux Empire Chiropractic Society, was selected as a board member of the South Dakota Chiropractors Association, and has won multiple national awards for clinical excellence and dedication to the chiropractic profession. He is a national speaker, author of Chiropractic Business Secrets, founder of Neuropathy Healthcare and Midwest Neuropathy Institute, and currently serves as the clinic director of Axiom Chiropractic and Neuropathy.

Overcoming FEAR . . .

On December 15, 2011, I was lying on an air mattress in a hospital next to my wife. All of a sudden, a loud, repetitive beeping noise woke me up, and fifteen nurses flooded the room. "All right, Stephanie, I need you to turn over. The baby's heart rate is dropping."

Have you ever had an event in your life where you went from calm and relaxed to 100 percent on but completely out of control of the situation?

I had just graduated from chiropractic school in 2010, and it seemed like I had it all. I had just married the woman of my dreams, who was totally out of my league. I quickly launched my chiropractic practice, was awarded the Rising Star Award by my state association, and sat on the board of the Sioux Empire Chiropractic Society. I was spiritually growing more than ever after finding a church where I could be completely authentic and vulnerable without being judged for my prior failures. But when I found out my wife was pregnant with my son, I was on top of the world!

The nurse was having my wife turn, move, and flip in every possible direction, but it didn't seem to help. But the worst part was, I couldn't do anything. I'm a man . . . I'm a fixer . . . I'm a health practitioner who was completely useless. "All right, his heart rate is still dropping. We have to get the baby out right now . . . prep for C-section!" And they rolled my beautiful wife and my unborn son out of the room without me even being able to say goodbye.

I stood there shocked and numb. Someone threw me a pair of oversized blue scrubs and a hairnet and then told me to put them on. I honestly don't remember putting them on, but once I was properly dressed, I remember being led out in the hallway, outside the door, where my wife was being prepped for emergency surgery. The nurse left, and suddenly I was all alone.

I vividly remember standing there, staring down the long, empty hallway, still numb to the situation. All of a sudden, I heard one of the most powerful questions I have ever heard in my entire life . . . "If I took your wife and your son today, are we still good?" This was not an audible voice, but it might as well have been. You see, I was spiritually growing so much, and I have heard of God speaking to people, but I didn't understand what that meant. I had never heard God's voice before, but I now know it was Him.

I remember looking at the tile floor for about five seconds (it could have been five minutes), and I softly but confidently said, "Yes." I remember the nurses opening the door and leading me into my wife being draped and prepped for surgery. I was looking into her terrified eyes and holding her shaking hands that were either from the shock or the medications. I'll never forget the look on her face. As they made the incision, I had no idea what to expect. Will I lose my son? Will I lose my wife? Will I really be okay if my son or my wife are taken away from me? I had so many plans for the future. I had so many dreams and unlived memories I had not yet witnessed. I wanted to be a good father and a supportive husband, but would that all be stripped from me? As they finished their incision, they reached inside my wife's stomach and pulled out this limp, tiny blue baby. Then it happened . . . He began to cry.

Have you ever had a moment in life where you had the feeling of complete terror and yet peace at the same time? It changes you. It changes how you look at the world. It changes how you approach life. It changes how you approach business. You look at FEAR through a different lens when someone says something about you or, even worse, when you circulate self-sabotaging doubt as an ongoing conversation in your mind. In powerful moments of pain, you don't care about anything else in life, and yet when you come out of it, you soon forget the level of transformation that it had on your life.

My healthy son continued to grow, and we eventually added two more beautiful girls to our family . . . I'm back on top of the world! However, the challenges didn't go away . . . they never do.

I happened to choose a profession that often is looked down on, minimized, and even called quacks by people who honestly have no clue what the training is. People didn't seem to understand what my profession did to help people. There was not a clear guideline in chiropractic school on how to share the message of what you do to a world that was told, "Drugs and surgery are your only option." Just so everyone knows, when you exit chiropractic school with $250,000 in student loans, you get your diploma and a slap on the backside telling you to go figure it out. The unfortunate part is that 50 percent fail in the first five years.

The FEAR of Public Speaking

I used to be terrified of public speaking, to the point where talking in front of two to three people would make my heart pound. One time in chiropractic school, we were going around the class introducing ourselves, and all I had to do was say my name, where I was from, and a famous person I'd like to meet. Simple enough, right? But as the turn to speak got closer and closer, my internal panic exponentially increased. My face turned red, my voice shook, and I felt like a bumbling fool after my turn was done.

Once I graduated from chiropractic school, I soon realized that people don't just flood to your clinic just because you are a chiropractor. I had to act quickly because I didn't know what to do and I didn't want to be one of the 50 percent that failed! I joined a coaching group that talked about the importance of getting your message out to the public, and since I am very coachable, I listened. They wanted me to promote myself through something that was by far the most painful thing for me to do . . . public speaking.

After I followed a framework for a presentation, people ended up walking up to me afterward and saying that I was really good. I wasn't sure if it was just them being kind or if it was true. But the tipping point for me was a patient who told me that if I had not stepped outside of my comfort zone and done a health talk, she would have ended her life. She had been to multiple medical doctors, neurologists, and specialists and fourteen chiropractors and had not gotten any relief. After twenty years of seeking help and over $1 million spent on her health, she was continuing to get worse. But when I gave my lecture, something clicked with her. She asked me, "How come no one has ever told me this before?" even though she worked at a hospital. She followed our protocol to the *T*, and I will never forget the day when she sat up and said, "Today, Dr. Wubben, I am 100 percent better."

The principle I learned is that to overcome your fear of public speaking, it can't be about you. But it goes both ways. One time I was giving a headspace lecture to a leadership group, and I wanted to impress them. As I was rattling off all of my awards and accolades to build credibility, it backfired. I came across as overconfident/ego driven because I was trying to impress them and make it be about me instead of serving them and helping them. On the comment sheet after the talk, the input was eye-opening. People can pick up on when you are talking about yourself . . . not helping them. The principle is still the same. It's not about you! It's about serving a person's needs with your unique talents and abilities.

Enter ClickFunnels . . .

I had already been lecturing for quite a few years at a chiropractic seminar that I had attended well over fifty times in ten years, and something strange happened. For the first time, it was not fulfilling. I called my wife and told her how unfulfilling it was to be at the seminar I usually rattle her ear off about. That night after talking to my wife, I was scrolling through Facebook and this energetic, fast-talking person popped up. His words in the ad spoke to me . . . so I clicked on it, and Russell Brunson entered my life. When he spoke, he spoke to every problem I was facing. He spoke to the conversation in my head and even questions that I had not thought of. He spoke to my soul. I decided to go deeper. Since I had time at the hotel, I watched his webinar. It spoke to my calling and why I was put on this earth. It was then I felt as though I had been given permission to capture the principles I had learned over the past decade and share them with the world.

I know you need to invest in yourself, and anything in the online world was by far my biggest weakness. I am an all-or-nothing individual, so if he offered it, I bought it all. I am not naive about where people have their attention and focus . . . it is online, and I wanted to learn from the best of the best.

I soon went to my first Funnel Hacking Live in 2019. Once my airplane landed in Nashville, I grabbed a Lyft, putting me in a car with three other strangers. I didn't know we were all heading to FHL . . . Just sitting next to the people in that Lyft, you could tell that there was something different about them. They seemed to have an excitement for life and an energy that was equally contagious.

Once we got out of the car after realizing we were all heading to the same place, we got checked in and registered for the event. The people checking me in were authentically excited to be there, unlike so many seminars I had been to in the past.

I ended up hanging out with a group of other people at FHL, and the energy was amazing. They were my people! They were excited about life, excited about why they were there, and authentically good people.

The next few days were amazing, and it was a no-brainer to sign up for the Two Comma Club Coaching. I showed up 100 percent to every coaching call and gave it my best. Then it happened . . . distraction! I got distracted by the unlimited possibilities. I made funnel after funnel after funnel . . . and I wasn't a millionaire in two weeks as I had planned. Even by the time the next FHL 2020 arrived, I had not yet reached my goals nor written my book. Not only that, but also my focus online was taking the focus away from my clinic. I didn't blame Russell or funnels because I knew my results were my responsibility. I already knew that my focus was split so much, but I signed up for coaching again, and I showed up to every session giving everything I had and didn't make any excuses . . . Then the world shut down.

This was a very pivotal moment in my life. My chiropractic practice was completely dependent on me doing outside lectures to acquire new patients, and I was quite good at it. But when the world no longer allowed you to go into businesses to give health talks, my marketing strategy was sunk. I was still considered an essential business since I was a Doctor of Chiropractic, but the writing was on the wall. I needed a new strategy. I wasn't using ClickFunnels for my business but rather for other business ventures that were parallel to my clinical skills and my calling.

A year prior I had done a 30-Day Stress Less challenge that was transformational for the people who did it, but I could not justify marketing it anymore because the money going out did not make up for the money coming in. So I decided to try to make it a fundraiser for nonprofits and split the profits . . . that did not work either.

The biggest thing I noticed was that my clinic was suffering because my staff had lost their leader. He was distracted. I went back to what my mentor Russell had told me. He said to first focus on one business until it hits $1 million. Then you can focus on the next. Here was the problem: my clinic had never collected $1M in a year. Not only that, but also I was so distracted before the world shut down that my momentum was driving my business straight into the ground.

At that time, I had to make a decision. During the Great Depression, most people remember hearing about all the businesses that failed, but the story in my head was different. I also knew that was also the time when some of the most powerful businesses exploded out of the Great Depression, and I made a decision to be the business that grew.

I dropped EVERYTHING that was a distraction and became a hermit. I focused on how to explode my practice and led my team in a way they both needed and deserved. The best way to explain it is like the movie

Paycheck with Ben Affleck where he locks himself in a vault to work on his project without any distraction. I didn't watch TV in the first place and wasn't really on social media, but I went nearly obsessive. I didn't watch anyone's webinars. I didn't check my email. I didn't respond to texts. I disappeared from all communication.

I took the principles I learned from the best real-life business school in the world (aka ClickFunnels) and ended up hiring people who were already getting results and good at making funnels/copy.

Then it happened . . . we grew 800 percent in a brick-and-mortar world where everyone else was struggling. We crossed the seven-figure mark. We grew so much as a business that I ended up needing an associate doctor to help out with the demand, along with more staff. The crazy part is that it took me over ten years to build a seven-figure practice, and I was able to get my associate doctor to that pace in three weeks after hiring her. Success leaves clues. I found out quickly that I needed yet another associate doctor to keep up with the volume. It's funny what happens when you put your head down.

The challenge I had was that during my business growth, I had recently surpassed a few mentors and didn't know who could coach me anymore. They started asking me lots of questions about what I was doing, but I was paying them . . . something wasn't right, and I knew I needed a new mentor and group of people to surround myself with.

By the time the world began to open back up, I was so focused and had so much momentum, I did not plan on going to Funnel Hacking Live even though it was arguably one of the best environments anyone could be in. It was about two weeks out from FHL, and at 2:30 in the morning, that same voice that asked, "If I take your wife and your son today, are we still good?" woke me up and said, "I want you to go to FHL." Since my son was born, there have been multiple times in my life that I have heard that small quiet voice, and every time I have been obedient, it has never been wrong yet. Without hesitation, I got up and walked across my house to my office. I opened my ridiculously full inbox to see an email to sign up for FHL and that there were only a few places left. It may or may not have been a marketing strategy, but I didn't care. I followed the link, paid, and received my confirmation to FHL 2021.

It's now 3:00 a.m. I'm sitting in silence in my dark office . . . thinking. I knew there was a reason I was called to FHL but wasn't exactly clear why. I knew one thing for sure, I didn't want to get distracted. I had such great momentum in my business and had been in the obsessive habit of saying no to everything. Even if Russell offered the Two Comma Club coaching again, I would have passed. Then a crazy thought popped into my mind. I told myself that the only way I would sign up for anything was if Russell reopened his $50K Inner Circle Mastermind. This made no sense at the time because the Inner Circle had been completely shut down with no signs of opening back up. It seemed silly at the time, but if all else failed, I would go to FHL and learn some amazing material, see some of my great friends, and get charged back up by my people.

FHL 2021 did not disappoint! Great speakers, powerful wisdom, and reconnecting with wonderful friends. It wasn't until the Two Comma Club award ceremony began with businesses that had collected over seven figures with ClickFunnels that my attitude changed. In the prior years, it was this nearly unattainable yet believable scenario where you wanted to visualize yourself on stage collecting the award. This time I was truly in awe and appreciation, recognizing the hard work and dedication that it took for individuals to cross seven figures as a business. Part of me was a bit envious, and I didn't apply for the award, but I decided that I was just going to enjoy the award ceremony.

Then I got a tap on the shoulder . . . it was Robbie Summers. In his soft yet gravelly voice with his best attempt to whisper, he said, "Hey, Justin, um . . . after this award ceremony, there is a little get-together. It may be for you and it may not, but if you want, here is an invite that will get you in the doors."

I already knew what it was. It was an invite to join the Inner Circle . . . and I was pretty sure I already knew the investment. The weird part, though, was the fact that Robbie had no clue that my clinic had passed the seven-figure mark when he handed me the invite. I went to the private gathering after the awards ceremony and showed my invitation, and we began to eat. I already knew the pitch was coming. Sure enough, Russell opened the Inner Circle back up. I was basically using my American Express to cut my chicken, I was so ready to join.

Since joining, I have continued to surround myself with people in the Inner Circle, and I realize there are so many untapped relationships and wisdom to both gain and share. These people are my people. Their challenges and victories are relatable.

We truly are a product of our environment, and once you get around these people, you realize that the individuals inside of Russell's Inner Circle are the kindest, most giving, and most authentic people you will ever meet.

The wisdom in the group is unbelievable, and you truly feel like you can solve nearly every problem a human ever has due to the different levels of deep experience.

In the meantime, I have been able to step out of the day-to-day patient care and let my staff maintain a seven-plus-figure flywheel practice. I continue to utilize and lean on the best of the best in the world to help me grow and launch different business ventures that serve both entrepreneurs and the chiropractic profession.

I choose to surround myself with some of the top entrepreneurs in the world because it pushes me outside of my comfort zone. I am not the smartest person in the room, but I realize my value to the world. The best part is that Russell's Inner Circle creates a secure, judgment-free environment. We come together to share what is working and what is not. We come together to share our victories without people trying to rip us down. We openly share our failures with the hopes of learning from each other's mistakes. Sharing new ideas creates new solutions when talking to someone who is changing the world. This is the power of a mastermind.

The reality is that sometimes you are going to get a tap on the shoulder . . . will you be ready? You may hear that small, quiet voice to do something difficult, and you must have faith in the process. What you need to do is find a solid group of people who are going in the same direction as you. Find people who are looking to change the world and do everything you can to both get around them and give value to them. Love them and love yourself because we will all fall short of perfection. Give each other grace and help others because we all need to be lifted up sometime. Follow principles founded in truth, and have a level of self-awareness of the things in life that are distracting you from your calling. Please understand that your calling in life is uniquely designed for you. Give yourself permission to say, "No for now, but not forever." Clearly define what you want in every category of life, but don't forget the people at home you are doing it for. They are your why . . . Just know that achieving your goals in life will take some time, but I guarantee it will be worth it!

In closing, I would love to share the entrepreneur's battle cry that was given to me in a flash by that soft, quiet voice at 3:00 a.m. many years ago. I hope it serves you the same way that it serves me . . .

Everything you do, you do with excellence, not perfection. You've failed more times than you've succeeded . . . You are an entrepreneur, and you've been called. Called to do the things that people say can't be done . . . to make a massive impact on others, authentically giving your best every time even though you may fall short of your personal goals. You put others first still knowing you must take care of yourself so you can help serve others. You fly to the seminars, meet with your mentors, mastermind with the best of the best knowing that success leaves clues. You follow principles . . . principles founded by faith . . . faith in your calling, faith in your God, knowing that your life is not just about you, it's about your call. Your calling to destroy fear and use your unique skills, talents, and abilities to be the person God created you to be. It's time for you to take one step closer and unleash your God-given potential!

—Dr. Justin G. Wubben

P.S. Russell, thank you for stepping out of your comfort zone and gathering us all together. You have created a movement and a legacy that will far outlive us all!

For a copy of *Chiropractic Business Secrets: 7 Business Principles They Didn't Teach You In Chiropractic School* visit:

<u>www.chiropracticbusinesssecrets.com</u>

DOUG BOUGHTON

My Favorite Band Told Me to Do It

2X Dream Car Winner & 2CC Award Winner | Client Acquisition Coach

Doug went from struggling restaurant server to ClickFunnels Dream Car Winner in his first two months full time online. After earning over $100,000 in affiliate commissions a few months later, he was able to pay off his entire student loan debt in full and present his mother with the student loan payoff notice that she had co-signed for him.

Now, CEO & Founder of the Fulltime Freedom Academy, Doug is on a mission to simplify client acquisition for online business owners.

Four years ago, the Dirty Heads helped me write my resignation letter and quit my job as a full-time restaurant server. The date was October

19, 2018. I had just left College Street Music Hall in New Haven, Connecticut.

On the drive home I sat in silence mumbling the encore lyrics to myself, "A-a-aye, I'm on vacation every single day because I love my occupation. A-a-aye, I'm on vacation, if you don't like your life then you should go and change it." Dirty Heads had just put on the best live performance I've seen from them, and all I could think of was how badly I wanted a change.

Although I had that night off, the first one in months, in the back of my mind, I knew I had to be up in a few hours to work a double on one of the busiest shifts of the week. I couldn't be further from loving my occupation. I took that song line literally in every sense of the word: "If you don't like your life, then you should go and change it."

More on this story to come, but for those of you who are just skimming through this chapter, I'd like to present to you the "CliffsNotes" version first.

To be continued . . .

How I Bootstrapped My Way into the Two Comma Club

Recently, I applied for the first-ever Bootstrap Entrepreneur of the year award. I am grateful to say I was able to make it to the final voting round for my category alongside a dear friend and personal mentor of mine, Blake Nubar, and the number one ClickFunnels affiliate, Keala Kenae.

When I was watching the trailer video on the application page for this award, there were three words that Russell said that really stuck out to me.

And I believe that these three words are the driving force behind every entrepreneur's big why.

Those three words he spoke were:

"Control My Vision."

I believe these words are so powerful because if we're not in control of our vision, then who is?

Four years ago, I set out on a mission to gain control over my big vision.

Up until that point, I had no control. What controlled me was my job, an unfulfilling schedule to adhere to, a six-figure student loan debt, and satisfying everyone else's vision for my life and what they saw being best for me.

I'd hear them say . . .

- "Doug, go back to school."

- "Finish your degree, Doug. You were so close."

- "When are you going to get a real job?"

- "How do you expect to pay back your student loans working in a restaurant?"

And, yes, that was always part of the plan until I realized that one day, life is going to pass me by, and at the end, I would look back and asked myself, "Where did the time go?"

And in that lack of control, there was always one voice that I'd hear to guide me in the right direction.

And that is the voice of my mom.

At the age of twenty-two, she was a single mother raising me and my two brothers on her own. Although we didn't have much, she always made sure we had everything we needed.

Watching her working multiple jobs, pursuing her degree, starting her own side businesses, volunteering in the community, and raising us really taught me everything I know about controlling my own destiny.

When I was growing up, I started to go down the wrong path and follow the older cool kids.

My mom pulled me aside one day and said, "You can lead or you can follow. You can't do both. Do what makes you happy."

To this day, those words continue to guide me.

From that day on, I knew there was no chance that I was going to have an easy time working for other people for an hourly wage.

Even during my years in college, instead of getting an internship like most of my friends, I started selling custom T-shirt designs to Greek life, cutting hair, and even selling my chapter outlines and exam study guides to my classmates.

When my senior year came, I was blindsided by some pretty devastating news. I was informed by the bursar's office that I couldn't secure a student loan to finish my final year of college.

After dropping out and moving back home, I was able to find a 100 percent–commission job going door to door and fell in love with continuing to be able to be in control of making my own income.

Six months later, I got the call that changed everything for me. The voice on the other line was someone from Sallie Mae, and they asked, "How do you plan on repaying your student loan balance of $114,000." It was more than double the amount of the original principle I thought I owed, which had more than doubled due to accrued interest.

I didn't know it at the time, and it might sound crazy, but this financial burden was a blessing in disguise.

It lit such a fire under me and would become the catalyst that pushed me on the path toward starting my own business so that I could pay that debt off as fast as possible.

I decided to take on a server position at a local restaurant which allowed me flexibility in creating my own schedule as I explored all kinds of online business ideas when I wasn't working long hours at the restaurant.

Through gaining experience in digital marketing and taking what I knew about the restaurant business, I started to help my employer with their website and run their digital marketing campaigns, and that's when I officially registered my LLC.

I started to branch out and take on as many clients as I could handle.

After years of dabbling in my online business ventures, I finally got the courage to put in my notice with the restaurant I was working at and took my online business full time.

That's about the time that I stumbled upon ClickFunnels and the One Funnel Away Challenge and learned how I could incorporate offering sales funnels into my services.

And that's when I made my big pivot. I realized I could sell sales funnels and start earning commissions every month from helping businesses get set up with ClickFunnels.

I launched my first funnel and made over $10,000 in ClickFunnels affiliate commissions in one month by selling the One Funnel Away Challenge. That next month, I went on to earn $27,000 in affiliate commissions, and it kept growing!

With that, I was able to hire my younger brother Jeremy full time to help me grow the business. Within six months, I was able to do something that I never thought would happen as fast as it did, and I presented my mom and Nonnie, who co-signed my student loans, with the loan payoff letter on Mother's Day.

Through the Funnel Hacking community I was able to connect with and make new friends who shared the same values that I have. I started flying to California for meetups and masterminds to surround myself with these other entrepreneurs that I met who were building seven-figure online businesses, after realizing that for me to grow faster, I had to break out of my comfort zone and do something I'd never done before.

I went back to Connecticut, donated everything I owned, loaded up what I could fit into my car, shipped it to San Diego, and made the big move. It allowed me to leave the same place I had lived my entire life so I could focus on myself, begin hiring a team, and go after the next big goal of earning the 2CC award.

For the first time in my life, I was fully free, and it gave me the idea for my new business name: Fulltime Freedom.

To date, I have been able to go from being buried in student loan debt to earning $1.75M in revenue, which just seems unreal to me, and I know that we're just getting started.

Now I'm on a mission to help spread Russell's word, to liberate other entrepreneurs with the tools, resources, and skills that will help them take their businesses full time and create the impact they desire.

Even now, it's still hard to say exactly where this is all going, but I see the ten-year vision, and the more it's starting to show its face, the more I'm able to give back to my tribe, my team, and the communities we're building. I visualize a nonprofit arm of the business where I can help build communities for families less fortunate and get more people involved in what we're doing together. It's all because of one company, one community, that led the way . . . and that's all of you over at ClickFunnels! Thank you for the guidance and support to create and control my vision.

Back to the Dirty Heads Story . . . Buckle Up!

Flashback to October of 2018, the night of the "resignation concert." I got home around 2:00 a.m. and began writing my resignation letter. I was waiting tables full time in a restaurant back in my hometown, Wallingford, Connecticut. In an industry notorious for no-call, no-shows and mid-shift walkouts, I knew that writing a letter wasn't common practice, but it made me feel better about communicating my reasoning. I just know from being on the other side how it affects an already short-staffed operation to just leave on short notice, and I didn't want that.

My situation was a little tricky. Not only were we short on waiters, but also our general manager had just left without giving notice a few days earlier. The owner had already approached me and dropped some hints that he was going to be making me an offer to manage the restaurant in the interim, and I had an inkling as to why.

Earlier that month, the owner approached me and asked me to send home all of the servers who were assigned to the Fall Wine Dinner. When I asked why, he mentioned that we didn't sell enough tickets to the event. Taking everything I knew about ClickFunnels and marketing that I had learned up to that point, I thought to myself, "If we just had an email list, we couldn't have sold this event out in one email." That's when the light bulb went off for me. At the time I was enrolled in the first-ever One Funnel Away Challenge launch, and I focused my attention on building out a funnel for the restaurant. I was able to get them an over 5,000 percent ROI! So at that point, I was already managing the website, running advertising campaigns, booking events, and leading shifts a few days a week.

Now, with the holidays upon us, and without a general manager in place, things were looking shaky at best. So I couldn't just walk out. I decided that I would go in the next day and hand him my notice for the end of that next month to give him time to hire a manager. That seemed pretty fair. He had given me a lot of opportunities, as he became my first client for my digital marketing agency. Everything worked out, and he even referred me to a few new clients to help me get started as I clocked out for good on November 30, 2018—my last day ever as an employee. To this day, he still uses the same ClickFunnels account I set him up with over four years ago. Pretty cool, right?

The Christmas Card Mix-Up

At the time, I was brand new to ClickFunnels, and I had the vision of becoming a Dream Car winner, Two Comma Club Award winner, and one day maybe even be able to join Russell's Inner Circle.

I was earning my first taste of passive income from the ClickFunnels affiliate program—a long ways away from the goal of making $1 million online. I mean I was earning a whole $38.80 per month from my one client's ClickFunnels account, but I was hungry for success. Honestly, it was really the massive burden of my $114,000 student loan debt that kept me motivated. I knew that if I kept pushing myself toward my goals, I could relieve my mother and Nonnie from the clutches of my own irresponsibility. You see, at the age of eighteen years old, I had no idea what I was asking them to sign. I begged them to cosign my student loans so I could attend a five-year business program at Drexel University. After I pleaded for months, they agreed. More on this later.

My initial plan: get one hundred local businesses to sign up to ClickFunnels with my affiliate link. I could build their sales funnel, charge them a monthly retainer to manage their account, and earn a commission from their ClickFunnels account. In one month, I was able to sign up my eighth client. I thought I would love self-employment, but instead, it felt like I had eight bosses now. I was getting calls and emails daily, far from what I thought would just be an easy retainer with maybe some updates every so often.

By mid-December, I was chasing checks trying to scrape up some money to pay my rent, get groceries, and cover my interest-only student loan payment. "Call me back after the holidays, and I'll cut you that check." This was the story from every one of my clients. I remember the embarrassment of Christmas Day that year when I showed up at my family's home empty-handed. Sitting in Nonnie's driveway with my head buried in the steering wheel, I thought maybe they wouldn't miss me if I didn't show up. I was in a pretty low place. I was negative in the bank and worried about having to crawl back to the restaurant with my tail between my legs and ask for my job back. It felt like nothing in the world could help pull me out of that slump.

I got home later that night and experienced a Christmas miracle. Well, to me, it was literally a dream come true. As I brought in a pile of mail that had been building up, a funky-looking envelope stood out. At that moment, I figured maybe it was another annual $25 Christmas check from my Grandma Tardiff. She always gets pretty creative with her holiday cards, and I love her for the kind gesture. But it wasn't. When I tore open the envelope, I saw a printout of an email with the words, "Congrats you're going to Funnel Hacking Live!" A close friend of mine knew my situation and bought me a ticket to my first-ever Funnel Hacking Live!

I didn't know it at the time, but that was the moment everything began to change for me. I realized there was no way I was going to be able to afford to fly to Tennessee and get a hotel in less than two months unless I really stepped my game up and got after it. I also knew I had to pivot away from done-for-you services for local businesses. My plan of serving one hundred clients just was not realistic. Even if I could get one hundred clients, I was already burned out from only having eight. So I asked myself, what do I love about this business model most? The only answer I could think of was, "I love getting that monthly check from ClickFunnels for my referrals." I started researching all the current Dream Car winners to see what they had done to earn their Dream Car Awards. I noticed they all had started to grow a community on Facebook. So I followed suit.

Battle of the Bonuses – A Race to McCall

At the time, the One Funnel Away Challenge was just picking up some huge traction. I had invested in it the previous month, but because of

124

phasing out of my server job and trying to keep up with my clients, I wasn't able to stay focused. I decided to join it again so I could build out my first affiliate funnel to promote the One Funnel Away Challenge.

Dave Woodward had just done a Facebook live announcing the six-month affiliate competition. They were going to fly the top ten affiliates who could sell the most One Funnel Away Challenges to Boise, Idaho, for a private mastermind with Russell and the whole team! I knew I had to go all in if I wanted to pull this off. As a brand-new affiliate with no following, I knew it was a long shot . . . but I had one advantage. Since I had no product of my own to sell, that could be my number one focus for the next six months, while the other well-known affiliates had their own courses and programs that they would be splitting their time between promoting. I got to work on my affiliate bonus and started marketing it as many hours a day as I could fit into my calendar.

Here's what I did first . . . I thought to myself, what prevented me from finishing the One Funnel Away Challenge on my first attempt? I asked myself, what kind of support could I have used to keep me more accountable to complete the thirty days and come out with an actual funnel built and launched? It hit me like a Stephen Larsen "BOOM" to the eardrums. Y'all original OFA-ers know what I'm talking about. I decided to make my new Facebook group an OFA accountability group. Anyone who signed up to the One Funnel Away challenge with my affiliate link would be able to attend my daily live zoom sessions, where I would show them exactly what I'm doing to implement what I learned from Stephen and Russell in real time each day of the challenge.

I then white-labeled my funnel template that they could use as their own bonus when they got sign-ups, and I would even help their people in our accountability sessions. It was a win-win-win. I was able to make my first $10,000 that first month of running my Facebook group after selling over one hundred people into the OFA challenge. Shane Larson recognized my "funnel audible" submission to be reviewed by Stephen Larsen on day thirty and asked me if I'd be able to jump on Zoom to meet Stephen and have my funnel reviewed live! The coolest part was Russell even made a surprise appearance that day where I got to meet him for the first time virtually. I was just so grateful for these two guys who have literally changed the trajectory of my life.

ClickFunnels Bought Me a Black BMW (and Paid Off My Student Loans)

After launching my first funnel, I used my commissions to attend my first Funnel Hacking Live ever, and it literally changed everything for me. I remember somehow getting up into the third row for the awards ceremony. I sat there in awe watching all of the Dream Car Winners and Two Comma Club Award Winners cross the stage to accept their awards, and I saw the vision. In that moment, I gained the belief in myself that this was real . . . this was possible for me. I left Funnel Hacking Live with my game plan fully mapped out and went home and got to work.

One thing Russell kept mentioning at Funnel Hacking Live was to start publishing every day for a year and not stop. I took that advice to heart and went for it. I continued going live in my group and publishing posts, and I even filmed my first webinar to sell the OFA challenge following Russell's Perfect Webinar framework. This started to bring in sales every day for me.

As my Facebook community grew, I would offer my new members my free course. The call to action in the modules would take them to my webinar. After sixty-six days of launching my webinar, I had sold over 270 One Funnel Away challenges, making me $27,000 in commissions, and I had officially signed up my one hundredth ClickFunnels affiliate. I submitted my application for the Dream Car Award and achieved the first of three major goals, all from just continuing to document my journey and providing value to my community. I was off to the races.

Next, I launched my first online course shortly after that, which brought in over $34,000 in course sales. Between ClickFunnels affiliate commissions and course sales, I made more in that one month than the entire previous year waiting tables. A few months later, I passed the six-figure mark and paid off my entire student loan debt on Mother's Day of 2019. It was a pretty amazing feeling when I presented the payoff note to my mother and Nonnie. It had been a pretty rough journey for them, even messing up their personal credit along the way because of my mistakes.

Ever See a Flying V of Boats?

Later that summer, the six-month One Funnel Away Challenge affiliate competition came to an end. Would you believe it . . . ? I was able to finish at the top of the leaderboard and earned a spot at the McCall mastermind! I was able to connect with the ClickFunnels team and the other top affiliates and even got to visit ClickFunnels headquarters to meet Russell for the first time. It was pretty awesome to hear about some of the things he was planning behind the scenes.

We drove a few hours north to McCall for the long weekend. Dave, Myles, and the entire crew rented eight jet skis and two boats for the ten of us to rip around the lake. That was probably one of the coolest things to be a part of, with a close second being us watching Dave's facial expressions as he tossed everyone around on the tube while Myles continuously cleared about twelve feet of wake with every jump. Impressive! Just sayin' . . .

I don't want to come off as braggy, but the "Flying V Boat Formation" was pretty epic. I was honored with a front-row seat on the lead boat . . . Captain Dave Woodward orchestrated the whole ordeal. Blake captured probably some of the most badassery of footage ClickFunnels has ever seen that day. Well, at least it felt that way in the moment.

Anyway, you're probably wondering what this has to do with anything, but it's a pivotal moment along the journey to Inner Circle. In fact, I believe without that weekend in McCall, I may have never ended up joining Russell's Two Comma Coaching Program.

How I "Snuck" in to Unlock the Secrets

After bunking up with the fellas in the Lake House for a week, I became pretty close with the crew. After hearing that I was going to be in Denver the same week as the Two Comma Coaching event Unlock the Secrets was happening, I got an invite to come check out the event as a guest.

At first, I felt a little out of place, as this only for Russell's coaching clients, and at the time, I wasn't in 2CCX yet. Not too long into day one of the event, I realized I had never felt so welcomed, understood, or part of something so amazing before. These were my people! I was able to make so many amazing connections and collaborations and left with so many huge breakthroughs that weekend.

I made the decision right then and there that I was going to enroll in Russell's 2CCX coaching program at the first opportunity I got.

Thinking back now, it's actually where I met some of my closest friends in the online world who are like family to me now. I ended up leaving with several podcast appearances, interview exchanges, and joint ventures and tons of memories.

Two Commas Baby, Baby!

Let me just say this . . . In the words of Biggie Smalls, "Damn right, I like the life I live 'cause I went from negative to positive . . . Don't let 'em hold you down. Reach for the stars . . ."

In all seriousness, going from negative in the bank . . . no car . . . and six figures of student loan debt . . . to living the life I've been able to achieve by surrounding myself with the right community and mentors, in such a short amount of time, has been one of the most humbling experiences of my entire life. If you are reading this and you are going for a goal that may seem a bit out of reach, just know you are a lot closer than you think. Keep the vision strong and your community stronger. Get around those who want to see you succeed. There is no better place to be than in the company of those leveling up around you.

Shortly after that weekend in Denver, I joined Russell's Two Comma Coaching Program, which helped me double down on 5-Day Challenges to fill my own program, the Fulltime Freedom Academy. Within a year of being in 2CCX, I was able to work with 2CCX coaches and earn my Two Comma Club Award just in time for Funnel Hacking Live 2021! It was official, two out of three major goals accomplished.

Full Count Bases Loaded

I'm no major sports fan, but I can imagine how it feels to be that guy on third base ready to slide into home, just to have the game taken away in split seconds.

I remember the day I heard the news. My vision faded, I lost my aim, and I really wasn't sure what my next move was going to be. I had just heard the news that Russell was closing down his Inner Circle. It felt like being tagged out at the plate. I was right there, about to go three for three on my major goals that I visualized at the beginning of my journey.

I had to change my entire trajectory of what I was working toward. I could have easily quit, as I contemplated doing several times. Then, an even bigger vision presented itself. That was to focus on serving the community I had built the best that I could.

My community became my new mission—to serve as many entrepreneurs and aspiring entrepreneurs as possible by documenting my journey to inspire, motivate through action, protect them from what doesn't work, and provide them with a plan that does.

That will always remain my priority. I began to focus on something bigger than myself, bigger than a monetary goal, and then something I didn't foresee happened. Russell reopened his inner circle! As soon as I heard the news, I was contacted by one of the coaches in 2CCX, as she knew I was waiting for that moment.

I honestly could not have achieved this without the support of my community, who helped me keep my vision strong even on the darker days. You might have days where you feel like your vision seems impossible, and I want to be here to stand as a reminder that they are not!

Create your vision, build daily habits, and execute on the systems to achieve the goals you have set for yourself. When that vision is cut short by something outside of your control, recalibrate and find a bigger purpose from it. It will drive you even further!

Since joining Inner Circle, I've started to go back to the fundamentals and completely restructured my company, team, systems, and offers. I have gone back to simplify everything. I went from having created over forty-two offers and selling four programs, down to only focusing on ONE. I have doubled down once more on live conversion events, niching down and helping entrepreneurs enroll one to many leveraging gamified challenges.

Russell, Jenny, the coaches, the ClickFunnels team, my fellow IC4Lifers . . . I am forever grateful for all of you. The mere fact that I am even here writing this chapter right now goes out to the dedication, imagination, and commitment of everyone involved. Big shout out to Justin Benton for bringing this all together.

The New Aim

Making over a million dollars in sales online is pretty remarkable. If you told me a few years back that this is something I would achieve, I definitely wouldn't have believed you.

However, I believe there comes a time when we must stop running away from pain as motivation and start running toward something so much greater than ourselves—the true *why* behind what we do. Find whatever that is, set the new aim, and make it far more impactful than money, and the universe will provide what you need to make it happen.

In the last year, I've continued to evolve my business and now am focused on helping my clients in my Fulltime Freedom Academy by incorporating passive revenue streams in their own online programs to increase their monthly recurring revenue.

To date, I've built an amazing community of my own, hired a team of nine amazing humans, impacted hundreds of our clients, and been fortunate to inspire thousands of our customers and audience members through my own journey.

We've even started planning our very own first house build as a team for April 2023 in Baja, Mexico, which I know will be the first of many to come.

What I am most excited about is meeting my entire team and clients at Funnel Hacking live this year so we can be together and bring it all full circle to where it all started.

I am forever grateful and am here to continue to grow this movement to show the world what they are truly capable of when they surround themselves with the right friends, community, and mentors.

And I am a #FunnelHacker for life!

RYAN JAYCOX AND JOE WOOD

How Crashing a Wedding Made Us Monthly Millionaires

Joe Wood and Ryan Jaycox are at the top of the game as global entrepreneurs and can often be seen and heard teaching on conference stages, TV, radio, and podcasts.

Together, they have received the coveted Two Comma Club X award multiple times, which is given by ClickFunnels to entrepreneurs that do over $10,000,000 in a single marketing funnel; they received their first one in less than fifteen months during the greatest pandemic the world has ever seen.

Between the two of them, they have also earned seven Two Comma Club awards (and counting) for doing over $1,000,000 in single funnels.

With a passion to give back and teach the business framework that has led to their success, Joe and Ryan founded Monthly Millionaire in 2021. This company is helping business owners of any industry create recurring revenue flows that afford a lifestyle of being able to fund their missions, live on vacations, and spend unlimited time with friends and family.

—

How Crashing a Wedding Made Us Monthly Millionaires

And the Lessons We Learned Along the Way

Let's set the record straight right now. The story you're about to read is so wild and so unusual that your first instinct will be to say, "That could never happen to me."

But in reality, we were YOU just a few short years ago!

Here's the story of how two ordinary guys with no extraordinary talents, education, or A-list contacts took the business world by storm and earned a combined *$47 million in ClickFunnel awards (in only 4 years)!*

Now, for the first time, we will reveal the lessons we learned along the way that every entrepreneur needs to know.

LESSON ONE: YOUR LIFE IS A SERIES OF DIVINE CONNECTIONS

The Wedding Invitation

It was like every other day as I walked to the mailbox, part of my daily routine to see what I would eventually put into the recycle bin. We all know any good mail now is email.

But this day was different. As I pulled out the various torn and half-bent coupon saver ads, I could see something was nearly hidden between the Valpak envelope and the utility bill: a wedding invitation. As surprised as I was to find the invitation, I was even more surprised to find out to which wedding I was invited. Sure, the couple belonged to the same church as my wife and I, and our pastor would be officiating, but we weren't close friends. But what the heck—I returned the RSVP with a yes, I would be there.

(*$47 Million Decision*)

The Wedding Day

Fast-forward a few months later, and my wife and I were standing in front of the bathroom mirror, wedding day ready!

But this is where the plot starts to twist.

Little did I know that about ten miles across town, at the same time we were admiring ourselves in that mirror, a meeting was happening with an unlikely impromptu invitation. It was our pastor, inviting his recently hired online campus pastor to the wedding he was about to officiate.

"Hey, Joe, I'm officiating a wedding tonight, and I want you and your wife to come along because there's someone coming I want to introduce you to," our pastor said.

Joe replied, "Um . . . I wasn't invited by the bride and groom. Are you suggesting that we CRASH A WEDDING?"

How was Joe going to convince his wife that she should, in a little more than one hour, find a dress, get ready, and go crash a wedding? (How he managed that is a lesson for another day)

Joe's very reluctant wife said, "I'm only doing this because Pastor David invited us."

And off they went and off we went to a wedding that was about to change our lives forever.

I pulled up to the valet, my wife and I got out (she looked awesome, by the way), and we walked down the steps of this beautiful ranch to the pre-party. I said, "Oh, there's Pastor David. Let's go say hi."

"Hey, Ryan, there's someone coming that I just invited as guests of mine specifically because I wanted you two to connect," he said. "His name is Joe Wood, and he's really smart with something called ClickFunnels. With your passion for business, I think you two would hit it off."

The Wedding Day Introduction

We immediately hit it off! It was like putting Russell Brunson in a room with Dan Kennedy. We talked about marketing and business strategy like two fifteen-year-old boys talking about the parts they were going to put on their first cars. Just after the ceremony, we all ditched the party and went out to dinner.

The story was being written.

But first, it's time for a STORY PAUSE: I'm going to interrupt your thought process right now because you may be thinking: "Wait, wait, wait, how does this all pertain to me? Your introduction at some wedding isn't going to solve the fact my business has only made $10,000."

Well, I'm glad you asked. You see, what was just described in the story above is no coincidence, and it's no happenstance. It's the miraculous happening around you each and every day.

You are surrounded by divine connections that in your hustle and rush, you're missing!

You're not even seeing it anymore.

Your steps are being ordered, your relationships are being arranged, and your opportunities are like floodgates being flung open. Are you ignoring these prompts?

Life is a series of divine connections at an appointed time. Being sensitive to these occurrences can open the door of favor like a flood in your life, bringing blessings that you never thought were possible.

Saying YES to the right invitations can and will change your life.

LESSON TWO: YOUR MOTIVES MATTER

Are you approaching every new business relationship with the thought, "What's in it for me?" Most of us are. But when Joe and I met on that wedding day, something interesting happened. We never once thought about how we could personally gain from the other. In fact, what we were most excited about was how our knowledge and experience could impact the Kingdom.

He wasn't just Joe Wood; he was pastor Joe Wood! He was an employee of the church, and I was a full-time businessman with a thriving marketing agency. Over those next several weeks, we would work together nearly every day, sketching and strategizing how we could help grow the church we were both connected in.

One particular day, though, another miracle invitation opened. It would put us both on a beautiful jet heading to strategize a famous Christian author's book.

Wait—"How much money did you get paid to do that?" you may ask.

Z E R O D O L L A R S.

In fact, we spent money to go there. Why? Because motives matter. Your motives matter. We weren't interested in how to become rich and wealthy; we were focused on our purpose.

What's your purpose?

Ours was to help more people live abundant lives here on Earth and know that Heaven was their home. The trip was fulfilling that purpose.

Over those two days of sketching the author's funnel, it was slowly revealing itself how naturally we worked together. It was like watching a Picasso being painted.

The irresistible offers, the order bumps, the upsells, the splinters, the payment options, all hitting that whiteboard for what would be an incredible masterpiece for the book.

Side note: The author of that book went on to make over $1 million on the funnel, much more than they would have ever made getting it published and selling it in bookstores. Funnels work!

But there is a major lesson to be learned here and one I had made mistakes with in the past. The lesson is that not everything you do not need to be focused on how everything you do can benefit you.

I know we all like to claim that we already operate in this mindset, but the truth is our own motives and ambitions often make our decisions, let's say—cloudy. When you can truly give to your purpose with an

138

honest heart, with no intention of receiving something in return, that is when your business can flourish!

Your motives matter.

LESSON THREE: YOU NEED AN ELEVATOR EXPERIENCE

Shortly before midnight that evening, Joe, my wife, and I, all exhausted after such an awesome two days, sat in the hotel lobby recapping the day. We would be flying back home in the morning.

I couldn't help but ask Joe, "I wonder if there's a possibility I could use a funnel and do some kind of a new business with it."

You see, I had never used ClickFunnels before, embarrassingly enough, and, as I've admitted to Russell, I used to make fun of people who were building a business with his software (don't judge me). No real business that makes money can be built without a WordPress website!

Joe told me, "Of course you can!" And over the next several hours, on tiny hotel napkins, we started sketching the future.

I will never forget that night. I walked into the elevator with my wife, looked over at her, and said, "If he's accurate in that sketch, our lives are about to change and will never be the same again." We had hope and a belief that we could use this incredible software called ClickFunnels to launch something NEW and successful!

Everyone's elevator experience is different, but until you have one, your business will be limited in its ability to grow. There must be that aha moment. It may be a meeting, it may be your next coaching call, or it could easily be the next Funnel Hacker Live event.

Something you hear may not only resonate with your mind, but also awaken your spirit.

LESSON FOUR: THERE'S NO PERFECT TIMING

As soon as Joe and I got back to our homes from that trip, we started putting in the work. We realized we were meant to build this new business that was sketched on those napkins, and we were meant to build it together.

A business partnership had been born, and we were burning the midnight oil to make the dream a reality. After about ninety days, we were READY TO LAUNCH! The funnel was built, the autoresponders were primed, the pixels were active—you know the drill.

And it couldn't have been more perfect timing, because the next thing we heard on the news was the president saying: "My fellow Americans, starting today, please do not leave your homes unless it's an emergency. There is a global pandemic, and the nation is shutting down."

Uh oh!

Did we perfectly time the exact launch of our business to be the very moment Americans were going to hunker in their homes, wash their groceries bags, keep their children home from school, and certainly not spend any additional money when they didn't know what the future held?

We sure did!

Have you ever heard the saying that there's no perfect time to have a baby? You're never going to be ready, and you'll never be fully prepared. We suggest to you today that there's no perfect timing to start, launch, and scale a business either.

Have you been waiting for the perfect time for your business? Have you said, "I will scale when (fill in the blank)"?

Well, what are you waiting for?

We quite literally couldn't have picked a worse moment to launch our business. This was the business we had worked so hard for, the business we knew was a divine appointment. This was supposed to be EASY!

"Ryan, we still have to launch the business today. We can't let this stop us," Joe said.

It's GO LIVE time!

And are you ready for this one?:

After thousands of hours poured into the funnel, countless sleepless nights, and the reading of every Russell book we could find to make sure we didn't miss a single step . . .

Drum roll . . .

We made $1,100.

$1,100! No, no, no, that couldn't be right. We had listened to everyone on stages, in books, and in interviews talk about their $500,000 one-day launches. "Joe," I begged, "check those numbers again. That can't be right."

That's not good at all!, I thought. What happened? I thought we were going to make a million dollars. Did we fail? Is our funnel bad? It's got to be the video on the opt-in page, right? No, it's the color of the button we are using on the page. Should we have used a two-step?

I mean, we could have made more money flipping burgers at a fast-food restaurant, with the hours we had put into this to only make $1,100? Had our leap of faith sent us plummeting to a disastrous flop?

LESSON FIVE: DON'T DISCOUNT HUMBLE BEGINNINGS

So many of us have the expectation that if it's meant to be, it's going to be exactly as we had planned. You've probably heard of these miracle funnel launches that did millions out the gate when they sent it to their list of two hundred people.

We are here to tell you, don't discount humble beginnings. Oak trees don't sprout up through the ground overnight, and neither do your funnels.

Disappointment leads to withdrawal. You're looking at those last two funnels and thinking exactly what we did: "Where did I go wrong?" May we suggest to you that it's possible you didn't go wrong; you just broke down before you broke through.

Humble beginnings challenge your belief systems and check how deeply you are rooted. That night we had two choices: disappointment or celebration. This was a test for us, and you're being tested in the same way right now as you read this.

How was $1,100 going to eventually lead to $47 million in awards for us?

This is why you can't judge or overanalyze your current results. Anything great takes time to build and scale. It's not to say that some of these miracle $500,000 launch stories don't have happy endings, but often they are bottle rocket businesses that spark, launch, explode, and hurtle back to earth.

Be of good cheer today if your business is operating more like an acorn than a rocket. These are the businesses that stand the test of time.

We didn't give up, and you shouldn't either.

LESSON SIX: YOU NEED A PROVEN FRAMEWORK

Each day, little by little, the company was growing. The $1,100 turned into $130,000 in total revenue. Then in just a few more months, we got our Two Comma Club Award!

For the sake of time, let's fast-forward slightly to the day we were collecting our Two Comma Club X for doing $10 million, and then, shortly after, to the turning point moment when we were achieving $1 million a month in business.

Monthly Millionaires!

Joe and I knew we had a system at this point. Every new product we launched for that e-commerce business would earn a Two Comma Club Award, some in as fast as ninety days! We were building a proven framework and, in the building of it, discovered that there were eight keys to launching and scaling a successful business.

It wasn't long before other businesses and entrepreneurs started contacting us. Remember, we weren't coaches or consultants; this was just a simple product-based e-commerce company.

Everyone started asking us questions:

"How did you do that?"

"How much for your framework?"

"Can you coach my business?"

"Will you map my funnel?"

For us, it definitely was easy to explain. We had unknowingly followed Eight Keys at the launch of our business and for each subsequent product.

"Wait, are other entrepreneurs trying to purchase our system?" I asked Joe. We had never even thought about that. We aren't coaches or consultants. We are just two ordinary guys having fun and building something awesome together to fuel our greater purpose and mission.

When divine opportunities open, step up and serve. And that's exactly what we did.

If only we knew where to even begin with a business model like that . . .

LESSON SEVEN: RUSSELL BRUNSON AND THE INNER CIRCLE DIFFERENCE

It was September 23, 2021, and there we were standing by the double doors outside of the auditorium at the Gaylord Palms hotel. We could hear the music cranking in the room, and the anticipation of everyone around us was pure ENERGY and EXCITEMENT.

We were officially at the Funnel Hacker Live conference! I had never seen anything like this before.

And there he was, Russell Brunson, on stage. This is the guy who created the software which I had once believed to be the worst business-building tool in the world. Yet there I was getting ready to cross the stage having earned multiple Two Comma Club awards and a Two Comma Club X using that same software. Ironic, right?

But on the stage that day, his words had life and meaning to me. I understood it.

They told us there was a special lunch for everyone in attendance that had earned a Two Comma Club award, so we eagerly went, and we learned there was this little club called Russell's Inner Circle and Category Kings, which we qualified for. They said, "This group is the next evolution of your business, and it will put you around the people that will speak into the next chapters of your life."

We were IN!

Remember all those entrepreneurs asking for our framework? Well, thanks to Inner Circle, we were ready! Before we knew it, we were hosting entrepreneurs across the country and had created something called our Monthly Millionaire One-Day Experience. This was paying tribute to what started it all for us from day one. We had no idea that the first day Joe and I spent mapping a funnel with an author (for free) would eventually become our next phase of business.

Now entrepreneurs are spending $110,000 a day just to sit in the room while we personally sketch and map their funnels, while others are buying our customized playbooks for $50,000. WOW!

Russell Brunson told us that you don't have a real business until you have subscriptions, so, like any smart business people, we took the advice and launched our Monthly Millionaire mentorship program where THOUSANDS of entrepreneurs are getting the help and guidance they need most!

And now here we are today, at Funnel Hacker Live 2022, collecting yet again more Two Comma Club and Two Comma Club X awards.

Would we be where we are without Russell Brunson's genius of the creation of ClickFunnels? Would we be crossing the stage yet again without the members of Inner Circle who have inspired us, educated us, and given us the tools we needed to achieve these incredible milestones?

Unlikely!

Thank you, Russell Brunson. Thank you, Inner Circle. And thank you, ClickFunnels community, where dreams take root, businesses come alive and purposes are accomplished.

Ryan Jaycox and Joe Wood

MonthlyMillionaire.com

ERIC THAYNE

From MySpace to Millions

Eric got his start selling online when he was thirteen years old by selling T-shirt designs to screamo bands on Myspace. He spent most of his high school and college years starting businesses, mostly in the creative arts like graphic design, music production, and filmmaking. He spent the better part of the next decade learning how to work with clients and generate word-of-mouth referrals for high-ticket services. But after so many years of trading time for money, he realized there had to be a better way. So in 2016, he created his first online sales funnel, selling an online course for videographers and filmmakers. In just a few years, he scaled this new business to over fourteen thousand paying customers in more than one hundred countries around the world and grew his revenue to multiple seven figures with low- and high-

ticket offers. Eric is a husband to his wife, Becca, and father to two girls. They currently live in Boise, Idaho.

—

I started my very first business when I was thirteen years old, selling T-shirt designs to emo bands on Myspace. I didn't know how powerful it was at the time. But I was communicating with people from all over the world and getting them to pay me real money over PayPal. Pretty incredible. Nowadays it seems every teenager is starting a business, but in 2003 that was not the case. I was the weird kid that didn't have a social life because I was always at home working on the computer. From a young age, I always had dreams of starting my own businesses or building big things. I didn't know what they would be, but I just started. Ever since I was really young, I was always doing artistic things. I started playing the piano and music when I was six or seven years old. I learned how to improvise and compose music. And I later started performing on the piano and recording music. I grew up drawing and doing graphic design. I did freelance work in brand design, developing websites, building iPhone apps, and more. I learned how to produce music, built two recording studios, and helped new artists gain a following on YouTube. I started making videos for weddings, real estate, commercials, and more. And I eventually built a production company making high-end videos for luxury hotels. Basically, throughout my high school and college years, my whole world was about figuring out what I loved to do and how to make money doing it. While my friends were doing interviews, getting jobs, and taking career counseling, I was dreaming about my next business. I was always self-employed and never wanted anything else because I couldn't stand having someone else telling me where I had to be and when and what to do. Most people—including my family—didn't understand it, and frankly, neither did I. But there was always something in me that just kept pushing me to keep going.

My journey to ClickFunnels, and eventually to the Inner Circle, began with puppies. I was at a meetup for YouTubers in Provo, Utah, for people to come and network and learn about how to grow YouTube channels. I was there because I had grown a YouTube music channel that I was working on where I made mashups of popular songs with some of my friends. I had a few videos that went viral, and I had gained about $30K subscribers, but I was mainly doing it for fun while running my video production business and recording studio full time. The main speaker at the event that night was Derral Eves (who, funny enough, also happens to be a member of the Inner Circle now), and he was speaking about how to monetize a channel and make money. And I was definitely intrigued by what he was saying. If I could find a way to make more money doing something else that I loved, then that would be a big win for me. But then another speaker got up and started sharing something I had never heard of before. He talked about how he had built a Facebook fan page called "I Love Labradors." He was posting pictures of Labrador puppies every single day, and people who loved Labradors were finding his page and following it completely organically without spending any money! Now that he had a big following, he could start selling products to those people and build a business out of it. That was when I really perked up. And I knew I had to try it. So I went home, hopped on my computer, and started building my own Facebook page—"I Love Golden Retrievers." To be clear, I had zero interest in golden retrievers or even puppies in general, but boy, did I get serious about posting puppy pictures on my new page every single day. I was determined to put this idea to work and see what I could make of it. Every day, I searched the internet for the cutest golden retriever pictures and posted them to my page. And the page grew fast. In a very short amount of time, I had gained thousands and thousands of new followers on this page who were all obsessed with golden retrievers—all except me, the owner of the page.

I thought it was pretty cool that the page grew so fast. But of course, after the novelty of it faded away, I didn't really have the passion for puppies that I needed to keep it going. But I saw what was possible. And I started asking myself, "What if I did this with something that I'm actually interested in?" And that was when the idea struck me. I had the idea that I could create some sort of online community or online course for filmmakers. I had been running a production company as a filmmaker and had made around six figures doing it. I had people asking me questions about how I created my style of work and how I got clients. So I knew I had some knowledge that I could share that would help other filmmakers do what I had done. Then I started thinking about the right strategy. Right around that time I saw a Facebook ad from a guy who was offering to help people build their coaching business online. I knew nothing about online coaching and honestly didn't even know what I was getting into, but it seemed like he might have some answers for me. So I signed up for a phone call with him, bought his program, and was on my way to becoming an online coach. I started learning how to build my first funnel, how to take sales calls, how to create email automations, and how to deliver a program to people. I created a live eight-week workshop called Cinema Mastery where I taught cinematography to filmmakers in eight live sessions. In the first two weeks, I signed up ten people in my new program, and I more than made back my investment with my mentor. Once the eight weeks were over, I took the recordings from the live calls, put them into a membership site, and then started selling them to more filmmakers using webinars. Over the next twelve months, I made more than six figures selling this course, but I was just getting started.

A few months later a friend reached out to me and invited me to go to a marketing conference called Funnel Hacking Live. I didn't know how I felt about going to a stuffy marketing conference, and I wasn't sure I wanted to spend the money on travel, hotel, and everything, but I decided if I was going to be a "marketer," I better start doing "marketer things." I agreed to get a ticket, and we decided we would figure out a way to split a hotel room to make it cheaper. Up until that point, I had always thought ClickFunnels was just a website builder. It was the software I was using to build my funnels, and that was all I knew. But at my first FHL in 2017, I realized I was totally wrong. FHL wasn't just some stuffy marketing conference; it was more like a party. There was loud music, people dancing, amazing talks by motivational speakers, and a vibe and energy you just couldn't get anywhere else. And more importantly than all that, I felt like for the first time in my life, I was surrounded by people like me and people that understood me— ambitious entrepreneurs who were trying to change the world, wanted to grow and excel, and had big dreams and aspirations. I watched as hundreds of people crossed the stage receiving a Two Comma Club Award for making a million dollars in their business. I could hardly believe that was possible. But when I left that year, I knew what my goal was. And I got back to work in my business trying to make it happen. With all the momentum that I felt from that first FHL, I was certain that next year I would be up on stage like everyone else.

But unfortunately, that didn't happen as I planned. A whole year went by. My business continued at a pretty steady pace, but I was nowhere near seven figures. It's hard to maintain the same energy and excitement you feel at an event for an entire year. So by the time FHL came around again, I had lost sight of my goal and was stuck in the grind of business again. But I still went back to FHL. I knew it was worth the time and the money to be around my people and get inspired again.

At FHL in 2018, Russell launched the brand-new Two Comma Club X coaching program. It had coaches, trainings, resources, and everything I needed to help me hit the Two Comma Club. I wanted it SO bad . . . but it was a LOT of money. I remember sitting in my chair— half the room had already emptied out for lunch—and I sat there with the order form clenched between my fingers, trying to decide if I should do it. It felt like a huge risk, I didn't have the money, but I had hope that if I put in the work, then I could figure it out. So in a moment of faith and chaos, I texted my wife, "Babe, I'm about to spend a lot of money, but don't worry, it will be OK." I filled out the form, ran to the back of the room, and turned it in. It was a flurry of emotions mixed with excitement and fear all in one.

When I got home from FHL, reality set in, and I had to figure out how to pay for this thing, so I got to work. I worked harder than I ever had before. I knew that if I just followed the steps of the program, I would be able to get my 2CC award next year. I worked hard, I showed up to the coaching calls, I got feedback on my funnels, and I went to the events. The very first 2CCX event I went to was in Phoenix, Arizona. I remember feeling extremely nervous walking into the networking party the first night—I didn't know ANYBODY. I awkwardly walked around and tried to start meeting people, one by one, little by little. Over that night, I met a few more people, then a bunch more throughout the event, and by the time it was over, I had tons of friends that I had connected with. I went home inspired, ready to get back to work again. I built a funnel for a $47 video lighting course that I was trying to sell with Facebook ads, but it cost me more to get somebody to buy it than what I would make, so I was LOSING money every single month on that funnel. And by the end of the year . . . I still wasn't anywhere near the Two Comma Club. I had been running this business for three years now and still couldn't hit my goal. Each year I sat in my chair at FHL watching other people walk across the stage and get their award, and I would tell myself, "Next year." And then a year would go by, and it still felt like I hadn't made any progress at all.

In January 2019, all of the 2CCX coaching program members were invited to go on a cruise with Russell, his team, and other Two Comma Club award winners. I was really excited to go on the cruise, but when it came to my business, I was about ready to throw in the towel. My business wasn't really growing, I was struggling to make anything work, and I had a funnel that was losing me money every day. But something Russell always said stuck in my mind: "Focus on one funnel, one offer, and one traffic source until you make a million dollars." So I kept at it. I still went on the cruise. I went out and had fun networking with everyone and doing fun activities during the day, and then I would go back to my room and try to figure out my funnel.

It was on the last day of the cruise that everything changed. And I didn't even know it. During the final networking party on the last night, I had a quick conversation with John Parkes, the head of traffic at ClickFunnels. I showed him my funnel, told him what was going on, and in a moment of desperation, asked him if he had any advice. He suggested a few little tweaks, and I decided I would try them. When I got home from the cruise, I went straight to my office, made those tweaks to my funnel, and started testing them. I had no idea what was about to happen. Immediately, my funnel went from LOSING money every day to MAKING money every day. It wasn't a lot, but it was profitable, and that was all I needed to keep me going. I wondered if there were other tweaks I could make to my funnel to help it even more, so I got on a call with Dave Lindenbaum, who was one of the 2CCX coaches. He gave me a laundry list of ideas to test on the funnel, and I got to work on those. I ran split test after split test, changing colors, copy, design, ads, and more. Sometimes the split tests would make the funnel convert better, and sometimes they would make it worse. But overall, eventually, things started growing.

In February 2019 I made around $15,000 in my business, but at a $3,000 loss. But that was when things started taking off. In March I made $30,000. In April, $50,000. And in May, we had our first six-figure MONTH ever. We made $100,000 in one MONTH. We were selling between fifty and one hundred copies of our course every single day. And after paying all of our expenses and a healthy salary for us, we were netting 50 percent profit margins. By August we crossed the million-dollar mark for our entire business and qualified for the Two

Comma Club Award. And not long after, our $47 course crossed over a million dollars all by itself. It took us three years to get just halfway to the 2CC, but then once everything clicked, we did the other half in just six months.

I stayed in 2CCX for another two years, learning and growing my business and building relationships with other entrepreneurs and the ClickFunnels team. And in 2021 there were rumors that Russell would be reopening the Inner Circle. I got a message from one of the 2CCX coaches saying that the Inner Circle was opening up again and they wanted me to be part of it. I talked to my wife about it, and we both decided that of all the investments we've made, the ClickFunnels community and its programs by far have given us the biggest returns. So it was a no-brainer for us to join the Inner Circle and continue that trend.

JUNIOR ANTHONY

FROM HOMELESS TO MILLIONAIRE: The Secrets To Building A Successful Online Empire

Junior Anthony is the founder and CEO of LiveSotori, a dynamic platform of online entrepreneurs achieving financial freedom and creating abundance in all aspects of life. He is a self-made multimillionaire that started with a single dollar to his name and an absolute will to succeed. Through his arduous journey in his early twenties and living through homelessness on the streets of New York City, Junior found his breakthrough and created massive wealth for himself.

—

I never expected my life to be like this. I mean, who would? As a regular kid from the hood, I didn't know any good. I wanted to be a rapper because I wanted to make money. I didn't really think about starting a business to actually create not only money but also impact.

I spent all the years after high school following this music career, and, yes, some may say I got a little taste of success, but I also tasted homelessness during that entire journey. I tasted a few misdemeanors that I racked up based on the fact that I simply did not have a stable household. (Funny story: I actually applied for a rental property recently. They almost denied me due to a trespassing charge. I was pretty much going to an abandoned house to sleep at that time. Funny how your past can actually catch up to you in the weirdest ways.)

At that time, I didn't imagine having the life that I have right now . . . making millions of dollars in business, helping countless people create income, having a passion for life, and being optimistic and excited to wake up every day. Right now I'm spending an entire month in a beautiful, gorgeous hotel in Xcaret, Mexico, a $2,000-per-night hotel. I didn't expect my life to be like this.

And it's crazy how it all started. So if you will, I would love to take you back in time to the pivotal moments in my life. I was once employed by this company that I will not name, partially because I don't remember them and partially because they shouldn't be remembered.

I worked under the drywall taping union, the same union that my grandfather committed his health and body to. He broke his body and ingested many cancer-producing chemicals like silica and other unknown, foreign particles through his nose. There is no surprise that he developed lung cancer. It's the same exact trade where I watched my father snap his Achilles tendon and be out of commission and unable to work for six months, which led to his house being foreclosed on and the catalyst to his divorce. He had to work twice as hard just to get back to where he was before, which was nowhere. I literally watched my father and grandfather do the same exact thing that I was getting into. I just wasn't smart at the time because I was so focused on money. If I had known better, I would have tucked my tail and run.

That's the same problem that most people have; they just focus on money, and they don't see that there are more things to life than just making money. If you're chasing money, then you will never get it. You will never have passion. You will never have fulfillment. Everyone I know that's making a lot of money, they're not making money because they are chasing money; they are making money because they care about change, impact, and freedom. (**Money hint**: chasing money is like chasing a cat. If you can figure out how to catch a cat, you can catch money.)

I was so committed to my job, it was unbelievable! I had never committed to anything the way I committed to this job. I would wake up and be at this job an hour before it started. Previously I was known as the person that was always late to work. So I made sure to change that identity. I showed up an hour early every morning. And I didn't start work at 7:00 a.m. when everyone else started. I started work thirty minutes earlier, at 6:30 in the morning.

While everyone was still getting their little breakfast in, I was working at 6:30. And on this particular fateful morning, I was actually rushing to go to the cellar to get started for work. The problem was that nothing was set up. Nothing was ready for me in that specific location. So instead of me sitting there and waiting for 7:00 to come, for my foreman (boss) to come and give me the instructions on what I needed to get done in the cellar, I decided to go back up those seven, eight, nine flights of stairs because the hoist operator didn't start working until 7:00 in the morning and I wanted to start working at 6:30 a.m. So as committed as I was, I picked up two fifty-pound buckets of compound and began to wobble toward the staircase. First down two steps, then up eighty-eight (I counted eleven steps per floor).

While I headed down the two steps of the platform, I stepped on a piece of protruding metal in the concrete. I felt my ankle and heard it crack. It was like an instant shock of terror that went through my brain. I was scared. I was petrified. But not for the reason most readers would think. I wasn't scared because I thought I had broken my ankle. I was scared because I thought this would prevent me from working, and if I didn't work, then I would pretty much be back to square zero, which is being homeless again.

So while being in this massive, paralyzing pain, I did my best to walk. Noticeably, I could not walk, and it did not take long before someone saw me and shouted, "Whoa! Whoa! What's going on?" and came rushing to my side. "Bro, what happened to your foot? Can you walk?" he asked. He was just a regular worker.

Right after, a rush of supervisors from the actual job site came to my side. When they arrived, they not only brought my job steward (the person responsible for keeping the union accountable) but they also brought the BIG BOSS, the owner of the company. Now the steward's responsibility is to literally make sure everyone in the union is protected. It's not to protect the bosses; it's to protect the union members and the integrity of the union. My bosses' job was to simply remain profitable.

"Hey, Junior, you should really go to the hospital. At least get it checked out, just in case." These were the exact words of my very concerned steward. Meanwhile, I am thinking, "Man, I don't want to go to the hospital, because if I go, they might say I need a cast on my foot. And if I have a cast on my foot, then I can't come back to work." Interrupting my train of thought was the voice of my boss, "Don't go to the hospital. You don't need to go to the hospital!"

At this moment I recalled a time when I fell off a nine-foot baker (think two ladders on opposite ends with a piece of wood in the middle to walk on). I was doing construction on a school building at this time and remember the injury that I had on my right shoulder; it wasn't nearly as bad as the emotional pain of getting laid off two days after my boss found out; this was after I hid my injury as long as I could to protect the company.

I decided to agree with the job steward. I went to the hospital just to make sure everything was okay. I assured my boss, "I don't care about collecting money. I don't want a disability. I want to work." My boss spoke with the driest tone, "Well, if you go, there will be consequences." And I was off in the cab with my job steward to the closest urgent care facility. During the entire cab ride, I was thinking, "What if I don't have a job again? Where will I be?" My car had gotten repossessed a few months prior, so I didn't have a car to be an Uber driver anymore. This was literally my only shot, my only hope.

Once at the hospital, they gave me an air cast and said, "Stay off your feet. We'll need to monitor it over the next few days." They told me to come back on Friday, and if everything checked out, they would give me a letter so I could go back to work on Monday. And that's what I did. I went home, stayed in bed for literally three to four days, put ice on my foot, and did every single thing I could to heal it as quickly as possible.

I kept it elevated with ice and heat packs and did everything else they said. When I went back to the urgent care on Friday, they asked, "How's your foot feeling?" And although I still had a little bit of pain, I said, "I don't feel anything. I feel amazing! Thank you very much!" And to my surprise, I got my doctor's note.

I was super excited because that meant on Monday, I got to return to work. For the entire weekend, I stayed off of my foot and kept it elevated, iced, and everything. Feeling super motivated, on Monday morning, I was back at work by 6:00. At about 6:15, I went down to the basement, where the boss had his office. This was one of the two bosses. He was young, only three years older than me, so I'd typically find him inside that room playing Fortnite. And I would sit with him and eat spinach. He used to call me Spinach Boy. Every day, all I would eat was spinach, raw spinach leaves. Truthfully, I didn't have enough money for anything else. A three-dollar bag of spinach could last me two days, so it made sense. Even when he would offer me a portion of his sandwich, I would stay true to my bag of spinach. Perhaps you can call that pride.

I knocked on the big, heavy metal door just as I normally would. I was expecting him to invite me in, me and my bag of spinach. But he didn't. He shut the door on me and my doctor's note. I was taken back by that. I thought we were cool, thought, "He's young, I'm young." I was still in shock at having the door slammed on me and unable to move. He opened the door back up and said, "You are a liability. Get off my job site!"

Those are words I will never forget. And he slammed the door in my face for a second time. At that moment, I knew. I knew I would never have a job ever again in my life. Thank God that I've been blessed with the opportunity to no longer need one.

Returning home was one of the longest train rides ever! I went back home and sat down, thinking, "What am I going to do? What am I going to do?" I was stuck. I didn't know what I was going to do. I didn't have anything.

That Christmas I ended up spending about two months with my mother in Trinidad. Now I had a girlfriend at the time. You see, apparently how race works in Middle Eastern countries is that you don't date black people. She is Middle Eastern and I'm black. She had these kinds of conversations with me, "Hey, you don't have any money. I can't bring you home to my family because I'll be shamed and disowned." And I understood it, but I still took her to her first Caribbean island, Trinidad, not only to meet my mother, but also to actually understand my culture and experience some things with us. We had an amazing time, but when we came back, she left me.

I was heartbroken, but instead of sitting around feeling sorry for myself, I decided to take action. (**Money insight:** When your sh*t hole becomes too painful to bear, that's when you will make a change!) I started doing research into how I could make money online. And it all started with this one question: "If you were stuck in a room with a computer and enough food to last you for thirty days, and in order for you to exit this room, you'd have to buy your freedom for $5,000, would you be able to do it?"

I sat down and thought about that question, and I thought, "Wait, how am I going to make $5,000 if I don't leave the room?" That opened up my mind to a book by Donald Trump that I read many years before, stating, "If you leave your house to make money, you are losing money." And I sat down and thought about this concept.

I was kinda floored by it, because I didn't know how I was gonna make $5,000 in thirty days without leaving the room. So I sat down, and I tried picking up stock and crypto and all these other things, but nothing worked. Well, it worked for a time, yes, but it wasn't really sticking.

Then I remembered this webinar that I watched. So I went back and looked through YouTube videos to find this webinar again because at that time, it was always popping up. I found it, and around this same time, my mother invited me to Miami to meet up after her cruise. I booked a flight to Florida with an $800 vacation check. That was all I had to my name at the time, no credit card, no debit card, just an $800 vacation check. I sat down, and I watched this webinar by Dan Henry, a really cool guy! It intrigued me how someone could actually make $25,000 a month by servicing five people at $5,000 each. I actually never thought of working like that, ever.

And that's how it all began, the journey I now know as my entrepreneurial journey. I started reading every single thing I could put my hands on: *Rich Dad Poor Dad, KPI, The 10X Rule,* and pretty much everything about business and sales. I was so determined I literally finished an entire book on the flight.

When I arrived in Miami, I figured I'd surprise my uncle. It was sad actually because he lived in a massive house there, and I figured he would house me for a few days, but he was like, "Yeah, no." I guess the joke was on me. That honestly did hurt me for a few. (**Money insight:** You will soon realize the person who will have the most impact on your success will be a complete stranger, not a family member.) Later on, I realized it was a blessing in disguise because it forced me to figure it out. I had to figure out what I was going to do in Miami for five days until my mother came back from her cruise.

During that time I found a motel that accepted cash. It was like $65 a night. I ended up spending about $300 on that motel. I was down to my last $200. I sat down and read three different books in like five days. My entire day was spent just immersing myself in knowledge and learning how to speak to people as well as understanding that there are businesses you can create.

And on the fourth day, my ex planned to visit and spend the entire day with me, but she got busy and didn't show up until later that night. So I actually decided to find some clients. I spent my whole day walking Biscayne Blvd., calling every single business that I saw. I told every business owner that I could do everything that I learned in the webinar! I was committed. I knew I could figure this thing out. Whether it was a dentist or a lawyer, a chiropractor or a gym. I even went to a Chevy car dealership, pitching the manager, telling them that I could run ads for them.

I did everything! And nothing, not a single thing happened for me. I missed my mother's call, so she ended up leaving me. So now I had to give my ex $100 to drive me from Miami all the way to Orlando.

I went back to New York. And I was back to my sh*t hole, back to my struggle, back to my uncertainty. And the only thing that was going for me at the time was the girl that I wanted to be with; we had just reconciled our relationship. During this time, I literally made thousands of phone calls, following up with every single person I encountered when I was in Miami. I was down to my last $10. I kept calling and calling. It wasn't until this one fateful day that I literally learned a very important lesson about life and business.

Because I had a very grumpy girlfriend when she didn't eat, my $10 quickly turned into $1 after we went to Panera Bread, where I bought her a Baja Mac and Cheese. When the teller handed me one dollar back, the only thought in my head was, "What's next? I can't live like this!"

Honestly, for a few moments, for a few seconds, I had thoughts like, "Well, if I died, who would notice?" Then I thought, "If I died, my grandmother would notice, but it'd probably take her a few weeks." I told my girlfriend, "Go sit down. I have to make a quick phone call." She went to sit down and wait for our order to be filled, and I went outside. Right between the outside door and the inside door, I picked up my phone and called the one lead that I felt was close to paying me for my services.

He answered, and I said, "Hey, how are you? This is John from Livefree CrossFit." Our conversation kind of went like, "Hey, man, I don't even know who you are; why am I going to pay you? You are probably going to take my money and run away." Because I had learned some things from these sales books that I was reading, I actually agreed with him, one of the first rules of sales. I agreed with him and addressed his concern. "You know what, you are right." I put my ego to the side. "You are absolutely right. I can actually just run away with your money the moment you pay me, but here is the thing, I want to build a relationship with you so you can continue paying us every single month for what we can do for you. How about if I do this for this month alone? You give half now, and you can give me the other half after you agree that I have done a good job for you."

It was dead silent. As uncomfortable as this silence was, I stayed quiet for as long as I had to because in one of the books that I had read, it said that the first person to speak in one of these silent stand-offs is the person that loses. I was determined to win. I did not say anything. The next thing that was said was from the mouth of John. He said, "OK, where do I send the money?" I told him, and I had my phone in my hand, and I got a payment notification. I looked at my hand, and I was only charging him five hundred a month, so I received about three hundred dollars upfront. Although it was only three hundred dollars, this proved to me that this concept actually works.

The biggest thing that separates a lot of people from succeeding and failing is their BELIEF. Once I believed, then I understood that this concept works. My entire life, my entire world changed. Belief is everything. Now that my belief changed, so did my reality. The first thing that I purchased with that new money was a beverage for my girlfriend at the time, and it felt great to be able to afford an overpriced cup of watered-down juice.

Now, at no time in this entire story did I mention that I actually had the skills to generate leads or traffic or run Facebook ads. The truth is I knew absolutely nothing about any of that, but I knew that if I had a client, a reason, a purpose for me to learn how to do this, I would fu**in' crush it, hands down. There would be nothing stopping me!

I sat at that table in Panera Bread, a completely different person than had previously entered, ignoring all conversations with my girlfriend. I couldn't shake the thought that I had spent all my life being friends with people who couldn't really help me. I can't even help me, but a business, a business has the resources available to help me get out of my situation.

I kept thinking, what if I make myself an asset, not to someone else, not to a good friend like Tommy or Lucy, but by being a great friend to a business? Where would that take me? I couldn't shake the thought. For the first time in my life, I felt as if I was really onto something.

From that moment forward, I decided to dedicate every single waking hour that I had to becoming a master of advertising. I committed to making my clients' business so successful, and I spent every hour of my day doing so. I had one client, and I spent at least twenty hours of my day servicing him. (**Money hack:** Most everything I learned came while being underpaid by this one client, but this allowed me to develop the skills necessary to become overpaid by all my future clients.)

Billy Gene, an amazing marketer, had a course called Genius Advantage. (I always admired his funny play on his last name.) This was my very first lesson on investment and having faith in the universe. Instead of me taking the little money that I made and putting it toward bills or food for the week, I purchased the training, a course to teach me how I could actually get results for my client. This was a very critical moment in my life and has set the foundations for many huge financial investments that I made in the future. (SPOILER ALERT: This moment pushed me to invest $50K into one training which brought me a return of over $90K in under ten minutes. Keep reading and I'll tell you all about it.)

Introducing the new Junior Anthony! "Hey! I just made some money, but I am going to take all that money and invest it into my education in hopes of making more money in the future." I had never done anything like that before. No one in my family had ever done anything like this before. But luckily for me, it worked!

Although what I was learning from Billy Gene didn't actually work and nearly cost me my client, I learned something else that was completely priceless. I learned how to stop being a little b**** and learned how to figure sh*t out. Who knew that spending $300 a day on a bunch of really crappy leads would get my client frustrated and force me into action.

Do you believe in infinite intelligence? So according to Napoleon Hill, "Faith is the only agency through which the cosmic force of infinite intelligence can be harnessed and used by man." The truth is, we all have the answers within us; we just need to awaken them. I remembered this ad, this ad of a funny fat cowboy guy with riddles and a dance talking about this thing. I couldn't remember, so I did exactly what I did previously with the Dan Henry webinar: I went searching on YouTube for ads, but it wasn't popping up, so I gave up. A few days later something popped up that prompted me to do a search on Google. This was literally my Google search: "What is the difference between a domain and hosting?" This was my biggest question, and I didn't understand it to save my life. Funny how in hindsight this search actually saved my life.

For anyone that is reading this who doesn't understand the concept of domain and hosting, allow me to literally break it down for you in the easiest way that I understood it. Your domain is your address, such as 123 Berlin Street. However, your domain has to be in a specific neighborhood, and that neighborhood would be your hosting. Example: My domain is livesotori.com, and I host my domain on clickfunnels.com.

Once I completed my search, I found the ad that I was looking for, and it turned out to be ClickFunnels. Now, I sat down and thought, "Sh*t, I don't have this money, and I am not getting paid any more money until I get this guy some results; how can I make more money so that I can afford this?" (**Money hack:** Most people cop out and say they don't have the money, but if you truthfully allow your mind to wander and you ask better questions, such as "How can I make money?" you will always get answers.)

An infinite intelligence moment occurred once again when I needed it the most. Meeting a complete stranger multiple times in the big city of New York prompted a conversation in which I was told, "Money is not physical; money is spiritual. If you get more aligned with your spirituality, you make more money." I didn't know crap about spirituality, but by now, I was getting used to the concept of figuring things out. And so I googled that too: "What is spirituality?" Then, I came across a bunch of different things, including another webinar by Vishen Lakhiani, the owner of Mindvalley, which then led me down a bunch of rabbit holes where I then came up with the name of

LiveSotori. (The soul only grows in two ways: one being Kensho, which means growing through pain, and the other being Satori, which means growing through insight).

 While sitting down and digesting all these concepts and really diving deep into what life really is and all these other things I grew up knowing nothing about, I asked myself a very important question, a very life-changing question that I am demanding every person reading this book right now ask themselves: "Why can't I get a client to pay me fifteen hundred dollars a month?" (**Note:** Everyone's number is different; for where I was in life, $1,500 was a dream). If I had a client paying me $1,500 a month, then this would solve my problem of not having any more resources to get the ClickFunnels account so that I can get results for my client.

When I asked this question, my brain literally spit out an answer in like a millisecond, saying, "Well, because you are going to have to give the money back." For a few seconds I agreed. I said, "Yeah, you're right!" While walking away from that conversation in my head, facing utter defeat, I thought, "Wait! What if I'm worth more than $1,500? Why would I need to return the money?" My brain stayed silent; it was the silence of victory. At that moment, I knew I had won that conversation.

The universe gives you everything you desire. And just like that, a few hours later, close to midnight, my phone rang. Surprise! Surprise! It was actually a client that I was trying to close; he literally called demanding that he get started with my services, "Come to the office tomorrow morning at 8:00!" I am sitting down in a dark room, thinking, "Wait, this is too weird. Like, what the heck! This must be a sign! OK, this is literally my chance to charge this guy fifteen hundred dollars." I couldn't sleep that night.

The morning came. I got dressed, tried my best to look good with whatever clothes I had, and then went to his office. We went straight to the back office and sat down, and I showed him some really cool things that I learned from a free two-week trial of ClickFunnels. I literally used ClickFunnels to pitch the idea of what was possible for him. As the conversation started progressing in my head, I was thinking, "I can't do $1,500, so I'll just do $750," convincing myself that it was a step up, and then he asked me the price.

It was one of the most nerve-racking moments in my life. I'm just glad I held my composure and remembered the conversation with myself the night prior. As sternly as possible, I replied, "$1500 a month." And once again, I remained silent. Being my first in-person sale, I attempted to make my face and body as calm as possible. I kept eye contact with him and did not say a word. He did the exact same thing that my first client did, except there was no skepticism. He just asked, "OK, where do I send the money?" I started freaking out! I thought, "Holy sh*t, this guy just said that he is about to pay me $1,500." I had never seen this much money at one time; this was crazy to me. I gave him my account information, and he sent it to me right then and there. I felt the payment notification on my phone, which was in my pocket, and although he told me to check to see if the payment was there, I nonchalantly said, "Yeah, I got the notification." I didn't check partially because I wanted to leave the perception of this being normal and partly because I would've probably cried. I hadn't eaten a meal in probably two days, and just like that, I could actually afford groceries. (**Sales tip:** Always ask for the sale. If your prospect says no or has an objection, you can always overcome it. Asking is a lot better than not asking. If you don't

171

ask, the answer will always be no.)

I didn't stop there, "Hey! Check this out. I want to help you get started right now. Last night when you called, I knew you were serious, so I went ahead and created your first website. I just need to fill in your contact information and get your domain, and it's all yours." I knew he didn't have a website, and that was one of the biggest things I was pitching to him. Once he saw that I had created his website, it was really easy to have him insert his credit card into this magical software, and just like that, I had a paid $297 subscription to ClickFunnels. (**Life hack:** always be prepared. It's easier to be prepared than to get prepared).

Not only was I then able to keep $1,500 for myself, but also I now had two clients with a ClickFunnels account that I needed to get better results for. Once I got back home, I dived deeply into ClickFunnels, fully committed to figuring things out by watching the videos and implementing them.

That is when I understood the idea of having a conversation between the ad and the offer. The problem with Facebook ads is that there is no conversation that bridges them, but with ClickFunnels, it allows me to take people from Facebook, bring them over to a landing page, have a conversation with them, and then take them to the next step. By that time, these leads were more qualified; this was a game changer for me and my clients.

Then I became a ClickFunnels addict, because just like that, this concept not only allowed me to get two clients, but a whole sh*tload of clients. I started literally racking up clients and charging them an insane amount of money to do work. I had clients of all calibers, such as a television station in New York. I had legendary clients that literally trained people like Rihanna, Oprah Winfrey, Nicole Kidman, and P. Diddy, just to name a few. I even worked for some boxing Hall of Famers, all possible due to the opportunities that ClickFunnels presented.

My entire life was changing so fast because of Russell Brunson, then CEO and cofounder of ClickFunnels. And I wanted to at least be able to tell him face-to-face how much he was changing my life, how I would probably be dead if it wasn't for him. If it wasn't for Russell Brunson, there would never be a Dan Henry; and if there was no Dan Henry, then I wouldn't have known that I could have clients. If it wasn't for Russell Brunson, there most likely wouldn't have been a Billy Gene, where I would still be stuck not knowing how to service my clients.

If there was no Russell Brunson, there would be no Junior Anthony, no LiveSotori. I wouldn't have been able to help thousands of people earn money online. If it wasn't for Russell Brunson, one of my students, Orit Bak, would probably either be dead or still a heroin addict. Thank you, Russell Brunson.

The year 2019 was a great year, until I got a call in November from my aunt. She was crying, and between her cries, I picked up the words, "Grandpa was diagnosed with stage three lung cancer."

I never really thought about the freedom of an online business, but then I was able to get on one of the next flights from New York to Florida and completely relocate without any hiccups; I realized that I didn't really have to be in any location. I could travel the world. I WAS FREE. Truthfully, I didn't really need any more clients; I was comfortable. The greatest thing about this entire thing was being able to answer a question I had asked myself a few years prior, "How can I make $5,000 without leaving my room?" I discovered that answer, and it's simple: by sending invoices to people.

I went to Florida pretty much with nothing. I just grabbed one backpack and hopped on a plane because I was intending to come back to New York, that is, until I saw the condition my grandfather was in. He was really bad, but luckily, over the next six months, his health began to improve, and he gained his weight back.

Then COVID happened. It was crazy because I even lost clients that I never thought would leave me for a million years; people were panicking. I mean, obviously, you could just move your business online. If your physical location is closed, figure out an online alternative, so when things open back up, you now have two different income streams. Always look for the positive alternative.

Example: Your gym is shut down because of the pandemic. A negative way of thinking would be, "I need to lower my expenses, fire people, do anything in my power to survive for the next few months until the government allows me to run my business again." A positive way of thinking would be, "Great! All of my competitors are panicking; how can I capitalize on this once-in-a-lifetime opportunity? Maybe I look around at other adjacent opportunities such as the market leader, Mirror (a smart fitness mirror), and mirror what they are doing (get it, mirror, Mirror). Or perhaps I can create an online exercise program, offer membership-based private intensity training, or pitch an exercise routine as a way to boost your immune system to directly combat any Covid infections, and the list can literally go on.

(**Money hack:** Don't ever retract. Always think of new ways to expand. In every world crisis, there are people who have turned a crisis into millions. My company, LiveSotori, is one of them. We started in May of 2020 in the beginning of the pandemic, and we made our first million in just nine months. Meanwhile, everyone was fearful of business and sat on their hands waiting for a sign.

On a very sunny, beautiful Florida day, a friend of mine reached out to me and asked me, "Hey, Junior! Where you at? I've been following you. You always been different. You no longer do music?" I replied nonchalantly, "No, I am just doing this online thing." At this point he had already put his music career on the back burner to be able to drive for Uber and Lyft to make money. (I already had experience in that department while I was homeless, so I gave him a little idea that added an extra $100 per day to his bank account, so he trusted my money-making abilities). He then asked me, "Hey! How can I do what you are doing? Can you help me? Can I work with you?" And of course, at that point in time, I had completely severed my relationship with all my friends, so I wasn't too eager to slow down and help him, but I did.

I had him start by having his own online business, because he could use that business to generate listeners for his music. It didn't take long for me to realize he lacked common sense and the ability to sell. Once I confirmed my beliefs, I regrouped with him and pointed him in another direction, to affiliate marketing. I told him that affiliate marketing gave him the ability to help someone else's business. I began showing him all types of different affiliate offers available, and then I literally took out my credit card and purchased an affiliate offer on Instagram so that he could understand how affiliate marketing works.

A few days passed, and unfortunately, just as I expected, he gave up on it. One thing I can say is entrepreneurship is not made for everybody. Everyone can do it, but some people just don't have the stick-to-itiveness required to make entrepreneurship work, especially online.

So then I started getting these notifications to join this group, thinking it's a cool accountability thing. I joined, then later realized it was just a bunch of people complaining about really small, trivial things. I always knew I was good at what I did, but It wasn't until I started seeing all of these people complaining about what was not working for them that I realized how advanced I had become. (**Money hack:** if you want to become really good at something, practice something called *assi-do-ity*, which is keeping your ass in your seat and doing it until you see results. I literally locked myself up in my basement so that I could be the best asset to my clients.)

To succeed, you need a high level of commitment. I literally studied Gary Halbert, an amazing copywriter. I watched TV only to watch commercials. (I would watch a commercial, and whenever the TV shows came up, I would go to another channel that showed the commercial so I could study them). I fully immersed myself in this entire marketing phenomenon.

Once I stepped back into the real world, I started seeing people asking the same simple questions. I started helping, more and more of these people every day. People started recognizing me within the community as the go-to guy, but the only problem here is I kept seeing the same faces coming back day after day, asking the same question. This older lady came to me asking me for help. And I told her exactly what to do, which was the same thing I was telling everyone else to do. This was the exact same thing that I do for my clients. She came back to me twenty-four hours later, and she had made a $2,000 sale using Blake Nubar's products. So I sat down, and I thought to myself, "Well, the thing that I'm helping everyone with clearly works if someone was able to use my method to make $2,000."

Once she came back to me asking me, "Hey! You literally made me $2,000 in twenty-four hours! What do I have to do next?" I began thinking, "How come everyone is not getting the same result?" And on that same exact day, I had this guy who sent me a bunch of messages, including his bank account statement showing that he only had $3 to his name. He was an American that lived in the Philippines.

He said, "My birthday is in the next two days, and if you can help me, it would mean the world not only for me but also for my kids!" Truthfully, the thing that I loved about him was that he didn't ask for money. He just asked for an opportunity to make money. Once I read his message, I prayed on it, and I thought, "Well, this lady just made $2,000 on an affiliate product, using the same information that I gave her, and it took her only twenty-four hours. And this guy desperately needs to make money. I also had all these people asking me all these things, and they were not getting any value out of it, probably because they were not paying for my help." So I had a realization, "What if I just charge for it and allow these people to be my affiliates? I teach them the same thing that I'm teaching now, and I help them to make money." And that's what I did.

So I launched my kickass offer the very next day. Believe it or not, I was able to help that guy make his first $100 online within twenty-four hours before his birthday. He was so happy! I helped a few other people to make money online as well. I got more and more people asking me, "Hey, Junior, can you help me make money? Can I join your team? Hey, I want to be an affiliate for you."

Before I knew it, I had an entire army of over a hundred active affiliates selling whichever product I recommended. I also realized that affiliate marketing isn't just a passive thing, but if treated properly, it could even be better and more profitable than starting a business. What if affiliate marketing can be the new normal, just like being a waiter or bartender or working in a retail store? What if affiliate marketing can be the thing that most people go to if they need to make money online or even just to make money in general? Instead of them getting a job, they just go into affiliate marketing, where they learn a lot more skills, such as sales, communication, and social skills? What if affiliate marketing could be that vehicle for them to achieve financial freedom?

I got tunnel vision serving people in affiliate marketing and fired my remaining clients. I became so dialed in, so obsessed with this concept of, "Hey, I used to be homeless, and now I'm able to help other people overcome their own personal problems, as well as elevate both their mindset and skillset."

Some people don't have homes. Some people don't have any money. Some people get divorced and lose it all. Some people lose their job and are left with nothing. With affiliate marketing, they can all rebuild their lives. I fell completely in love with this new concept.

During my first Annual SotoriLive Family Growth Reunion event in August 2021, I noticed Funnel Hacking Live was only a few weeks away. So I decided to bring some of my Sotorians (LiveSotori students) to FHL.

The challenge was having about forty to fifty people that were with me in August and now, a pop-up event with literally two weeks' notice. We had about twelve people come to FHL in 2021. While being there, I was able to receive my Two Comma Club Award, which was so amazing. I was able to shake hands with Russell Brunson, the guy that had changed my entire life. That actually blew my mind!

Then I met Robbie Summers, who then told me about this other opportunity. He didn't tell me much, but he told me enough to pique my interest. I thought to myself, "Well, the more training I get, the better I am and the better I can serve my students and community."

I forgot exactly how, but I found myself in this Two Comma Club Award winner lunch with no voice left. (We made a lot of noise not only for all award winners but also for all presenters). We sat down, and Russell actually came back into the room. He gave a speech and then offered this thing called the Inner Circle. Apparently, he had shut it down but brought it back this year. (I keep telling people I am the luckiest person alive). I made a commitment to do whatever it took to be among the GOATs. Then, I signed up.

It was like $50,000, and at that time, I had never spent $50,000 on anything in my life, so that was scary. That was my single biggest purchase, but because of that experience, I have made so many other big purchases after that, which have benefited my life tremendously. As a result of me being in the Inner Circle, I have now been able to provide high-ticket offers. I was awarded the Two Comma Club selling low-ticket items, which I later found out was an extremely difficult approach.

Being in the Inner Circle, I was able to make $90,000 in about ten minutes. I have been able to raise the prices of my training for my students literally by fivefold. It would have never been possible if I didn't get the mindset training from people like Robbie or if I didn't get access to the belief from Russell. In the Inner Circle I have met and befriended amazing people such as Bart and Sunny Miller, Justin Benton, Erik Sorenson, Nate Armstrong, AJ Rivera, Kristin Mirelle, Myron Golden, Damon Burton, and even Russell Brunson. The list goes on.

My life has changed completely from being in the Inner Circle with Russell. We literally had Russell Brunson present at our Second Annual SotoriLive Family Growth Reunion, which is still mind-boggling to me, even while writing this.

I have seen myself in his promotional videos and sales videos. It is so crazy how my life could literally go from me being homeless, not having anything, sleeping in my car, and almost freezing to death, to now having pretty much anything that I want.

I wrote this chapter in paradise, aka Xcaret, Mexico. And it means the world to me to have had the ability to coach and help bring over forty Sotorians (who otherwise couldn't afford it) to this luxury resort, made possible because of affiliate marketing. All of these things were possible because of Russell Brunson, because I trusted him, because I joined the Inner Circle. If you are thinking about joining the Inner Circle, now is the time. And if you have yet to reach the status of Inner Circle, do whatever you have to do to get there.

When Russell offered me the $50K price point and I saw there was another price point for another $150K, I think I went up to Coach Vince and said, "Hey, Coach! I don't want to buy this one. Can I buy the one for $150K because everything that I have belongs to Russell?"

Obviously, he told me no. "Darn it!" The $150K is only for the Two Comma Club X winners.

I have that much appreciation and gratitude for Russell, Todd, the ClickFunnels team and the entire Inner Circle Family. If you go into it with the mindset of gratitude, to give back, to serve and be part of something bigger than yourself, like me, you will be able to accomplish greatness in a short period of time, such as being featured in *Forbes*, having priceless experiences, collaborating with like-minded multimillionaires, being able to change many lives, and having one of my students go from homeless to literally making $20K in one month. One of my other students, Trang Nguyen, literally lost her entire business because of Covid and ended up making $160K the next year. I've been blessed to have all of these amazing experiences. (**Money insight:** Your network equals your "net worth." Show me your friends, and I'll show you your future.)

It is all going to start with you being committed, serious, determined, and driven, not focusing on the money but focusing on the impact, focusing on the legacy, focusing on what you want to leave for the world and the message you want to show.

If you take away only one thing from my chapter, let it be this: "All you need in life is a dollar and a dream." Thank you.

STEPHANIE DOVE BLAKE

From High School Dropout to Seven-Figure Entrepreneur: A Homeschooling Momma's Story

Stephanie Dove Blake is a 2 Comma Club award winning, recognized marketer, speaker, author, and coach with a docket of praise from industry-shifting marketing experts like Russell Brunson, Billy Gene, and Julie Chenell. But perhaps more importantly to her, she's helped hundreds of her clients build their businesses and make the impact they're destined for.

Stephanie started her agency in 2016 as a struggling homeschooling momma of 4. Despite all odds, this high school dropout, techie-geek grew a 7-figure agency from scratch and has made waves in the industry.

But accolades and accomplishments are one thing; what makes Stephanie a true unicorn is her love for people paired with a fierce dedication to building a business while keeping her family first.

Stephanie brings passion, strategy, inspiration and brilliant creativity to whatever she puts her hands to. Stephanie is the wife to a red-bearded hero, mother to 4 out-of-the-box blessings and a lover of all things Jesus, marketing, Back to the Future, Princess Bride & BlueBell Ice Cream.

My road to the Inner Circle looks much less like a road and more like an almost-indistinguishable-to-anyone-else path because, well, my journey to the current destination was a highly unlikely one.

Fatherless.

Poor.

High school dropout.

Unseen.

Trauma, and lots of it.

I wasn't a poster child for future success by any stretch. I was much more likely to end up building a life of drugs than funnels. So if you're reading this right now and you know you've never fit the mold and never plan to . . . high five, I see you. Here's to forging our own path to success.

When I think back now, I can see it. Little hints and clues that I have been an entrepreneur from the beginning. But it wasn't until Funnel

Hacking Live 2016 that I finally realized that I belong to this 1 percent crazy group of entrepreneurs . . . thanks, Russell!

Up until that point I think I thought I was just on a roll . . . I was "lucky" . . . a string of back-to-back blessings . . . and it was DEFINITELY going to blow up in my face at any moment!

At that point I had just started an agency using funnels, and our WHOLE life had changed. I'm talking serious life-change. We went from barely making it with my husband working two jobs, with me working from home while homeschooling our four children, to making six figures in under six months and bringing my husband home.

I've now scaled that agency to seven figures, built an incredible team of thirteen, and serve our clients from all over the US.

But how did that happen? And how did I end up in the Inner Circle?

In 2016 I found this incredible funnel hacking world all because of a funnel. I believe it was the *DotCom Secrets* book funnel. On the back end of that funnel, I remember seeing a video with Russell talking to a bunch of people on a panel on a stage. He was interviewing these people about what had happened in their lives since they had started building funnels for others.

Story after story, I was blown away. I still remember staring at the screen and kind of feeling almost like a heat rash on my face. I don't know if others feel this, but it's when you know that you've happened upon something that could potentially change your life. At the end of the video, there was an invitation to apply to become a ClickFunnels CERTIFIED Funnel Builder.

It's so funny to me now because I now recognize that there was no real "application" process that I had to be approved into. At that time I had no idea about any sales tactics, so when I received the email that I had been "accepted" into the program, I was over the moon.

I had given my heart and soul in this application process, and I got in. I was then invited to get on the phone with someone at ClickFunnels, and they proceeded to talk to me about my dreams and goals. They connected the dots for me on how becoming a CF Certified Funnel Builder could be the key to making my dreams come true.

And then they dropped the price tag.

$10,000.

$10,000?

I remember feeling the blood drain from my face as I stared off into the white curtains in my room, my brain scrambling . . . "Did he just say $10,000 dollars?"

I didn't have a thousand dollars to my name. We were living paycheck to paycheck. There were things that were broken in our house that we couldn't afford to get fixed: a bathroom with no hot water, our fence was falling down from a windstorm . . . How in the world could I figure out how to get $10,000 when we were not sure we could pay the mortgage some months?

I was determined. I knew this program was going to be the key to me being able to stay at home with my children and homeschool, all while bringing in more money for our family.

I was *supposed* to be in this program. I can't explain it. I knew that I knew that I know that I needed to be in this program, but the reality was we didn't have the money. I thought through the items we had to sell in our home . . . DEFINITELY not enough money from our second-hand furniture. I talked to my husband about getting a credit card and seeing if we could get one with a high enough credit limit to use. We both decided that wasn't an option for us.

I was supposed to get back with the sales guy the next day with my payment choice. I felt this sinking feeling going to bed that night. I was like, "I'm missing out on a huge opportunity. I believe in myself, and I know that if I could just get into this program and get the skills, I could change our lives."

I woke up the next morning and was still battling in my mind, searching for a way to make it happen. And then it hit me. I had this epiphany, and I decided I knew what I needed to do to get the money.

I decided that I could sell enough stuff online and I could get about $1,000. And then, get this . . . (I'm still in awe that I was brave enough to do this while simultaneously cringing inside that I took action on this hair-brained idea) . . . I was going to reach out to three contacts that I had been doing some work for. I felt like these people could easily let go of $3,000 and wouldn't miss it.

What if I wrote those three people and told them about the opportunity that was in front of me and then asked them to invest in me in return for six months of funnel work in the future.

If all three people said yes at $3K each plus my $1K, then I'd have the money I needed!

So I did it. I wrote the email. And the CRAZIEST thing happened.

One of them wrote back and said he wanted to give me the FULL $10,000! As I read his words, I remember I was shaking. I couldn't believe it. I kept saying to myself, "This is gonna happen. This is *really* gonna happen. I'm gonna do this!"

This contact chose to believe in me and wrote me a check for $10,000. I had never spent more than maybe $37 or $47 online on any kind of learning of anything. It was far beyond me to think about spending even a thousand dollars on something online.

Then there I was with this $10,000 check and was going to go plop it down and give it to Russell Brunson so I could build funnels?

Of COURSE I was!

Truly, it was one of the best decisions I've ever made. It laid a solid foundation of knowledge that enabled me to unlock talents and gifts inside myself that I didn't know were there.

I began learning about different types of funnels, offers, direct response copy, funnel design, and more. It was like a master's degree in digital marketing.

I'd had recent success building a funnel and running ads for a chiropractor for free. Now that I was armed with this knowledge, it helped me have the confidence to do a webinar with that chiropractor client for OTHER chiropractors. Our first webinar together, there were ten chiropractors on the call. Nine out of ten of those guys signed up, and I had my first $7,000 day in my agency.

It was a $7K day that had started with cooking breakfast for my four children, doing homeschooling lessons for the first part of the day, checking accounts during nap time, and then doing the webinar that evening.

I continued to grow my agency to six figures within six months and hired my first employee by the end of the year. Fast forward to now (2022), and we have thirteen employees and serve chiropractors all over the country.

The *beautiful thing* about being an entrepreneur is that we are high-achieving creators.

And . . . the *difficult thing* about being an entrepreneur is that we are high-achieving creators.

As my agency began to grow, I began to say yes to every fun/creative/interesting opportunity that came up. We ran ads for e-comm, infopreneurs, locally based businesses, coaches . . . I was funnel happy, and there were so many people to serve and courses to create!

The BOT craze happened, and I was among the few proud bot-preneurs who created a course on how to build and sell bots. It was awesome, and I loved every minute of that journey . . . and then there was a Facebook Ads course . . . and a Pixel course for bloggers . . . and a funnel-building service for wedding creatives . . .

Before I knew it, I was working sixty- to seventy-hour weeks while still trying to homeschool my children.

I had "yes'd" my way into a big mess.

I was a successful, multi-six-figure business owner who low-key was questioning her entire business existence. I built this business so that I could be with my kids at home, and now, it was keeping me from my kids. This was NOT the freedom lifestyle that I had envisioned.

A dear entrepreneur friend of mine once told me . . . "You know, Stephanie, starting a business is a lot like going to a pet store and picking out a really cute baby alligator. It's adorable at first, and it starts growing, and you teach it a few tricks, and then one day, you wake up and you realize that your cute baby alligator is now as BIG AS YOU! And it's gnawing on your leg and threatening to swallow you WHOLE!"

When he told me this, it stuck . . . and I thought that there was no way I would build a business that would swallow me whole.

BUT THERE I WAS! I had worked so hard and built an amazing team of rock stars, but even though they were incredible, I still found myself working sixty to seventy hours a week.

No matter how many times I thought I'd finally have a break and have stopped all of the things that were fighting and vying for my time . . .

. . . there I'd be. Staring at my screen . . . my to-do list still sitting there . . .

I knew I had worked my tail off that day, but yet I didn't work on the things that I knew were going to grow my business.

I knew things had to change drastically.

Thankfully Russell had sold me into a $20K program called Two Comma Club X in March of 2018. I was listening to all the advice except to focus on ONE funnel, and it showed. Through that program a solution was solidified in my brain because of a training that we received from Alex Charfen.

He told us, "What got you here will kill you going forward." We had to adapt, eliminate pressure and noise in our lives, and learn how to get out of our business so we could work ON it and not IN it.

That confirmed it. I had to cut off all the fluff, shut down my courses, let go of all of my nonchiropractor clients, and hire an integrator. At that point my team and I were running ads for a few of the biggest names in the industry. To niche back down was going to cut tens of thousands of dollars off from my agency. But I was convinced it was the only path to setting things straight, freeing my time, and helping my business get back to what I had dreamed it could be.

I started working on cutting away the fluff, but the biggest key was going to be getting an A player into my business to help me manage it. I knew that I needed to hire someone with WAY more consistency and all the things I was not, to help me create and implement systems into my business that I knew would change everything.

I hired a friend to become my integrator, and the results were incredible! She and I went to work together, implementing, changing, adapting, and ultimately creating the systems that freed me from the prison that I'd built.

And I'm proud to say that I went from those soul-sucking sixty to seventy hours per week to working in my business just five to ten hours in about a month and a half!

This story is important because in 2019 right as I had just freed myself, Russell asked if I would join the 2CCX coaching team and help coach hundreds of entrepreneurs in their journey in a part-time capacity.

That was an immediate yes for me. I couldn't wait to get in there and start serving my Funnel Hacker family. The experience that I had coaching in this program unlocked something within me. I had no idea that I would love coaching as much as I did. I was able to champion people who were like me and help them find pathways to make their dreams happen.

It was like magic for my soul. So after the program switched from contract labor coaches to employed coaches, I continued on in my coaching journey on my own by taking on three coaching clients per quarter.

During that time, I was able to help three of my clients reach seven figures in less than ten months. The confidence and revenue that came from this period of coaching leveled up my ability to believe and dream.

Over the course of my journey, I've seen my ability to dream BIG dreams expand exponentially. Stephanie, eight years ago, would have NEVER imagined building a six figure business . . . much less building it to seven figures, coaching others to do the same, joining the Inner Circle, and speaking on the Funnel Hacking Live stage.

I look back now, and I'm so very grateful! So much gratitude goes to Russell for saying yes to showing up for his audience. I joke around with the staff at ClickFunnels that they need to rename Russell's female avatar Stephanie.

It all started with Russell saying YES to showing up for the people he was called to: the "Stephanies" of the world who might not know that their "different" is what will set them apart, that they have the capacity within them to change the world in a way that only they can . . . and their tribe is waiting on THEM to show up.

So friend and fellow Funnel Hacker . . . what are you waiting for?

One foot in front of the other . . .

Conquering one fear at a time . . .

Solving problem after problem . . . relentlessly . . .

Because it's what you were born to do! If I can do this, so can YOU! All you have to do is choose to show up and play all out and not quit!

And remember, you never LOSE. You only WIN or you LEARN something (Nelson Mandela).

See you in the Inner Circle! ;)

Stephanie Dove Blake

www.stephaniedoveblake.com

SAM KWAK

From Near Deportation to Millionaire

Since 2019, the Kwak Brothers have built successful real estate investment companies, educational courses, coaching programs, and software to help emerging real estate professionals grow their own real estate investing businesses. Today, the Kwak Brothers are on a mission to help every family achieve financial peace of mind.

—

The Kwak Brothers Story

Our Backstory

It took us twelve visa applications to get to the United States, become illegal immigrants and almost get deported, and then ultimately join the military, being flat out broke and riddled with debt. But a moment of redemption and transformation happened that allowed us to build a multi-million dollar business, which is where we are today as Inner Circle members. From broke and poor immigrants to a manifestation of the American dream, here is our story. It was all because of the grace of God and His leading.

My name is Sam Kwak. My brother, Daniel, and I were originally born in South Korea in the early '90s. We were born to a dad who was a church pastor (and still is) and a mom who was a piano teacher who is now retired. We grew up in a small town with less than two hundred residents. It was a small farm town in where you had two corner stores, a church, and an elementary school.

Our journey to the United States began in 1999. My dad was called to pastor a church here in the United States, specifically, a church for Korean American immigrants in Chicago, Illinois.

To enter the United States legally, we had to apply for a specific visa that allowed my parents to work here as members of the clergy. Each time we applied for the visa, we kept getting denied.

But still, my parents firmly believed that they had a calling and a mission to serve Korean American immigrants. They were relentless and persistent. Denial after denial, my parents kept applying for the visa even if it cost fees each time. Each time, the entire family would go to the US embassy to be interviewed and explain why we wanted to enter the United States.

Then, on the twelfth try, the US finally granted our visa. I remember that day as if it was yesterday. My dad walked downstairs from the second-floor office to go pick up the mail. Inside the mailbox was a thick envelope. Just imagine something like a FedEx envelope. My dad slowly opened the envelope. Inside contained our passports, each for our four-member family. But this time, it was different. My dad paused each time he opened one passport after another. He hurried inside and yelled, "WE GOT IT!"

As a young child, this taught me a lesson that if you want something in life, you persist and persevere. Even today, I believe that I can accomplish anything as long as I put enough time and energy into it. But most importantly, when you surround yourself with others who have either gone before you or they are in the pursuit of the same mission, your chance of accomplishing your goals increases exponentially!

After the announcement, all I remember afterward is packing all of our belongings into a large box—everything we owned. I had to tell my friends at school that I was leaving soon for the United States. Then on December 8, 1999, we boarded the plane from the Gimpo International Airport in Seoul, South Korea.

As soon as we arrived here at O'Hare International Airport, we drove to a small apartment in Chicago, Illinois, and that began our journey here in the United States.

Fast-forward to twelve years later, I graduated from high school, and I wasn't sure what to do with my life. I decided to join the United States Army because I wanted something challenging in my life, and I wanted to get away from home as much as I could. At the same time, I did want to go to college primarily because of parental pressure. So I decided to join the Army Reserve so that I could still go to college and be a member of the military at the same time.

It was after my first semester of college that I realized that I wanted to start my own business. Honestly, the thought came to me out of nowhere. Today, I call it God tapping on my shoulder with an idea. I didn't give up on school but rather started the business in between homework and class.

Just like Russell, I got obsessed with the idea of being able to sell my services and products from my dorm room. I was trying to make this work. I remember having to refund my first client because I screwed up delivering it. I was terrified, but that didn't stop me from persisting and finding my next client.

In 2014, I read a book called *Rich Dad Poor Dad* by Robert Kiyosaki that opened a whole new world of finance and entrepreneurship for me. I never knew that it was possible to own real estate as a business to ultimately create income without a huge ongoing investment of time. This led me to slowly discontinue the business I had built for the past two years and begin diving into real estate investing. I got obsessed. I read every book that I could get my hands on. I watched every YouTube video and listened to every podcast there was back in 2014 so that I could formulate my first steps into this business.

But as you can imagine, I was only twenty-two years old at the time. I had zero savings and no credit history. No bank was ever going to loan me money, and I didn't have money for a down payment to do my first real estate deal.

It wasn't until 2015 that I got connected with a local community of real estate investors where I began to build relationships with some of the top players in the area. This is when I quickly realized the power of association. I realized that who I choose to associate with could determine my success. This is the same mindset I had that led me to join Russell's Inner Circle mastermind. I'll unpack more on this in just a moment.

As I began to build relationships with some of the top players in the area, I even offered to work for free just so that I could learn as much as possible. I would show up nearly every day to shadow what these people did. I assimilated much of their styles, strategies, tactics, and how they would approach potential opportunities. I did this for almost three years while still trying to pay the rent and bills on top of it.

It wasn't until April of 2017 that my brother and I closed our first real estate deal ever! We were twenty-five and twenty-three years old at the time. We managed to acquire four properties as a portfolio for our first deal. It was all because of the strategies, tactics, and business models we learned from the top players that mentored us. We are eternally grateful for them.

That same year, we bought over $5 million worth of real estate, and the rest is history. And because of our success, we were able to grow our affiliate marketing business at the time, selling real estate courses. We were doing six figures just from selling real estate education as a marketing affiliate. And the more success we had with our affiliate marketing business, the more I fell in love with marketing.

I increasingly became more familiar with ideas like webinars, opt-ins, building landing pages, and so on.

And it was late 2018 when I heard the name Russell Brunson for the first time.

At first, I thought Russell was one of "those gurus" out there until I saw his presentation at Grant Cardone's 10X Conference. And when I saw how he closed the stadium with a legendary table rush, I couldn't believe it.

I know what a table rush looked like. Every week when I did live presentations as an affiliate, I would see a line form up to get people signed up for the next steps. But this. This was something else.

I literally saw people running and some nearly tripping over people. This could not have been hired actors doing this. Somehow I thought Russell hypnotized these people to run to the back to sign up for Russell's offer on stage. But it was all real.

So I immediately thought to myself, "I have to know what this guy knows about presenting." Russell was a genius.

At first, I didn't buy Russell's offer on stage. I cared more about the fact that Russell was able to get a huge crowd *sprinting* with their credit cards in their hand.

But then, when Russell came out with an offer to show others how he pulled it off, I told myself, "I'm in!" This was the 10X Secrets.

I took out my credit card to buy. I put my credit number down, and something weird happened. It didn't give me a confirmation page, but instead, it asked me if I was going to buy this other offer that he had. I was so confused, but at the same time, I had a "holy smokes" moment. He offered the very slide template he used to close the room. So I bought that too!

Later that evening, I began diving into the program. Minute by minute, I was taking notes. I wrote down action steps that I could take. With everything I learned, I went back to my own affiliate business at the time to begin implementing it.

But there was a problem.

The compliance officer of the company that we were affiliates with just released several guidelines of what we could and couldn't do to promote the educational program. If we wanted to use our own materials, we had to get everything approved. Word quickly spread that the compliance officer would deny many of the materials that the other affiliates wanted to use. My brother and I also had a growing YouTube channel at the time with almost thirty thousand subscribers. The compliance officer also wanted to restrict us on what we were allowed to publish.

My brother and I thought we were affiliates, not employees.

I really wanted to use Russell's Perfect Webinar framework to promote the educational programs of an affiliate, but I had a feeling that we were going to get denied. The compliance officer even denied materials that came from some of the top affiliates that were making more money than us at the time. I thought to myself, "There's no way we're going to be able to use the Perfect Webinar framework with these guys."

In just a few days, after many hours of prayer, my brother and I decided that we were going to start our own real estate education company. "Why not?" we thought. After all, we had closed millions of dollars of deals, and we know what it took. We had the framework and the strategies to teach so that we could help others duplicate our success even faster.

So because my desire to use the Perfect Webinar framework was SO strong, we decided to end our six-figure relationship as an affiliate so that we could start our own company.

We wanted to be free to use the marketing and sales strategies that Russell taught. We believed that his framework trumped whatever framework we were using at the time.

From then on, I bought all of Russell's books, starting with *Expert Secrets*.

On January 1, 2019, we officially launched our very own company. It was the second week of January when we decided to do a live webinar for almost three hundred people with our very own perfect webinar. The whole thing was about an hour, and we had almost twenty people join our program.

It was one of the most freeing things I've ever done in my life.

The fact that we were able to create a program from scratch and ultimately use our own webinars was incredibly exhilarating. It was incredibly freeing to me.

However, I still didn't buy into ClickFunnels yet. I was stubbornly trying to be as cheap as possible by not using ClickFunnels because I thought it cost "too much money" at $97 a month at the time. So instead, I built our entire course and member area inside of a WordPress theme. And boy, this was a big mistake.

First, the entire site crashed at one point. I remember being in Los Angeles to consult a client in person. Then I got a text saying that our entire site had crashed and that none of my students could get in. I remember my body tensed up so severely that certain parts of my body get tender if the same emotions come up. I dropped everything I was doing and went back to my hotel room to fix the issue.

It turns out that I accidentally deleted the entire server. The only backup I had was a version of the site that was still underdeveloped. So I spent the next hours putting it back together. I even brought the laptop into the computer as I was trying to fix the issue AND drive back to the airport at the same time. Don't try this.

Even when I got to the gate, I was still working on bringing the site back to life.

That was one issue, but I remember our refund rate was up to 15 percent because our students couldn't navigate the site properly. They would tell me that the site was too complicated to use. They couldn't figure out where to go to start watching the classes.

That's when I decided to throw my hands up and surrender to the idea of signing up for ClickFunnels. As soon as we switched and brought everything into ClickFunnels, our refunds went down to only 5 percent. That 10 percent of the difference probably cost me more than $97 a month that I could have paid instead. Plus, all those hours and the physical stress that I had to endure left me exhausted. It was not worth it.

So as I plunged deeper into the ClickFunnels world, I heard Russell talk about the Two Comma Club award. I remember thinking to myself, "There's no way I'm going to get that award. I'm too far out. It's going to take forever to get that."

All I could focus on was day-by-day improving my funnel, my service, and my business and serving my customers to the best of my ability. I decided to hire my first sales rep at the time. It was one of the best decisions I made in my life. This sales rep, Joel, is now my VP of sales and owns part of the company I started in 2019.

But something happened in late 2019 that changed my business forever.

Through the Funnel Hacker community, I've begun learning from people who were part of the Two Comma Club and the Inner Circle. They were telling me that I should raise my prices and I needed to narrow down my offer to a specific quantifiable end result.

We raised our prices from $497 to $1,497 by the end of December 2019. We started to focus on servicing one aspect of our business, and we got very clear on the result we wanted to help our clients achieve. Then in early 2020, we raised the prices again from $1,497 to $1,997. From $1,997 to $2,997. We kept raising our prices, but people kept buying. We finally ended the year 2020 with our price being $3,997.

By far, the decision to keep raising prices helped us achieve our Two Comma Club Award. It was only a year and a half ago when I was riddled with doubt and a lack of confidence. I never thought I would be able to win the Two Comma Club Award that quickly, in less than eighteen months. My belief in limiting thinking has been shattered.

During the 2021 Funnel Hacking Live, Russell invited all of the Two Comma Club winners to join the Inner Circle after it was closed. This moment of decision goes right back to 2015 when I decided to rub shoulders with some of the top players in my area as it pertains to real estate. I knew that If I associated myself with other Two Comma Club award winners, I could quickly solve roadblocks and challenges through people who overcame them in the past. Equally, I knew there would be people who were going through challenges that I overcame before.

Of course, the "lower brain" side of me was trembling because of the financial commitment to be part of the mastermind. But my "higher brain" side knew this was the only logical decision to break through to the next level of my business.

So despite my fear, I pressed on. Every part of my lower brain was telling me that I was crazy. I remember telling Daniel, "Holy crap, I can't believe we just signed up for Russell's Inner Circle!" It took me a few days to process that decision.

But because we made that decision, our business grew another 50 percent from 2021 to 2022. And my goal is to increase our business again by 100 percent by the end of 2023, effectively doubling our business. That would in turn qualify us for the Two Comma Club X Award.

More specifically, I remember jumping on a call with Robbie Summers to see if there was anything in our process that caused friction for our prospects from becoming clients. A little tweak that Robbie suggested increased our opt-in rates for forms that included phone numbers. And the best part is, we had real phone numbers coming in, not fake numbers!

That is allowing my sales team to make effective outbound calls which translates to more qualified appointments and sales.

It was those little tweaks and adjustments that made a big impact on our revenue.

In another instance, my brother and I decided to launch another high-ticket offer as part of the value ladder. We wanted to increase our belief and credibility, so we decided to launch a five-day challenge to help our students get quick results. The only problem was that I never launched a challenge in my life! Thankfully, there were a handful of Inner Circle members that won Two Comma Club Awards through challenges. They were incredibly gracious and generous in offering their own time to help put a challenge together. Which has certainly helped us generate even more sales for our high ticket coaching offer.

While these instances may not seem like a huge leap forward, I count them as inflection points that create the biggest results in the big picture. I am more than happy to say that our financial commitment to join the Inner Circle Mastermind has certainly paid off, and it will continue to pay dividends.

What was also interesting is that there were Two Comma Club Award winners that didn't decide to join the Inner Circle. I remember meeting them and befriending them, and I expected I would see them again in Boise. But it turns out that they didn't join. By no means am I shaming or judging them for not joining. Everyone is going through a different set of circumstances, and understandably, not everyone can join.

But I often wonder about those who did have the financial resources to join but chose not to. Have they made a decision not to grow their business? Did they feel like they'd arrived? Did they join another mastermind group? Whatever the case, I sincerely hope and wish them well.

However, I realized at that moment that some people choose to create their own barriers to the growth they want. In other words, some people let their lower brain hijack their more logical higher brain, which keeps them from making powerful decisions that lead to powerful results. Unfortunately, the sticker shock of joining the Inner Circle mastermind overtook some individuals.

For me, joining the Inner Circle has led to deeper friendships, new ideas, and improvements to existing ideas. This, by far, has led my business to grow and continue to grow because of the momentum I was able to build. I know it will do the same for many who are considering joining, but they must overcome fear and the hold of their lower brain making the decision.

Ultimately, I believe the journey of growing one's business is actually a journey of pushing beyond fear, limited thinking, beliefs, and outlook on life. I truly believe that if an entrepreneur cannot master his or her own inner challenges, they will have a hard time mastering the outer challenges.

So think of joining the Inner Circle as a way to break through the next level of YOUR abilities to overcome fear. The faster you can overcome the next big fear, the faster you can apply those new fear-busting muscles to grow your business as well.

ANISSA HOLMES

From Average to WOW! The Secrets I Learned to Achieve Multiple Six-Figure Months!

Founder of the Delivering WOW Platinum Coaching Program for practice owners and teams, Business Quick Start Program for pre-startups and associates, and the Delivering WOW Marketing program, Dr. Anissa Holmes helps practices grow by focusing on leadership, effective case presentation, schedule and systems optimization, and implementing high-return marketing. While others are helping their clients have multiple six-figure years, she is actually helping her clients have multiple six-figure months.

Dr. Holmes has been named one of Ultradent's Female Icons of Dentistry and Dental Product Report's TOP 25 Women in Dentistry, and has been featured in top publications such as Dental Economics,

Dentistry IQ, Dental Products Report, and Entrepreneur Magazine. Dr. Holmes is also the author of the bestselling book, **Delivering WOW: How Dentists Can Build a Fascinating Brand and Achieve More While Working Less.**

In addition to coaching and being an International Dental Speaker, including being the business keynote for the 2022 AACD annual session and the business speaker for Catapult Education, Dr. Holmes has been a featured speaker at Social Media Marketing World and Funnel Hacking Live. Dr. Holmes is also dentistry's leading digital marketing expert, having trained over five thousand practices to leverage social media to effectively grow their practices, and her **Delivering WOW Dental Podcast** *has listeners in over 125 countries.*

—

My journey to entrepreneurship began at a very early age. I remember being at the pediatrician with my dad. At the end of the appointment, despite the nurse providing my immunization, my dad wrote the check to the doctor. I remember being very curious and asking my dad, "Dad, why did you write the check to the doctor? He did not even see me." He smiled, looked at me, and said, "Well, that's because the doctor owns the business." I simply responded that I needed to be the doctor.

Fast-forward fifteen years later, once I had created a successful multi-million dollar dental practice that was running like a well-oiled machine, with a duplicatable processes, my then business coach,

Marcia, asked me one question that challenged me to think about my future path as an entrepreneur.

She said, "I know your office manager is now running your practice as COO. I know your team are all leaders. I know that you are known all over your community for impeccable service and community impact, and I know that you have discovered little-known ways to get fifty to eighty patients a month for your practice while spending less than $500 a month. My next question is . . . what's next for you? What will be your legacy?"

I thought long and hard and decided to write a book so that I could share the exact steps of how I accomplished success in my practice in such a short time with other colleagues. As I was writing my first book, *Delivering WOW, How Dentists Can Build a Fascinating Brand and Achieve More While Working Less*, I knew that a problem that I would need to solve is to how to have other doctors know about my book so I could help them, so I launched the Delivering WOW Podcast, making me the first female dentist podcaster in the dental industry.

As a result of relationships created through my podcast, including being interviewed on other dental podcasts, dentists started to hear about my success with social media. A few months later, a doctor reached out to me and asked me to teach him Facebook. I told him quite simply I do not teach Facebook. However, he and others kept emailing me, insisting that I teach them how I was getting my results. After listening to one of my mentors, I made the decision to start one of the first online courses in the dental industry, a Facebook marketing course.

As I began searching for platforms to host my course, someone recommended that I check out ClickFunnels, which led me to register for Funnel Hacker Live. Like many of you out there, I thought that when I attended the ClickFunnels annual conference, Funnel Hacking Live, that I would be learning more about how to use the software. However, as I attended my first Funnel Hacking Live, I realized that the event was so much more. I also noticed that there were patterns most of the speakers on stage followed.

Everyone on stage was in different industries, but they were all impacting the lives of hundreds of thousands of people. Everyone on the stage was using their creativity to create products and services that had never been created before. Everyone on stage had made over a million dollars, most within a year of beginning their journey online, and most were giving large sums of money to charity.

This is also what I wanted, to help thousands of people, to provide more for my family, to make an impact.

There was also one other pattern. Most of the speakers were all in Russell's Inner Circle.

At that year's event, they were not promoting Inner Circle, but I kept hearing the speakers talk about being a part of it. I knew I needed to find a way to be in that circle.

I remember also being at the Starbucks behind Kailyn Poulin, who was a speaker that year, asking how I could get into the program. She shared that there was an application process online.

I also remember talking to Rachel Pederson at the table at the Funnel Hackathon. (She was also a first-time attendee.) I said, Rachel, this is a pattern. We've got to find a way to get into Russell's Inner Circle.

She said, I have an idea. I just met Derek Wilson, who works for Russell, and we can ask him what the steps are to get in?

At that point I was just starting to make money from my Facebook course, and I had done three or four online business acceleration bootcamps. Money was coming in here and there, but I had not made a lot of money online. However, I made a decision to put the $25,000 Inner Circle fee on my credit card.

Again, Inner Circle was not advertised at this particular event. But I made a decision that I was not leaving until I found a way to get into that circle.

Rachel and I also challenged each other to both be on stage the next year together getting our Two Comma Club Award.

A month later, as I was sitting in Boise, Russell asked me one question that allowed me not only to pay off my Inner Circle investment but also to nearly 10x my investment within the first month. That question was, "What is it that people are asking you for that you currently aren't providing?" I shared that a Dr. Rizvi out of Fort Lauderdale had asked me to coach her year around. She had been a part of my Business Boot Camps that taught leadership, how to empower your team, strategic partnership marketing, case acceptance, effective systems to scale, and knowing your numbers. At the end of boot camp, she asked me if I had a "what's next" to help her and her team implement more and faster in a year-round program.

Russell said, "If people are asking you for something and you are not providing it, then you should listen. What I recommend is that you go to your hotel room tonight and send out an email to anyone who has been in your past boot camps. Let them know that you have a year-long program where you can help them not just for four months but all year long. You will not only train them and their teams, but also you will be able to bring them all together as a community."

So I went back to my hotel room and did just that. Two weeks later, I had ten doctors that joined my program, which generated over $200,000 of revenue. It's so interesting how one turn of the knob that you are not aware of can change everything for your business. The next year, the moment was captured perfectly as we were both on stage, one behind the other, getting our awards.

That initial coaching program has now led to Delivering WOW Dental Education, a multi-million dollar dental consulting firm where we're helping hundreds of practices a year grow and scale faster. Most practices are easily growing revenue and profits by 40 to 50 percent per year, and because we empower and train their office managers to be COOs and train the entire team, including financial coordinators, schedulers, and front and back desk teams through proven proprietary frameworks, as well as help with marketing and funnels, the doctors no longer have to micromanage, let things slip through the cracks, or have to carry the burden of trying to do everything themselves. This allows them to have greater income and wealth to take care of their teams, have time to spend with their families, and be able to create a bigger impact.

My inner circle journey has not only allowed me to learn how to create better programs, become findable, and elevate my mindset to think bigger, but also it has allowed me to create friendships with like-minded entrepreneurs who also believe that any idea is possible. We believe that we can change the world, and we are doing just that.

The road to entrepreneurship has been and will continue to be an exciting one. Being able to take my creative ideas and execute them without limits, create products and services that have never been created in my industry, and develop frameworks to help my clients get results faster and faster than ever before has been the biggest reward. As I tell my doctors and teams, there are always shortcuts to get where you want to go faster, and the quicker you do it, the longer you can enjoy it.

MARK STERN

*From Broke to Boxes: How Direct Mail and ClickFunnels Helped
Me Launch a Two Comma Business in Less Than One Year*

*Mark Stern is the founder of the Custom Box Agency and TeleportQR.
Recently, he was featured in Forbes as one of the Next 1,000
Entrepreneurs Redefining the American Dream.*

*Before becoming an entrepreneur, Mark was a top-ranked strategy
consultant at Deloitte Consulting, the world's largest consulting firm.*

*Mark holds an MBA from Duke University. He is a five-time Spartan
Trifecta holder, South-by-Southwest Start-up Mentor, and lifetime lover
of tacos and BBQ. Mark currently lives in Austin, Texas.*

Mark Stern

Inside the Inner Circle:

Hear the Incredible Journeys and Insights from Inside the Inner Circle

I live for the moments when you realize nothing will ever be the same again.

For many, it's those key milestones in life . . .

- Graduating from high school

- Getting married to the love of your life

- The birth of your firstborn child

- The loss of a loved one

These moments are precious and should be cherished. And with the mixed emotions that come with them, a new, unexpected journey reveals itself in front of you.

For my entrepreneurial journey, these moments all came unexpectedly.

Alone on an Island

It started in November 2013 at a conference in the Dominican Republic. I took a leap of faith and attended Mind Valley's A-Fest.

You see, I had no business being at that conference. I came across a YouTube video about it, and it looked fun.

At the time I was a strategy consultant at Deloitte Consulting, the world's largest consulting firm. I had just graduated with an MBA from Duke University, and I was $165,000 in student loan debt.

I was happy at my job, and I had a six-figure salary. I had spent the last year and a half traveling every single week to my clients, and A-Fest was simply meant to be a vacation.

And although I tried to get some friends to come with me, I ended up heading to this conference alone. I knew nobody there.

I was not prepared for what happened next.

When I arrived at A-Fest, I was surrounded by entrepreneurs who showed up in the world differently. They were not restricted by a corporate agenda—they set their own terms.

They created their own impact, and they had the flexibility to navigate this one life in a way that filled their souls.

It was also the first time I was exposed to digital marketing. Yanik Silver, Noah Kagan, Andre Chaperon, and several other marketers were among the 250 attendees.

The experience shattered all the previous beliefs I had about living a fulfilling life.

You see, I believed that there was one pathway to success . . .

- Graduate high school . . . go to college

- Graduate college . . . get the dream job

- After a few years, go to graduate school . . .

- Graduate grad school and land the big lifelong job . . .

I not only followed this pathway until my early thirties, but also would often joke that I was the poster child for Corporate America.

I was student body president of my high school, college, and graduate school.

Between undergrad and graduate school, I landed my dream job doing national marketing campaigns for some of the biggest beverage brands on the market.

I got my master's in business administration (MBA) from my dream school, Duke University.

Afterward, I received an offer from a leading consulting firm doing retail, travel, hospitality, and leisure strategy consulting.

I was happy in the bubble I lived in.

Flash-forward to A-Fest, and in one weekend, that bubble shattered.

I had been exposed to something that I had never experienced before, something that none of my family or friends had experienced either.

I was alone on an island with the realization that nothing would ever be the same again.

It was the start of my journey into entrepreneurship.

Alone at a Conference

Whether you're an introvert or an extrovert, or both to some degree, one of the easiest leaps of faith you can take is simply attending a conference alone.

In small groups, I'd classify myself as an extrovert, but in large crowds, I definitely get overwhelmed pretty easily.

Too often we don't take advantage of the adventure right in front of us because we're waiting for someone else to do it with us. The reality is that you are on your own journey, and so are they. If you need to wait until they're ready to get started, you may be holding yourself back. More importantly, you may be holding back those who need what you have to offer.

In 2015, I attended Digital Marketer's Traffic and Conversion Summit. For three days, I immersed myself in the event, but it was one particular breakout session that stuck with me years after attending.

In this breakout, a marketer named Russell Brunson took the stage to demonstrate how to build a sales funnel in less than seven minutes using the ClickFunnels platform.

I had never heard of Russell before, but he did something in that thirty-minute session that I had never experienced before.

He made me believe that if I quit my job that day, I'd be just fine.

He made me believe that I could be successful as an entrepreneur.

In 2016, I started my first ClickFunnels account, and in 2017 I attended my first Funnel Hacking Live in Dallas, Texas.

Plata o Plomo: Burning Down the Ships

I'd love to tell you that I discovered digital marketing in 2013 and Russell Brunson in 2015 . . .

And then I quit my job and launched a seven-figure agency.

But that's not how my story played out.

It took me until 2018 to finally leave Corporate America and go all in on entrepreneurship. There were two key factors for this delay:

- I was $165,000 in debt from getting my MBA at Duke

- By contract, everything I produced within and outside of the firm was owned by Deloitte

In a nutshell, if I were to start a business or side hustle while employed with Deloitte, the firm had the right to seize the business.

This was a common measure taken by top consulting firms and technology companies, especially after the Enron scandal in 2001.

And while I do not believe the firm would actually seize the intellectual property (IP), the idea that they could take my business away was enough to stifle an entrepreneurial spirit.

So I continued to do what I loved to do . . . dream:

- Dream of the business I could create and the impact it would have on others' lives

- Attend conferences to surround myself with like-minded people

- Purchase courses and programs on different popular marketing topics

- Join coaching programs even though I had absolutely no business

I lived on the periphery of the dream. But it wasn't until 2017 that I realized that all the actions I was taking were simply a panacea for the underlying issue at hand.

I felt trapped in Corporate America. It wasn't meant to be my path.

That's when I had my *plata o plomo* moment. Do or die.

On December 27, 2017, I woke up in the middle of the night with tears in my eyes and an eerie premonition—something I had never experienced before.

It was the realization that if I did not leave my corporate job, it would kill me.

And that's all I needed to be pushed over the edge.

On January 3, 2018, I reached out to my partner at Deloitte and put in my formal resignation.

Did I know what I'd do next?

Nope. I had no idea. All I knew was that when I freed up the space in my brain to create again, I'd figure it out.

And that's what I did.

I stayed active at Deloitte until May 2018 (we'll call it a four-month notice), and at Funnel Hacking Live in Orlando later that month, I joined the Two Comma Club X Coaching Program.

THE FIRST YEAR

During my first year in Two Comma Club X, I focused my business on building virtual events.

In October 2017, I launched the CLICKpreneur Summit, a virtual event targeting people in Corporate America looking to transition into the digital marketing place.

The event had forty-plus speakers, and it spotlighted many individuals within the TCCX and ClickFunnels Community.

By the time the event was over, I had . . .

- Gone from zero to over two thousand people on my email list

- Gone from zero to seven hundred plus people in my Facebook group

- Generated over forty hours of video content

- Launched my first multi-five-figure event

- Pre-sold a coaching program on creating virtual events

I had gone from having no presence online to starting to build strong relationships with other entrepreneurs in the space.

I started getting invited to speak in groups, on podcasts, and at other virtual events.

By taking action, I started to build confidence in the foundational elements of becoming an entrepreneur.

With all the content generated from the event, I wanted to create something original . . . something that people could hold.

So I took all the interviews from the CLICKpreneur Summit, transcribed them, and put them into a publication called *Entrepreneur Elements.*

Once printed, I sent a copy to all the forty-plus speakers, and that's when the magic started to happen.

When the speakers received their copy in the mail, they started to share it with their own communities via social media. This created incredible social proof and organic buzz. It also increased my visibility and authority online.

Little did I know at the time that this would be the precursor to my Two Comma Club business—more on that to come shortly.

In May 2019, I launched another virtual event—High Ticket Online. This event featured twelve all-star entrepreneurs, including Eileen Wilder and Fran Harris.

With all the content generated from this event, I launched an evergreen product called The Official Black Box of High Ticket Online.

When this box launched to market, we had 92 percent of the speakers take pictures or do unboxing videos with the box contents.

This activity created even more organic buzz, which brought in additional sales. It even solidified the power of direct mail and physical products to complement a digital experience.

From that point forward, every time we launched a virtual event with a client, we would complement it with a physical box experience.

The Custom Box Challenge

While the virtual event business was getting traction, other entrepreneurs kept on reaching out, inquiring about how we were producing our custom boxes.

In mid-to-late 2019, we'd entertain calls weekly to help other entrepreneurs do what we did with our own experiences.

The problem was that our core business was not custom boxes . . . it was virtual events.

So on October 24, 2019, I went public on my Facebook page announcing that I was launching a five-day challenge on creating your first custom box experience.

The goal of the challenge was simply to "buy back" my time so I could focus on the core business— virtual events. I wanted a place to send people if they were interested in learning more about boxes.

The entire challenge was designed in less than twenty-four hours, and it would not have come together without the help and support of my Two Comma Club X Coach.

Together, we laid out the strategy for the event, including . . .

- The funnel strategy and core offer

- The layout for the five-day challenge

- Opportunities for bumps and one-time offers (OTOs)

- Promotion strategy

And the best part . . . it took off. It really put me on the map as an expert on custom boxes and experience design. It gave people an easy outlet to refer me.

But that's when the unexpected happened.

While I built the challenge to buy back my time so I could focus on virtual events, the complete opposite ended up happening.

When people went through the Custom Box Challenge, they didn't want to build their own boxes. They wanted me to build the boxes for them.

And so, the Custom Box Agency was born.

THE AGE OF COVID

In early 2020, the rise of the COVID pandemic changed the face of business as we know it.

When the world went into quarantine in March 2020, the events industry was flipped upside down. All live conferences, concerts, sporting events, and even schools/universities went on lockdown. With the absence of in-person events, all local market event planners became "virtual event experts." So what was once a "blue ocean" for me quickly became bloody red with competition.

Everything in my business changed back in May 2020 when my mentor and fellow Inner Circle member, Bart Miller, challenged me with three words:

WHO ARE YOU?

It was the single greatest piece of advice that made the biggest impact on my business.

And I had two businesses that were starting to come to life . . .

A coaching and done-for-you service for virtual events.

And a new agency on building custom boxes.

I had just started to work with Bart when he made a simple observation.

You see, Bart had reached out to some of my peers and asked them the question, "Who is Mark?"

Half of the responses highlighted that I did virtual events. The other half indicated that I worked on custom boxes.

To the market, I was perceived as 50 percent one thing and 50 percent another, and this was not a good thing. When you try to be a little bit of everything, you'll quickly discover that you're a whole lotta nothing since you cannot clearly articulate your real value.

"Are you the virtual event guy or the custom box guy?"

And that was it.

I made the decision to go "all in" on custom boxes. And that one decision truly changed my life.

When someone searches for recommendations, whether via word of mouth or via social media, for people who do custom boxes, it made it universally *so much* easier for other people to recommend me.

It also had another added benefit.

I no longer needed to think about launching virtual events. I could dedicate all my mental capacity to how custom boxes can enhance the customer experience.

I could test new concepts and develop a point of view that was so focused on my craft that it continued to help differentiate me in the marketplace.

Flash forward to a year later, and Custom Box Agency passed one million dollars in annual revenue. We were officially a multi-seven-figure agency, and the best part is that we did not spend one dime on paid traffic.

Our business has grown organically. It has grown from word of mouth.

From Two Comma to Inner Circle

When Russell decided to reopen the Inner Circle in September 2021, it was simply a no-brainer for me.

Russell and the ClickFunnels Community have been instrumental to my journey, and they've filled up my "entrepreneurial cup" in more ways than one. I could not be more grateful to be a part of the legacy he's creating.

When it comes to the people that the community attracts, they're absolutely world-class. I've loved watching my fellow peers in TCCX ascend up into Inner Circle, and nothing excites me more than seeing the impact they've created.

I no longer have to travel this journey alone. I get to surround myself with my people.

Since joining the Inner Circle, the Custom Box Agency continues to expand its impact in the marketplace.

When I think back to the past two years, it's a surreal and humbling experience to reflect on the journey I've been on.

We grew the Custom Box Agency to a multi-seven-figure business in less than two years, and we did it via word of mouth only.

At the time this chapter was written, we have not spent a dime on paid traffic. We also have no investors.

And in that time, we've . . .

- Produced well over one hundred custom box and mailer experiences

- Built a team of twenty-plus employees throughout the US and globe

- Launched a warehouse and fulfillment center in Austin, Texas

- Launched two software platforms: TeleportQR and CBA Dash (inventory management platform)

- Shipped tens of thousands of boxes and mailers all across the globe

We've also been recognized by *Forbes* as one of the Next 1,000 Entrepreneurs Redefining the American Dream and received two ClickFunnels Two Comma Club Awards.

We've even been featured in best-selling books and publications for our work.

And we're just getting started.

I highlight these achievements for one reason only.

Your life can change overnight.

Two years ago, I didn't have a business. I didn't have any Two Comma Club Awards. I was an aspiring entrepreneur who was trying to figure it out.

And in many ways, I still believe I'm an aspiring entrepreneur.

The greatest mindset shift I had was realized by others before I was able to see it myself.

So here's the secret . . .

The world around you wants you to succeed. We want you to win.

People need what you have to offer.

Your worst enemy is the small voice between your ears.

It's you, and you need to get out of your own way.

And until you realize that, you simply won't be ready for what's next.

I needed a mentor to call me out when I got in a self-sabotaging head space.

I needed masterminds and communities of like-minded entrepreneurs to help guide me through the unknown.

But for me, experience is at the heart of what simplifies transformation.

And I'm honored to be surrounded every day by a team, a community, and clients who inspire me all the time.

Final Thoughts

When it comes to entrepreneurship, never forget that people need what you have to offer.

Here are a few tips to keep you focused on the road to Two Comma Club and the Inner Circle:

1. **Stay focused:** It's easy to want to launch multiple businesses or jump to the next shiny object. Make it EASY for other people to promote you, so lead with being known for ONE THING.

2. **Know your why:** Why do you do what you do? With the correct "why," you'll have an endless source of motivation that will be your catalyst during tough times

3. **Find your people | join a community:** Entrepreneurship can feel like riding a roller coaster at times. Find a community of peers who can support you during the highs and lows.

4. **Find a mentor:** Search for someone who can truly invest the time to "get into your business." A good mentor will be able to keep you accountable, diagnose challenges you face, and guide you back on the right track.

5. **Expand your mindset:** Create daily rituals that focus on empowering your mind and belief systems. Eighty percent of the game is believing that you are worthy of a seven-figure and beyond business.

6. **Build a team:** Although you may think you cannot afford it, sometimes you cannot afford NOT to have a team. When I started to grow my team, I feared that I wouldn't be able to sustain them for long. The reality is with the right team, I gained more freedom to GROW my business.

7. **Define a clear customer journey:** The customer experience is everything to me. Create a clear path to show your customers how you'll take them from where they are today to where they want to be.

8. **Be your best case study:** With the Custom Box Agency, our "client zero" was us. We tested custom boxes on ourselves well

before we started building them for our clients. We became our own case study. You can do the same. Show others what you're capable of doing.

9. **Have an abundant mindset:** You are your greatest competitive edge. Someone can steal your ideas, but they will never be able to represent them in the same capacity as you because they are not you. This is a game that we can all win in. Give value—it'll come back to you tenfold.

10. **Increase your visibility:** You may have the greatest product or service, but if no one knows you exist, so what? There are people who need what you have to offer. Increase your visibility via whatever means feels most natural to you, and as you put the right systems in place, expand that footprint.

BILL ALLEN

The 7 Figure Flipping Blueprint: Lessons Learned from the World's Leading House Flipping Mentor

Bill Allen, a navy pilot and real estate professional, is the CEO and owner of 7 Figure Flipping and host of the 7 Figure Flipping Podcast, where he leads the top house flipping and wholesaling mentoring groups in the world. Just a few years ago, he was stuck flipping one or two houses per year and doing all the work himself, but since then, he's built a systematized business that runs without him. His wholesaling and flipping company, Blackjack Real Estate, is based out of Nashville, Tennessee, and does over one hundred deals a year throughout the Southeast.

You know what the really cool thing is? Since you are reading this book, you have probably heard of Russell Brunson, his Inner Circle, ClickFunnels, and Funnel Hacking Live! That wasn't the case when I was pulled into this supernatural world with the 1 percent Crazy Funnel Hackers! I got here a different way than most, which I really hope gets you excited because the journey is far from linear; it's very dynamic. Often, we don't know what God has in store for us until we reach our destination and are able to look back and see all the little things that had to happen to get us there. That's what my story looks like, and I wouldn't trade it for the world!

My name is Bill Allen, and I describe myself as a nerdy engineer that loves numbers, data, and testing things, but I'm also able to hold my own socially in a crowd and make friends somewhat quickly in new places. I believe that is from growing up a navy brat then spending twenty years in the navy myself. During my navy career, I moved fifteen times, and I always had to quickly meet new people and attempt to fit into my new environment. I flew helicopters and airplanes for the navy, and one of my biggest accomplishments was becoming a test pilot and flying over forty different varieties of aircraft. I was also lucky enough to meet my wife, Lucy, while I was stationed in England during my time at test pilot school.

Shortly after we got married, we had our first son, Will, and that was the moment I realized that I wanted more from life than simply flying for the navy and deploying every few years. I wanted to be home with them as much as possible and control my TIME. That is where I turned to real estate in hopes of starting a house-flipping business that would give me financial freedom and eventually time freedom. I had moderate success the first few years, flipping one house a year and making over

$40K on each of them. (That was half of my salary with the navy.) However, it was really just a second job, and I was spending more time at the properties and less time with my family. That had to change!

That's when I started listening to a house-flipping podcast by a guy named Justin Williams. He was flipping over one hundred houses a year and not going to see them and not doing the work himself, and he was spending more time with his family than ever! He said he had set up "systems and processes" to allow him to build his business around his life and not vice versa. This is where the name Russell Brunson first entered my world. Justin called him his "marketing mentor" on the show, and to be honest, the first time I heard his name, I thought Justin was talking about the guy who owned Virgin Airways. I didn't think much of it at the time and just focused on learning as much as I could about real estate from the podcast. After a few months of listening to the show, Justin rolled out a brand-new program called 7 Figure Flipping. This program was a mastermind group focused on showing people how to build a million-dollar-a-year house-flipping or wholesaling business. I wanted to be a millionaire one day, but I had never even heard of someone who was doing that in ONE YEAR! At the time, I had been brainwashed by everyone online to not pay for coaching and to believe that you could find everything you needed online for FREE. So when I found out that the price tag for this 7 Figure Flipping Mastermind Group was $25K a year, I was shocked and immediately put off.

After a lot of deliberation, listening to more podcasts of people who were joining the group, and some discussion with my first and best mentor, my dad, I decided to JUMP and join 7 Figure Flipping. I was one of the first of twenty people to jump in, and that year was amazing.

It wasn't easy, but I went from a solopreneur flipping one house a year to a team of four who did 67 houses the first eight months! The next year I grew the team to nine, and we flipped and wholesaled 135 houses. The year after it was 187, and then we did over 200 houses the next few years. Our gross profit went from $700K to over $3M per year in just a few years. All because I said YES to myself, invested in my future, applied the tools and strategies I was given, and trusted my coach and the process. It wasn't easy, but it was simple, and it worked!

I tell you all of this because I believe my story is a little different than the others you will read in this book. I built a successful real estate investing business while flying full time for the navy and really had no idea who Russell Brunson was, what ClickFunnels did, or the fact that a ton of Funnel Hackers from around the world congregated once a year to go to an event called Funnel Hacking Live. Nor did I know that most of what I was learning was trickling down from a mastermind group called the Inner Circle. We had an event called Flip Hacking Live, for goodness sake! Looking back, it's very clear that our world at 7 Figure Flipping was modeled after Russell's world. And if it hadn't been for Justin being in Russell's Inner Circle Mastermind, there is no way that I would be where I am today. I was a product of this Inner Circle group without even knowing it, and because of that, I will be forever grateful for Russell and everything he does! How many other people are out there, just like me, whose lives have been changed because of what their coaches are learning HERE? Maybe you have, too, and you are only now realizing that! This is the impact that's possible from what you can do. It's incredible.

My house-flipping business, Blackjack Real Estate, became so successful that a year after I joined 7 Figure Flipping, Justin Williams asked me to be a coach for him in the program. A year after that, he asked me to become the COO of the company and run things for him. I was so excited to jump into 7 Figure Flipping that I hired a COO for my real estate company, left my active-duty navy flying job after fifteen years of service, joined the navy reserves, and jumped into the coaching and mastermind business with Justin full time. This is when I finally started to learn more about what ClickFunnels was and the impact this community had on us started to become clear. However, Justin was always in charge of the marketing side of the business, and I stayed in my lane of sales, fulfillment, events, and finance.

In 2019, Funnel Hacking Live was in Nashville, and I was asked to come to represent Operation Underground Railroad at their booth in the hallway. I lived in Nashville and was the Tennessee director of volunteers for OUR at the time. Justin was attending the event that year, so in between breaks I sat with him to watch some of the presentations. I was literally blown away by the community, the content, and the life-changing experience of that event. This was the start of me jumping into Russell's books, podcasts, and content. I started devouring everything that he had to offer, and that was the start of the next-level transformation in my life as a business owner and entrepreneur.

This is a much longer story, but less than a year later, I ended up buying the entire company from Justin Williams and became the new owner of 7 Figure Flipping. I was always the behind-the-scenes guy. I was never out in front running the 7 Figure Flipping Podcast, selling our mastermind programs from stage at our event Flip Hacking Live, or leading the marketing team and coming up with new ideas to bring people into our world. But Funnell Hacking Live 2020 changed my life big time! I was the new owner of this coaching company, I was seeing the world through a whole different lens, and I was dedicated to growing our presence as the #1 real estate mastermind in the world. As I sat in the audience watching these amazing presenters, I wrote in my notes: "I will be on that stage one day as a speaker." I didn't know how, I didn't know when, but I felt called to this dream. Not for my ego, not for show, but to be a part of something so much bigger than me and to contribute to a movement that has made such an impact on me and my life!

That year, at FHL 2020 in Nashville, I received my first Two Comma Club Award for 7 Figure Flipping. This award wasn't just for running Justin's 7 Figure Flipping company as the new owner; it was due to all the hard work and changes I put into it after buying the company just six months prior. And when Russell made his offer for coaching that year, I was the FIRST one running to the back table to buy it. I knew this was the community for me, and I was going to soak up every ounce of value it had to offer, no matter the level!

Over the next two years, I took 7 Figure Flipping from doing about $2M per year in revenue to nearly four times that with what I was learning. I grew quickly and built up my confidence in marketing via email and our podcast, selling from stage, and fulfillment. I created new levels of my value ladder, built out life-changing events, and modeled what Russell was doing inside of his coaching community. At this point, it wasn't an indirect impact that Russell was having on me and my business, it was direct, and I was the one translating it into action. This is where the spark turned into a flame. I truly believe that I am one of the best in the world at taking a concept, going deep on it, and implementing it quickly and efficiently in my companies for a huge return. I have an ability to quickly see trends and patterns when I look at data, kind of like Neo in *The Matrix* when he can just see the lines of code when he's looking around.

At this point, I was quickly becoming a successful mastermind owner, but I was incredibly lonely in business. I didn't have anyone inside my company or in my mastermind programs to talk to about ideas, strategy, vision, and direction. They were running real estate investment companies, and I was running a digital marketing company selling information and community. So I set out to look for a mastermind group for ME . . . and unfortunately, Russell had closed his Inner Circle group a year or so before I started my search. I knew that was the place for me, that he was the coach for me, but it just wasn't open. I honestly thought it was some sort of secret underground group that was really meeting, and I just couldn't get in, so I applied every few months to the wait list just in case. But no calls! Meanwhile, I researched other groups and asked around to find out what else was out there, but nothing fit my core values. After almost two years of looking, I nearly gave up and almost threw in the towel. That was when I got a video message from a number I didn't recognize!

It was a woman named Sarah who worked for Russell saying that my name came up in a meeting they were having. It said Russell was opening his Inner Circle again and if I was interested to respond to her. I couldn't write back fast enough, saying, "I'm in." She slowed me down a bit and sent me a calendar link to book a call with Robbie, the one who was going to be checking to make sure we were a good fit. I scheduled my call for the next day and could barely sleep that night. I knew the cost of the group going into the call, but I also knew the value that Russell and his whole company had already provided to me the previous years for next to nothing in payment. I owe millions of dollars of ideas to them!

On my call, Robbie asked me about my business size, revenue, goals, and more. It took about ten minutes for me to tell him that, and then as he was going into the benefits of the group, I simply stopped him and said, "Robbie, this will probably be the easiest sale you have ever made . . . I'm in. Just send me the link to pay!" But his response was different. He told me about this other higher-level group called the Category Kings and said he felt that I would be a good fit for that group. Instead of $50K a year, this group was $150K a year! Along with a higher price tag, it had higher revenue and experience requirements to apply. It only took me a second to respond, saying, "If you will let me into that group . . . I'm in. Just send me the link to pay!" I always want to be the dumbest person in the room, making the least money, because when I'm there, I know I have the most to learn and grow. It's what I've done ever since I joined that first 7 Figure Flipping real estate mastermind for $25K, and it hasn't led me astray yet.

Over this past year in the Inner Circle, I have made so many amazing friends, grown my business and myself, and have hit goals and dreams I didn't even know were possible. It's all because of the support and the vision that these other amazing business owners provide. I never thought I would ever be able to find a way to give back to this community; there are just so many amazing people who are on the tip of the spear in marketing. I haven't had a lot of original and creative thoughts in my life, and I'm really just best at taking other people's ideas and creating a Frankenstein model of what they are all doing to implement in my business. However, this year, the Inner Circle has allowed me to see the matrix and go deeper on one concept that I feel impacts everything we do: the Hero's Journey. I would argue that I know this concept better than 99.9 percent of the people on this planet, and I now see the world and business through that lens.

I've decided that the next phase of my development is to go deeper here and to bring this concept from the movies over to the world of entrepreneurs and the 1 percent crazies out there just like you! We can change the world, and with the right tools at our disposal, there is no stopping us! By going deeper in this Hero's Journey concept and combining it with some other strategies taught by Russell, I've been able to make a Frankenstein model to show other business owners how they can be better leaders, better husbands and wives, and better mothers and fathers; never lose a customer again; and have their current customers achieve success faster in their programs and sprinting up their value ladder! Yes, all that is available in this one framework, and I'm happy to say that my dream from FHL 2020 is coming true. I will be presenting on this topic at Funnel Hacking Live 2022, and I can't wait to do just that. Every action starts with a dream, and mine was to speak on the big stage one day. That dream became a vision, the vision became a plan, the plan became a goal, and that goal became actions. What is your dream?

My dream came true because I said yes to this group. I said yes to being uncomfortable, and I stared fear in the eye and used courage to push through. But really all I did was believe in myself and say YES to ME. You can do that same thing, and the Inner Circle, Funnel Hacking Live, and ClickFunnels can help you get there just like it did for me. I look forward to meeting you at an upcoming Inner Circle meeting because I have no plans of going anywhere anytime soon!

RICH FORGET

OOOYAAA LIFE'$ GOOD

Rich Forget is a French Canadian entrepreneur that has founded, acquired, and sold five-, six-, and seven-figure businesses in different markets. In his twenty-plus years of experience, he has put his companies on the Profit 500: Canada's Fastest-Growing Companies, managed one hundred-plus employees, and received different awards as an entrepreneur.

His passions are entrepreneurship, sales and marketing, and real estate. If you ask him what's his biggest accomplishment, he will tell you: "My family." He's in love with his wife, and he traveled around the world with his three kids while homeschooling.

Even if he has ADHD, dyslexia, dysorthography, and anxiety and is gifted, he's always happy . . .

If you ask him WHY, his response will be: "Because OOOYAAA, life's good!"

If you want to know more about him:

www.fb.com/oooyaaafunnelhacker.

Here's a thirty-second video that explains his world:

OOOYAAA (https://www.facebook.com/watch/?v=947640335673637).

—

My journey into Russell's world!

Who Needs Goals?

I'm the kind of guy who needs challenges and needs GOALS! Since 2000, my entrepreneurship life is driven by GOALS.

After having sold one of my businesses, I traveled with my family all around the world (yep, homeschooling!), and I was doing real estate investing.

Call for Help

One day, Ghislain, one of my friends, asked me to help him with his business. My answer was: "I don't want to work, but I'll have a look!"

HHMMMM . . . Lot of things to do! . . . Just for the fun, I decided to help him.

Funnel Hacking Live

Publicity

While I was in his business, I saw the publicity of a marketing event called Funnel Hacking Live.

Hummm, I thought. OK, GO! It could be cool to go to the USA (don't forget, My name is Rich Forget from Canada!) and learn new stuff (I love to learn and I love marketing!).

Event

When I arrived at the event . . . OOOYAAA! I was freaking out! The energy is perfect, and the content is good . . .

<u>My New Goal</u>

BOOM, I had discovered my next challenge, my new GOAL: I wanted to be the first French Canadian to get the Two Comma Club Award!

Telling My Friend

When I went back to Quebec, I called my friend and asked him: "Do you want to bring your business to the next level? I want to bring your business to $1M/year with funnels in the next year! I love you, and I want to help you. ARE YOU IN?"

His response: "YESSSS!"

Let's Dive in to Russell's World

I was ALL IN: Russell was my new GURU.

I'll do what Russell says:

- Books (PDF/audio/paper): *Expert Secrets/DotCom Secrets/ Traffic Secrets*

- 2CCX coaching/One Funnel Away Challenge (v1)

Two Comma Club Award = Check!

Eighteen months after this commitment, YESSSS, my challenge was completed successfully!

I had made $1M with funnels! Even if the market was tiny (French people in Quebec/Canada)!

My Question: What's Next? <u>What's My Next Goal?</u>

After this accomplishment, I asked myself: "OK, what's next?" Because I'm an entrepreneur, I need ONE GOAL to be high performing!

3 Two Comma Club Awards? Why Not?

On to my next target: two more Two Comma Club Awards!

I needed to prove to myself that the first award wasn't luck, but it was a process, a "recipe."

I love marketing and technologies. At that time, I had already sold one marketing company and one technologies company . . . I know that market.

I Called 2 Friends: "ARE YOU READY?"

I called two of my friends: "Do you want to take your business to the next level? I want to take your business to $1M/year with funnels. I did it one time, and now I need to prove that I have a recipe and redo it with two other businesses. I love you, and I want to help you. ARE YOU IN?" (Yep, I know, it's basically the same question I asked my friend Ghislain a few months earlier!)

I Got Two Answers:

1. Friend #1: Video marketing agency: YESSSS!

2. Friend #2: Real estate SaaS: YESSSS!

COOL, now I have a new goal! Take two more businesses to $1M/year with funnels. OOOYAAA, LET'S DO THIS!

FHL 2021

While I was working on my NEW GOAL, I went to FHL 21, and Russell announced that the doors of the Inner Circle were reopening . . . WHAT? HMMMMM interesting. Can I get in? Should I jump in? Not sure. I went out to grab a coffee, as I was too excited!

Mike Schmidt - Should I Talk to Him?

BAMMMMMM, when I walked out of the coffee shop, I saw one of the FHL 21 speakers, MIKE SCHMIDT. He was there, alone, walking . . .

This is my chance: "Excuse me, sir, can I talk to you about Inner Circle?" His response (very calm): "SURE." After this talk, I knew that I was adding another goal on top of my other goal!

I wanted to be part of a tribe of people like me: the 1 percent CRAZY ONE! ENTREPRENEURS THAT WANT TO HAVE IMPACT AND CHANGE THE WORLD.

Inner Circle—Here I Am!

A few hours later, I was IN! This legendary tribe. WOW! Now I was allowed to wear the Inner Circle shirt and chill with other CRAZY people that were excited like me!

What a year! INNER CIRCLE plus my energy to generate two other Two Comma Club Awards for my friends!

How to Focus? Business Framework

I have few businesses, and I needed to focus to achieve my goals! How did I do that? By having a FRAMEWORK! The OOOYAAA framework. (BTW, this is my personal framework. It's not for sale!)

Even if I have twenty-plus years of experience as an entrepreneur, I always learn from other people with different backstories. Sharing experiences is so important! I have talked with incredible people in the Inner Circle, and this helped me to improve my frameworks. Look at the next section to find out how I'm managing a few businesses and how the people of the Inner Circle or the people of Russell's world impact it.

OOOYAAA!!!! + 2 Two Comma Club Award for My Wall!

At the FHL 22, I'll be on the stage to receive two more Two Comma Club Awards from Russell Brunson! We received the confirmation a few months ago!

OK, now I have accomplished my two goals! WOW!

Recipe or Framework?

With three Two Comma Club Awards, I can confirm: I'm not lucky! Generating $1M/year is a process, a "recipe"! Russell Brunson will tell you: it's a FRAMEWORK!

What's Next? Something Big

What's my next project . . . ? I have something in my mind . . . BIG . . . Very BIG . . . it will be my BIGGEST project ever. It will have IMPACT on hundreds of thousands of lives with funnels!

When I talked to Fabio Soares (one of the Inner Circle tribe), he told me: "WOW, that's so genius! IT'S BIG, and it's a lot of work!" My response was: "Just watch me!"

If you want to know what's next, go to www.oooyaaa.ca/InnerCircle.

Experience Sharing

I'm different . . . Nope. I'm bizarre . . . Nope. I'm in my world, the OOOYAAA world! I'll share with you my "golden rules" that help me to become happy as an entrepreneur, husband, and dad and keep the right balance between my personal life and my businesses.

3- OOOYAAA FRAMEWORK

I'm not a coach, I'm not the best, I'm just a guy that has developed his structure to be happy, rich, and able to be present with his family! So, please, don't throw rocks at me. I never went to university ;-)

I have 5 big pillars:

1. Alignment: Personal first, business second

2. Businesses: The machine to keep control

3. Sales and marketing: Doing money while sleeping

4. Humans around you: Family/friends/business partner

5. Me first: Focus on my mental and bodily health!

This is the result of twenty-plus years of experience, and I continue to improve it—even as I write this!

Russell's World and Inner Circle Impact

I have added a few pictures of people that had an impact on my framework. You'll see people from the Inner Circle and/or other people from Russell's world.

3.1 Alignment: Personal First, Business second

Quote: "Know your *why* and you'll never work again!"

Backstory:

Being an entrepreneur is not always easy, and you can have "surprises" like being fired from your own business, becoming depressed because you have one hundred employees, losing all your money, losing your best friend, working eighty hours per week, etc. Yep, this is a short list of my "surprises"!

After fifteen years of entrepreneurship, I have realized the following:

- I wasn't happy . . . Why? Because I was doing business to make CA$H.

- My businesses weren't aligned with my personal vision . . . Why? Because I didn't have a personal vision!

- My businesses were first and I was second (maybe third or more!)

- I was a slave of my own creation!

Transformation:

At that time, I was starting my family with my INCREDIBLE WIFE Catherine, and I decided to take back control of my life. The first step was to figure out why I was in this situation and what should I do or change to be a happy entrepreneur, happy husband, and happy dad.

Long story short, here are the four pillars that I have built to create my new life:

1. My big *why*: Identify why I wanted to build businesses.

2. My personal plan: Visualize me in ten years and write down SMART objectives by category.

3. My flow: Identify my flow and stay in that state as much as possible.

4. My values: Identify my values and be true to them.

Result:

I have used these four pillars, and now, I know why I have few businesses. They are always in correlation with my personal plan, I'm very often in the flow (You can ask my wife!), and I follow my values.

Now I can share with you that I'm a happy entrepreneur (eight businesses), happy husband (ten plus years marriage), and happy dad. I travel all around the world with my three kids, and I'm there for them.

Russell's World and Inner Circle Impact

Russell Brunson: his origin story	Dave Woodward: his life, his vision, his happiness, the human . . .
Basha J Katour: his origin story and vision	Justin Benton: his origin story, his mission, the human

- Reference (Books):

    o *The Big Why* by Michael Winter

    o *Flow* by Mihaly Csikszentmihalyi

    o *The Secret* by Rhonda Byrne

3.2 Businesses: The Machine to Keep Control!

Quote: "If you don't have goals, you'll work to realize the goals of someone else!"

Backstory:

In the last twenty-plus years of entrepreneurship, I have built, acquired, sold, and closed businesses of 5-six to seven figures. Yep, I'm that kind of guy ;-)

I started entrepreneurship very young, and I think "sooner is better" to start a business because it's an advantage not to have a lot of expenses (house$, car$, kid$, etc.)

My pleasure is in the growth of businesses. Because I love to sleep at night instead of freaking out about ABC in one of my businesses, I use "my machine" to stay on top of my game.

One business is difficult to manage, but when you have few, you can't manage them without difficulties! This is why I try to systematize my companies to fit in my machine!

Transformation:

My machine has 4 pillars:

1) Business plan: Yep! I said it! l create it, follow it, and adjust it down the road!

2) Decision taker: I take decisions quickly by asking myself my three golden questions!

3) System: Process and documentation/people/time and project management. VERY important.

4) Cash is king: Profit first and cashflow second.

Result:

By using my machine, I can see the results VS the objectives, make decisions to scale or revise, communicate with the people on my team and generate passive income.

RUSSELL'S WORLD AND INNER CIRCLE IMPACT

James P Friel: his robot brain and process!	Bradley Gibb: $$$$ produce/profit/protect
Edward: Finance: you need to know the law and have fun!	Jr: his origin story, his mission, and his business plan

3.3 Sales and Marketing: Making Money While Sleeping!

Quote: "I'm not selling, but they are buying!"

Backstory – Church Star:

When I was very young, I loved trading stuff with my friends (toys, hockey cards, NFL stickers, etc.), I loved to negotiate (You can ask my parents!), I loved selling things to make money. On top of that, I loved to speak in front of an audience! At the church, I was reading the Bible (with a microphone!) in front of everybody! In my mind, I wasn't a rock star. Nope, I was more than that, I was a church star!

First Step as a Real Entrepreneur

Very young, I knew that I wanted to become an entrepreneur (like my mom and my aunt). When I started my first web agency, I found out that it was easier to speak to someone at the church versus a prospect I was trying to sell to.

Learning Sales and Marketing

I have specialized in sales and marketing. My objective: find out how a prospect thinks in his brain and adjust my message so the brain of my prospect will understand my message and his hand will write me a check ;-) It became my passion! I didn't know it at that time, but I found my flow!

What? It's Payday? AGAIN?

Down the road, I have discovered that if you want to create a real business with employees, you need to generate more money for the paycheck of employees. They need $$$ to feed their family or to buy the new game Warcraft 2 or Counter Strike or Quake 2 or Red Alert (GEEK stuff!). I was ready to make everything with web technologies to generate $$$ because I had a payday every two weeks!

My business was surviving, but very fast, it became complicated to support lots of different clients, different technologies, different source codes, different pricing, different, different, different . . .

Focus

With years of experience, I have discovered that I needed to focus on one market instead of anybody with money to create a website! A few months later, I was the expert in my market and, I was able to sell the same thing to different clients! WOW! Same price for them, but less time for me to install my CMS (content management system) for each client!

Expansion Time!

My recipe was simple!: be visible where my prospects was looking (web portal and specialized newspaper)/identify prospects/contact them —contact them, contact them, contact them (Did I say contact them?) Sell/install/repeat! A few years later, I sold this company and I was ready for my next challenge, my next goal! A technology business! (This is another story!)

Transformation:

Since 2000, I have generated millions of sales in my businesses with my system/process, but Russell's framework has helped me to simplify it!

Here're my 5 pillars:

1. Avatar: Focus on him, know him more than he does! Know his pain and the result that he wants.

2. Expert: Position yourself with your expertise AND your successes AND your experience.

3. Sales machine: Stop selling your time for money. You need to generate $$$ while you sleep.

4. Value ladder/offers: Create irresistible offer (with amazing copy) in your value ladder, test it, adjust it, repeat.

5. Be visible: You only need to be where your prospects are looking! Traffic and @ are the key.

Result:

Here is my result: three Two Comma Club Awards!

RUSSELL'S WORLD AND INNER CIRCLE IMPACT

Peng Joon: wow on traffic and video content	Jim Edward: the unicorn of copywriting, his humor is hilarious
Marley Jaxx: the human, her brain for video marketing	Lamar Tyler: his mission, his business model, the human
Alie Berk: her family vision and her experience sharing Pedro Adao: experience sharing on challenge	Steve Larsen: his brain on how to create an irresistible offer and his entrepreneur transformation since he was Funnel Builder at CF Anissa Holmes: experience sharing on Summit
Stephanie Blake: the human, her energy, her drive, her knowledge, her willingness to help—one word: WOW	Damon Burton: his brain, his humor, his geekiness, his vibe
Richmond Dinh: his energy, his structure, his experience sharing and . . . his smile!	

3.4 Human Around You: Family/Friends/Business Partner

Quote: "You're the average of the five people spend the most time with" (Jim Rohn).

Backstory:

When you're an entrepreneur, you only have twenty-four hours in a day! Yep, you're different because those twenty-four are passing faster than "normal people's"! You're passionate, you're in the flow, and you forget to take care of the people around you.

It's precisely what happened to me! I had fun building growing companies and was even in the Profit 500 Canadian's Fastest-Growing Companies. I was in a parallel world where time flies. It was cool, but step-by-step:

- My wife and kids were having fun without me. Basically, my wife was a single mom and my kids were doing their thing without Daddy.

- My personal friends stopped calling me because my answer to their calls was: "Sorry, I have an important meeting/project and I can't go with you . . . Next time."

- I had started to replace my personal friends with business friends.

- The relationship with my business partner became tense.

- We started to hire B players instead of A players because we had contracts with clients.

Basically, I was becoming a terrible husband, terrible dad, and terrible friend, but I was a successful entrepreneur with issues finding employees even if I had three full-time HR employees and a head hunter.

Transformation:

As you can read, I needed to change my lifestyle and my thinking and start taking care of the people who still loved me again.

My framework has 3 pillars:

1) Family: I take care of my wife Catherine (the most amazing human on the earth), and I'm present for my kids.

2) Friends: I now keep a balance between personal and business friends.

3) Business partners: I hire A players or no players.

Result:

Family: My wife and I are still in love after ten-plus years of marriage. I see my three kids growing, and I take one on one time with each one of them. Last summer we traveled for two months in Europe. I plan time for my friends. After all of those years in entrepreneurship, I can confirm that I prefer a small business (thirteen employees or less) and connecting with my employees and business partners.

Resources:

- Who not how: Dan Sullivan

RUSSELL'S WORLD AND INNER CIRCLE IMPACT

Zak Harlow: his brain, his thinking, his vision, his family values, and his Texan accent!	Alex Durand/Dany Therrien: my French Canadian partners in the Inner Circle!
AJ Rivera and Mike Schmi: Wow, what an origin story! Thanks for everything!	

3.5 Focus On Me (My Mental and Body Health!)

Quote: "Mental health . . . is not a destination, but a process. It's about how you drive, not where you're going" (Noam Shpancer, PhD).

Backstory:

Managing growing companies became a "drug" for me, and I became a JUNKY of my own companies. When I wasn't working at the office, my brain was spinning and was thinking about ABC very important things! In that situation, it's easy to forget to take care of yourself. Breakfast, lunch, dinner at the restaurant, cocktail, gala, short nights, sleep at the office, no time for sport, my suit was shrinking, no time for me, all-in business!

One day at a conference, one speaker said: "Your body isn't like a car. You can't change all the pieces. If it's broken, it's broken forever. Is the RPM of your body in the red or yellow zone for a long time . . . ?"

OOPS, I was pushing my body to the limit and I didn't know it! I started to take care of myself.

Transformation:

My framework has 4 pillars:

1) Knowing myself: I did few psychometric tests to understand myself and how to communicate with others.

2) Mindset: I have chosen to be happy and optimistic and eliminate the bad energies from my life.

3) Body: Sport is important for the body AND for the brain!

4) Presence: I try to be in the moment (having ADHD, it's a little bit difficult).

Result:

It's a never-ending story! Often, I forget to think about myself! It's always a work in progress. I do meditation (thanks <use 2!), and sometimes I take pills to be in the moment. My mindset is ALWAYS on fire! I'm happy and I know that I'm lucky!

RUSSELL'S WORLD AND INNER CIRCLE IMPACT

Myron Golden: his mindset, his stories	Mandy Keene: her expertise on the DISC test

LAUREN GOLDEN

The Secret to Achieving Financial Success without Sacrificing Your Freedom

Lauren Golden is the fearless leader of The Free Mama Movement and a thriving community of tens of thousands of women. Her mission is simple: to ensure that no mother ever has to choose between family and financial stability. Lauren is also a #1 international best-selling author and a Two Comma Club Award winner, whose business and life experience has made her a popular choice for guest speaking events, sharing the stage with the likes of Tony Robbins and Russell Brunson. Lauren is most passionate about helping people get comfortable with the uncomfortable in pursuit of living a totally awesome, guilt-free life.

Learn more about how she teaches moms how to start and run a successful virtual business at thefreemama.com.

Six years ago, I was a work-from-home wife and mom of two living in Kansas.

To be fair, those things are still true today, although I now have three kids. And because of the story you're about to read, my bank account, health, and lifestyle look completely different.

I am completely different.

I also have a few more accolades to my name, which is kind of cool, not because I'm special, but because **I went for it**.

I am the leader of The Free Mama Movement, a thriving community of over forty thousand extraordinary women.

I work part-time and travel often (we've taken our kids to over thirty states in our RV!)

I'm a #1 international best-selling author and a Two Comma Club Award winner.

I've shared the stage with the likes of Tony Robbins and Russell Brunson.

I've been on the cover of a magazine, on the news, and featured by media outlets.

I'm also a member of Russell's Inner Circle.

This is the story of how I got there and what you should take away from my story to reach your own goals while enjoying the process and staying true to yourself.

From December 2017 to June 2019, I made over $1 million in revenue in my business from course sales of my program, The Free Mama Movement.

It took eighteen months.

And while this wasn't record-breaking by ClickFunnels standards, I did this profitably, without any full-time employees, from a brand-new business (and as a brand-new business owner), with no email list or social media following, and with a baby on my lap—literally.

Russell always talks about being One Funnel Away, and in my story, it was my very first funnel that led to my first Two Comma Club Award. (It should be noted that I hear this is quite uncommon.)

While the journey to my first million dollars was exciting, relatively quick, and full of head-down, hard-working days, the journey to Inner Circle is a deeper tale of personal development, mistakes and courage, grit and resilience, and pure determination.

But let's go back to 2017.

I had been freelancing for a few years when I came across the world of automation, digital products, and business coaching.

I knew I wanted more. More security. More significance.

I also wanted to help more people, moms in particular, get out of the status quo of their jobs (where there is almost no support for work-life balance) to create a career on their own terms that allowed them to show up as the parents they wanted to be.

My mission was to help moms uncover the path that I had discovered a few years prior: that they don't have to choose between family and financial stability.

As someone who had already worked hard to replace her salary freelancing in a fraction of the hours demanded by an employer, I wanted a way to build this impact-driven business where I didn't destroy my sanity or newly designed family life in the process.

I needed *leverage*.

After nine months of talking myself out of it, telling myself I wasn't ready or good enough, I finally reached my do-or-die moment. I had to try, or I had to quit talking about it.

In September of 2017, I hired Liz Benny, perhaps one of Russell Brunson's earliest success stories and founding Inner Circle members, to be my business coach. I was terrified. It was about ten times more money than I had spent on anything. Ever. But if I was going to go for it, I knew that **investing in a mentor who had done it before was going to save me a lot of time and struggle.**

Her Ultimate Kapow membership was built with this goal in mind: make a lot of money, make a lot of impact, and earn a million dollars with a digital course.

Let's go.

I was the last person to join her mastermind that year but came in with the most speed.

I didn't have a lot of time to sit and consider making back my investment. I had spent money I didn't have (a maxed-out credit card and payment plan), and it was go time. There was no room for "maybe this will work" or "I'll wait until I feel ready."

Failure was not an option.

For the first few months of the program, I made sacrifices to work whenever I could. I had a baby, a three-year-old, and a five-year-old at home while still freelancing full time to pay the bills.

Late at night, early in the morning, and any guilt-free second I could carve out in between, I was putting together my (very ugly) slide deck for my very first webinar to launch The Free Mama Movement, a program to teach moms how to start a virtual assistant business from home.

After the slides were designed and rehearsed, the email sequences were written and set up inside the ClickFunnels platform, and the Zoom webinar was integrated, I was ready to finally launch my very own Perfect Webinar (about three to four weeks' time).

I sure as heck didn't feel ready, but I was prepared.

The problem was that I had absolutely no audience whatsoever to show up. I started running paid traffic because I needed speed. Ads were the fastest way to get the numbers into my funnel to even know if it was working (converting) or what levers to pull (messaging, offer, etc.).

So after giving my webinar to *no one* (not a typo) for seven consecutive weeks, always tweaking and growing, I decided to go all in and crank up my ad spend to ensure that I had enough people registered to have enough even on the webinar to figure out if a conversion would happen.

This was it. Seriously, I was out of money (and almost out of belief and energy). I showed up and delivered that webinar to about a dozen people live.

And no one bought my course . . .

Until a few days before Christmas, I made my first course purchase on an email follow-up sequence. And a day or so later, another one.

Holy moly. It worked.

My funnel *was working*.

I reinvested the money that I made to pay off part of the credit card and did it again.

Third sale, fourth, fifth, eighth. Again! By mid-January of 2018, I had paid off my credit card and reinvested additional funds into hiring a copywriter who could undoubtedly outperform the copy I had originally drafted off of Swipe Copy. I earned back that investment in just two days.

From that first sale through March 2018, I worked the hardest I've worked in my life. Every day I was serving my own freelancing clients, and I spent mornings, nights, and weekends building out the modules of my program. Yes, I sold it before I created it, and I highly recommend you do this too! I recorded, edited, and uploaded my own videos. I made all of the worksheets and daily emails. I did it all.

This season of head-down, get-it-done, no-excuses work lasted twelve weeks. Hustling isn't something I subscribe to, and it will lead to burnout 100 percent of the time. With that being said, the work I put into those few months continues to generate money in my business today, nearly five years later!

When you work hard, do it intentionally. When you create, know how you'll leverage it. Hold yourself accountable to your boundaries . . . there's always more to do.

By February 2018, I had the first five-figure month of my entire life. This was something that as a school administrator where I earned a modest $50,000 a year, I never thought was possible.

The first week of March, just one week later, I had my first five-figure week!

The glass ceiling shattered.

Beliefs changed.

All the while I was growing and nurturing my Facebook group. The more I showed up and served these women, the more my program sales increased because of the amazing testimonials and social proof. After a few months, I didn't even have to show up or publish every day because the women showed up for each other.

To facilitate my rapid growth, I gave my program away to a few women in my community who couldn't afford it, and they worked off the investment by helping me with administrative tasks. I ended up hiring one of them as my virtual assistant to help with all the back-end support for my growing community and support email.

By May 2018, it was clear that I had built a machine! The Facebook ads and group fed my funnel, and my funnel fed the community. I was earning enough money to leave my freelancing clients and dedicate my part-time working hours to The Free Mama exclusively. Plus, I had help!

I knew this was the perfect time to pursue another dream of mine: becoming an author! I collaborated with a ghostwriter to start writing my first book, The Free Mama: How to Work from Home, Control Your Schedule, and Make More Money.

I took quite a bit of the summer off, mostly just showing up for coaching calls and meeting with my writer.

Up until this point, I had channeled all of my marketing efforts into a Facebook group. This turned out to be both incredibly brilliant (laser-focused and committed) and totally naive (all my eggs in one basket).

By the time my oldest was back in school, I hit what was probably my first major setback in being an online business owner when I lost my Facebook ads account. Now I would love to tell you that I recovered quickly and got my account back and everything was great, but that would be a lie.

The truth is, I wasn't prepared for a challenge like this in my business. I was completely blindsided and had pretty much no experience adapting quickly (a skill that is important for all business owners to learn, the impact of COVID-19 being a super obvious example).

No, instead I curled up into the fetal position and cried.

In between bawling sessions, I reached out to my coach via Voxer with the attitude of, "Well, I guess the jig is up. I had a great run while it lasted."

I know. Not my highest self.

My coach reminded me that perhaps there were other solutions to my now cut-off traffic supply. Maybe one Facebook ad account didn't have the ability to overthrow The Free Mama Movement.

Hmm.

Sadly, I hadn't been looking at it that way . . . yet.

This was the beginning of a new belief system for me: **Things don't happen to you, they happen *for* you.**

I made the decision to become a resilient problem-solver (a skill that's served me well ever since).

I hired a social media manager with the pure goal of "looking alive" on other platforms and supplemented with some Pinterest ads, and a few months later, we birthed FreeMamaTV, my YouTube channel, which now has over thirty-five thousand subscribers, generates the majority of our organic lead generation, and provides completely passive income each month from our channel monetization.

In December of 2018, I published my book, and because of the support of my community, it became an international best-seller before I even woke up at 6:00 a.m. on launch day!

But truthfully, it didn't feel like I thought it would. It felt like another checkmark. I rapidly moved the goal posts and set a bigger goal. I didn't take the time to stop and acknowledge the work I was doing as I was doing it. **I didn't enjoy the journey because I was only focused on the destination.**

By January 2019, I was aware of how different I'd become.

I no longer believed making money was difficult.

You have a market you're passionate about serving. You solve a problem with an irresistible offer. You fulfill that commitment to your buyers. You sell to those people again.

That's a business.

And my role in my business was evolving pretty substantially.

While I wore every single hat when I first began, I now spent the majority of my time managing my team and creating content.

Outsourcing is the ultimate leverage (right alongside funnels and automation). I had to learn how to hire people and fire people. I made some mistakes and did a few things really well. I'm always learning and growing when it comes to the team.

I was no longer building a funnel, I was building a company, and the Two Comma Club Award was no longer something I dreamed of achieving because I knew it was only a matter of time.

As the months to the million-dollar mark got closer and my money mindset shifted, I also realized that I had become disconnected from why I actually started.

Sure, I had wanted to feel more secure, and thanks to my funnel, I had paid off over six figures in debt that first year.

But I also cared greatly about impact and fulfillment. I was incredibly aware of my personal and business values, and connection had to be at the core of what I did.

So at the beginning of 2019, I set out to travel to a different state each month to meet my Free Mamas in real life. I got to hear story after story about how freelancing was changing these women's lives.

While it certainly wasn't sustainable for my family of littles to have me gone on these trips so often, it was my favorite year in business to date because of the relationships I formed with my students.

It was on one of these trips, at an Airbnb in St. Louis, Missouri, that I watched my Stripe account flash over to $1 million.

I did it.

I actually did it.

I had done the thing that part of me always knew I could do (or I probably wouldn't have actually tried), but part of me was not so sure this could really be possible for someone like me . . . a mom from Kansas.

That day wasn't about the money at all. The million dollars did not compute like the thousands of lives that it represented, especially my own. I was changed. My family was different. We were debt-free and safe.

I had transformed into an influencer, a boss, and a thought leader because I'd had the courage to show up over and over again.

The Two Comma Club Award on my wall does not represent a million dollars in sales from one funnel. It represents who I became in the process of getting it.

And yet when that moment came, I wasn't shouting it from the rooftops.

I was afraid people would think I was bragging. I was insecure that people would think I didn't genuinely care about my students or helping people.

I wasn't quite sure who to share this accomplishment with, because it felt so personal. It wasn't until a few months later at my first annual event in October 2019 that I publicly announced that I had won a Two Comma Club Award.

I cried and celebrated with my community of Free Mamas, the community I had built and encouraged to share in moments just like this. It was a true moment of leadership to practice what I preached (even though I was terrified and uncomfortable): **celebrate your wins, no matter how big or small.**

At Funnel Hacking Live 2020, I walked across the stage and got my photo with Todd and Russell and the coveted award, and I felt proud.

And then . . .

The pandemic hit.

Everything changed in my business and life. I spent months serving my audience above and beyond, often for free. Moms were educators overnight, myself included, and isolation left us all feeling more alone than ever.

For a few months, my sales skyrocketed, because suddenly everyone had to learn how to work from home. I learned how to host a virtual event, the adaptable business owner I now was.

I launched programs because I thought I should. Or worse, because someone else told me that they thought I should. I had outgrown the frameworks that had once made me a lot of money, yet I was struggling to trust myself as a business owner.

Behind the scenes, my family was going through some major life events. A death. A move. Serious mental health concerns.

Through the struggle, I felt myself changing once again; this time it was extremely personal. I started allowing myself to slow down. To feel more. To focus on being present, instead of focusing on a future goal. I asked myself for the first time in a while, "What do I actually want?" At the same time, it felt like things were falling apart on the inside. I was receiving recognition for what I had created at The Free Mama: magazines, interviews, awards.

Something kept drawing me back to Russell's world, and that same spring I got a Voxer message from Russell inviting me to speak at Funnel Hacking Live.

Now, in case you don't know the numbers on this, only 2 percent of Funnel Hackers have earned the Two Comma Club Award. (Likewise, only 2 percent of female-owned businesses ever cross the million-dollar mark.)

But even fewer Two Comma Club Award winners get one of the lucky spots to speak on Russell's stage.

I was honored and humbled, and, if I'm honest with you, I *felt* deserving. I had worked hard and served my face off within my community, and it felt so good to be recognized by someone I admired so much and whose knowledge had played such a significant role in my own success. I wasn't nervous about speaking on stage; I was nervous about making Russell proud!

A month before Funnel Hacking Live, the Marketing Secrets team shared with a select group of people that they were reopening Russell's Inner Circle program. I was possibly the easiest sell of all time, ready to sign up and call myself a part of this prestigious group.

Much like the Two Comma Club Award, however, joining Russell's Inner Circle is a story of becoming, not an achievement. While you have to have a million dollars in revenue to qualify for this group, doing so will require you to become an entirely different person.

From the outside looking in, I felt as though the Inner Circle was the "cool kids" club. The members had everything figured out about business and life. They had "made it." It was the ultimate goal!

Now that I'm here, I know that isn't true. Don't get me wrong, there are some extraordinary, brilliant, generous, and even cool people, but no one has it all together all the time.

We all have gifts. We all have challenges. We all also have these things in common:

- We don't give up.

- We take extreme ownership and responsibility.

- We get up (or rebuild, or redesign, or repitch, or rewrite) over and over and over again.

- We care about our humans and know our reputation ultimately lies in how well we serve them.

- We give back freely, whether it be time, knowledge, or access.

I'm grateful for the opportunity to sit in this space and for every single lesson and connection that brought me to this place and made me the woman of conviction and transparency I am today.

Russell's tagline is you're only One Funnel Away, and I think most people presume he's talking about being one funnel away from success, whether it's your first, life-changing online sale or your one-millionth dollar online.

But the truth is (and I think Russell knows this too), the one funnel away, the Two Comma Club Award, and even Inner Circle isn't just about money.

It's about our ability to change lives, and it starts with your own.

Being a business owner is hard (*almost* as hard as being a mom).

You'll have to make sacrifices most won't understand. You'll feel pressure from clients and team members. You'll be stretched beyond your comfort zone, and at times, beyond your capacity.

But it's so worth it.

You just need the unwavering courage to go for it.

Saving you a seat in the Inner Circle.

Lauren Golden

ALLIE BJERK

Unleashing Your Potential: The Secrets to Achieving Success in Life and Business

Allie Bjerk is a visibility strategist, coach, and consultant. Allie has helped hundreds of business owners create the visibility strategies and marketing plans behind growing super-profitable businesses for balanced and prosperous lives. Allie has taken her marketing agency experience and used it to lead entrepreneurs towards their goals through her transformational programs.

Allie's mission is to help entrepreneurs to show up authentically, owning their expertise and not shrinking down from their big dreams. Her focus on inner-work, confidence, consistency, captivation and clarity has set her work apart from other marketers and strategists, who focus on tactics and algorithms over the relationships. Allie spent 4 years working for corporate web development and Internet marketing agencies before launching her business. She managed the SEO and

Social Media departments, teaching marketing and training new agency employees. Allie left her corporate marketing career after the birth of her first baby and a battle with debilitating postpartum anxiety that served as the catalyst for her to transform her life and never look back. She now lives an adventure and travel-filled life based in Northern Minnesota with her husband and three young children.

"I didn't sign up for this." I thought. With my back against the door of our laundry room, I sunk to the floor, dizzy from sobbing. I couldn't do it anymore. The house was a disaster: I had a pile of dishes to finish, clutter on seemingly every surface of my home, and a bed covered in laundry.

My baby was fussing, wanting to nurse again, and her toddler brother had just dropped an entire carton of eggs onto the floor out of the refrigerator—into which I had repeatedly asked him not to climb. My husband was working out of town for the third night this week, and I wasn't sure how many more nights we had to go. I was utterly exhausted, mentally fried, and completely alone.

Up to that point, I'd spent most of my adult life in indecision and unhappiness, feeling like I was floating from day to day, year to year.

I did everything "right": got the degree, married the guy, bought the house, had the kids—yet I was miserable. I hated my job, I was in a ton of debt, and I had a really hard time coming to grips with the reality that this was it.

This was life. This was my reality. Working forty-plus hours per week, counting the hours until Friday, and screwing around on Facebook when my boss wasn't around.

I was miserable and searching for something . . . ANYTHING that would make me less miserable—more money and a different job seemed like it could help.

I considered going back to school for something else, like nursing. I was stuck in a $35K-per-year job as an SEO manager for a web agency, and I figured if I went back to school for nursing, I could at least double my salary and make $70K per year . . . worth a shot, right? Both of my siblings are medical doctors, so I figured it was an option.

One problem, though: I hate blood.

I signed up at the local community college for a fast-track nursing degree, since I already had a bachelor's and had started classes.

We were super broke, trying to balance being new homeowners, having student loans and babies . . . so I thought, "Maybe I could start doing some SEO, graphic design, and social media management jobs on the side to earn extra income."

My first clients had an unlimited retainer of services for just $250 bucks per month. Yes, seriously.

And surprisingly, it only took me THREE months of saying I was (sorta) open for business to have a full client roster and to have completely replaced AND gone above and beyond my current salary working for someone else.

It was like a lightbulb went off. I didn't have to deal with hospitals, clinicals, blood, OR overnight shifts . . . and I could still do what I loved, making more than my original plan of $70K per year.

I went to BNI meetings at 6:00 a.m. I networked. I shook hands and met all of the local business owners and landed a couple amazing clients . . . and eventually, I quit my job.

Over the next five years, I kept expanding my skillset.

I realized that social media management alone wasn't enough.

So I taught myself ads.

Then I learned ads alone were not enough, so I taught myself about sales funnels.

As a side project, I had even started my own Etsy shop selling nursery printables and wedding invitations, and I remember telling my mom proudly that I'd made $1,000 in one month from Etsy!

I discovered this world of online businesses, experts, and coaches existed, and I knew I wanted to shift from working locally to serving online businesses, but I had one major problem.

I was terrified of video calls. Like, hated them with a fire of a thousand suns. If a potential client wanted to meet on video, I would be like, "Nope, not doing it. Guess we're not a good fit."

I felt awkward and uncomfortable, and my biggest fear was that my internet would be shoddy, my face would freeze in a dumb expression on the screen, or I'd be left sitting there by myself, saying, "Can you hear me now?" (So what? It happens!)

In order to face my fear, I decided to go into Facebook groups and ask other entrepreneurs to meet with me for a coffee chat, "just for fun." I ended up scheduling thirty coffee chats in two weeks with other entrepreneurs, and even though I wanted to cancel every single one of them, I showed up, and by the end, not only was "popping onto a video call" easy, but also I started looking forward to them. The connections I made actually propelled my ads management business into true existence, and it laid the foundation for me to start using video in my marketing.

The referrals started flying in, and I was doing better than I'd ever expected to do as a service provider.

I was comfortably behind the scenes of many different online businesses, running their ads, building their funnels, planning their launches . . .

But I started feeling somewhat unfulfilled (that darn nagging voice of growth was rearing its head again), and I dreamed of having my own line of digital products, coaching, and courses—but I had a really hard time putting myself front and center. Sure, I'd design products and halfsies launch them, but without a lot of focus, they never really took off (weird, right?).

I blamed my inability to be a personal brand or blamed my lack of confidence and then went back to working with clients.

I was always aware that Inner Circle existed, but I never thought it would be possible for *me*, a Minnesota mother of three, to see the level of success where it would make sense for me to join . . . so I always kept that dream on the back burner, never wanting to get my hopes up that it could actually be possible.

After a couple years of wanting to do my own thing and almost growing to resent my clients (ouch), I had a horrible client experience where the client pushed through a $6,000 chargeback unexpectedly on work that had already been completed.

How was I going to walk into the kitchen to tell my husband that I had screwed up again and that $6K was going to be pulled from our account in the morning?

I had no clients in the pipeline, no other money coming in, no savings, and completely maxed-out credit cards. My bank account was about to go negative.

That was my "back against the wall" moment, my do or die. I had to REALLY actually launch something and mean it this time.

I dusted off one of my old digital products (a social media calendar with 365 ideas for live streams), and found a secret credit card I'd kept hidden from myself with an $8,000 limit . . . and I started my own ads, for the first time. I hit publish on my ads and basically curled up in the fetal position on my couch, knowing I was spending money by the minute that I definitely didn't have.

The next day, I was running an errand with my husband, and my phone pinged with a sale.

Someone had bought my $27 calendar from my ads! AND they bought my order bump and one-time offer too. I'd just made $164 while shopping. What?

"This was definitely a mistake. There's no way they did that on purpose. They're probably going to ask for a refund any second," I remember thinking. I watched my phone carefully for the refund email, and much to my surprise. It never came. But more sales notifications came.

That very first day, I tripled the return on my ad spend. So I doubled what I was spending for day two . . . "Let's see how hard I can push this," I remember thinking. And again, my phone pinged all day with sales. That day was a 5X ROAS day.

Within two weeks of starting those ads, I'd make $10K—the most I'd ever made in a single week. Which was enough to cover my $6K chargeback and get my account back into the black.

I kept scaling my ads, and I had made half a million dollars in six months. By then, people were asking how I'd done it and asking if I'd teach them. I built a $997 course and put it behind an evergreen funnel and waited for sales. (You might be noticing a "comfort level" theme here.)

A friend of mine came across the recorded webinar and messaged me saying, "Allie . . . this needs to be a LIVE webinar, and you need to sell this as a $6K group program. Minimum."

Nope. Not for me. I COULD NOT run a group program. I'm NOT comfortable leading a Zoom room with thirty-plus people expecting me to have the answers every week.

"C'mon, Allie, I'll build the tech; you just come give your presentation and pitch."

So I gave it a shot. That first launch of my group program, I made $130K in one day. I mean, $27 offers are great, but $6K sales are even more fun.

We hit a million in revenue in just ten months from that fateful chargeback evening.

I remember googling "Russell Brunson Inner Circle" around that time and learning that it had been closed down. I remember being so bummed and feeling like I'd missed my chance to learn from Russell Brunson directly.

I continued #doingthework and growing my group program and ended up making about $4M in revenue from that program. When Covid hit, it was a really hard time for me. My husband continued working outside of the house, and I was trying to manage distance learning and managing a team with a payroll of $80K per month, and I basically burned everything to the ground. I stopped doing weekly webinars and relied ONLY on the sales of my Tiny Offers because I felt like I was drowning.

For most of 2020 and 2021, I felt like I was in survival mode. I was struggling and felt horrible that I'd had to let a few team members go. I had almost entirely stopped actively and consistently marketing my higher-ticket programs. (Thank goodness for ads and Tiny Offers because they gave me the space I needed to process all of those "unprecedented events" and not go out of business.) I even stopped journaling. I started drinking a giant glass of red wine every afternoon (after surviving my kids' messy distance learning schedules for the day), and I put on a ton of weight and felt super depressed, unsure of how I was going to move forward. I went from being a strict vegan to eating just about anything we had in the house—aaaaallll the snacks. I remember feeling super ashamed and almost helpless (with no idea how to dig myself back out) in those moments.

Slowly, as the world started opening back up in Minnesota, I started to feel more like myself, and I started getting excited about growing my business again. I went back to being alcohol-free, eating healthy, and exercising at the gym once it opened back up. (Side note, I learned from Inner Circle that movement is SO important for those that are a high D on the DISC scale—thanks, Coach Mandy Keene!)

I started recognizing that there are seasons in business, and I gave myself grace for getting through a slump and being stronger by the end. There was only one way to go from there, and that was back up.

Then in late 2021, at the same time FHL was going on in Florida (I hadn't gone that year because my kids were sick), I read a book by Alex Hormozi called *$100M Offers* (maybe you've heard of it? ;)) and it completely rejuvenated my passion for my business. After reading that book, I created a brand-new $15K VIP offer and launched it to my list the next day, and sold out the spots I'd opened up (in just twenty-four hours) for a cash injection of $100K!

Meanwhile, I had been living vicariously through friends that were at FHL, and a few of them sent me excited messages saying, "INNER CIRCLE IS BACK OPEN!"

I responded immediately: "WHERE DO I SUBMIT MY APPLICATION?"

Without thinking twice, I filled out the app and patiently waited for my call with Robbie. If I hadn't read the book and launched the new $15K offer when I did, I probably wouldn't have been able to join.

I had my credit card sitting on the table before I even hopped on that Zoom call and told Robbie, "This is gonna be your easiest sale today, I bet."

I'm so grateful that I was able to join Inner Circle, and the timing couldn't have been better. My momentum and growth as a leader have grown exponentially since surrounding myself with such a high caliber of peers, and I know that the lack of peer accountability and community was part of the reason I had struggled so much throughout the lockdowns.

I've seen myself in an entirely different light after speaking on stages at 2CCX Coaching Events, and I'm immensely grateful for the opportunities and the growth. Something Russell said that really stuck with me is that it's not about the money, but WHO YOU BECOME on the way to being able to make (manage AND keep) the money.

I'm working on things now that the old "$250/mo. Retainer Allie" couldn't even imagine being capable of doing. Not only am I still running my $6K offer, but I've also launched a $25K mastermind full of inspiring and amazing students. I'm also working on a few top-secret membership projects that are going to completely revolutionize the peer-to-peer learning industry, writing a book, and planning for hosting more in-person workshops in the future while getting on more stages to share inspiration with others.

One of my favorite taglines for my program is "Dream Big. Start Tiny," because that's exactly how my journey began. I started with one tiny step at a time, slowly inching out of my comfort zone and expanding more and more until I barely recognize previous versions of myself.

I hope my story inspires you to start tiny and to give yourself grace if you're in one of the challenging seasons. This brings me to the end of my Inner Circle story, and I hope that it can be the beginning of **your** own Inner Circle story.

JOSHUA STEPHENS

From Pig Farmer to Eight-Figure CEO: The Power of Faith & Rising from Adversity

Joshua Stephens is the CEO of Kings Loot, a luxury wallet company. Growing up in Arizona, Joshua worked many jobs, from pig farming to selling cookware door-to-door. In 2018, Joshua and his family relocated to Colorado for him to attend Bible college.

While in school, the idea for the first Kings Loot wallet was birthed. Joshua and his wife invested their life savings into this dream. Starting at tradeshows, the company took a massive hit during the pandemic.

ClickFunnels was the answer Joshua needed to take his business online and scale. In 2020, Joshua won the Two Comma Club Award for hitting a million dollars in revenue. Today, Kings Loot is an eight-figure business with nine employees. Recently, Joshua acquired his second company, Kingship Fulfillment.

He has been married to his wife, Jessica, for a decade and has three beautiful daughters. Joshua wakes up every day excited to live life abundantly.

—

Today, I run an eight-figure business called Kings Loot. We design modern and minimal products that help change the way you see yourself. Before I could be where I am today, I had to change the way I saw myself, and that was a long journey. Let me take you to the beginning.

From a young age, I had an entrepreneurial spirit. My grandfather was an entrepreneur. He was in the molding business. During his lifetime, he started and sold three different molding mills and employed hundreds of people. He had a relentless drive, and it was really my inspiration for getting started in business.

For me, my own entrepreneurial journey started at nineteen. I was really into music and invented a cross-shaped guitar. I would go to big music festivals like Spirit West Coast in California, and I would sell these guitars. I quickly realized that this would be a hard business to scale because I was making them all by hand. From there, I dabbled in a lot of different things: pig farming, selling cookware, and real estate. I was busting my tail working crazy hours to earn the life I wanted and, in the process, sacrificing the one thing that was the most important to me—my family.

At the age of twenty-two, I married my high-school sweetheart, Jessica. We had been best friends growing up, and our friendship developed into something more. The foundation of our relationship was God, and she was the one person I trusted with everything. We built our life in Arizona and had our first daughter two years after getting married. I was working for a cell phone company, and right before my first daughter was born, I got fired. From there, I started pig farming and got a job working as a physical therapist tech. Right before the birth of my second daughter, I got fired again. After being fired twice, I realized that I didn't have any security in a job and I didn't want to have to depend on anyone else.

Soon after, I got the opportunity to work for a direct sales company and did really well. In the first month I made $14,000 in commission, and after ninety days, I won an all-expense trip to Puerto Vallarta. I was ranked as one of the top two sales representatives in the United States for this company. I was a driver, I was going so hard. There was no rest. I was addicted to the chase. I was doing multiple jobs at the same time and got involved in real estate too. That's when my wife served me with a divorce. I was actually served twice. They were both very well deserved. My children were like, "Daddy's never home. We never see Daddy," and they were little at the time. It was literally the grace of God that changed my wife's mind to stay with me.

Things began to change for me in 2017 when I met this man who carried himself differently. I went on a business trip to Montreal, Canada. The second night I was there, I went out with this man, Aram.

Aram is Armenian and a good-looking dude. We were at dinner, and these two French girls started hitting on him and wanted him to go home with them, and he refused them. I was shocked. They left, and I asked him, "What's wrong with you?" He was twenty-five years old and single. In my mind, I didn't understand why he was refusing them. He told me, "I just love my Father. I can't do that to Him." This man not only professed to know God, but also he was a living example of a relationship with Him, and I had never seen that.

This was monumental to me because it went against my experience in the church. I became a Christian at fifteen years old. My first pastor cheated on his wife in the church. The second church I went to, that wife left the pastor and that church split. It happened again at the third church I went to. My whole entry into Christianity was infidelity. It was seeing men who professed one thing but lived another.

When I met Aram, I encountered the real gospel at work in someone's life, and that was attractive. I wanted to have what he had because it was so real. From there, we started a friendship, and one year later, in March 2018, he invited me to a men's conference at Charis Bible College in Woodland Park, Colorado. I got there, and I was in a room full of men praying in tongues. I was like, "What the heck is going on here?" It was like nothing I had seen before. I had never been exposed to the spirit movement.

I was sitting in this conference, and I looked out the window and could see this beautiful mountain, Pikes Peak. I had this feeling of familiarity. For two years, I had been having this dream of my family and I holding hands and walking in the mountains. Up until this point, I had never understood the dream. I just knew that it filled me with so much peace.

I realized, "Wow, that's the mountain from my dreams." I asked the Lord, "Am I supposed to move here?" Immediately I felt like, yes, this was where I was supposed to be. At this point, I wasn't spirit-filled. I had been a Christian for ten years and hadn't seen any growth in my life. I was stuck, but I felt this yearning in my heart.

I went home and told my wife, "We're moving to Colorado," and surprisingly, she was all for it. She wanted out of Arizona. We sold our home and packed up all of our belongings, and by June of that year, we were in Colorado. I thought I was going to do real estate in Colorado. I'd go to Bible college for four hours during the day and then flip houses at night. I had this whole plan, but when I went to buy a house, I kept getting outbid by $50,000 to $60,000 over asking. I just got exhausted. I gave up, and the Lord told me, "Joshua, you need to rest." It went against every fiber in my being. I didn't think I could just do nothing. I thought I always had to be doing something. It was the hardest thing for me to do. I still had some income coming in from a rental house in Arizona, and the Lord told me to sell that too. I was like, "Whoa, whoa, whoa, Lord, you want me to not work and sell the only income that I have?" He was like, "Yes." I was thinking, "Okay, this is crazy, but I'll do it."

I was going to school four hours a day and coming home to an empty house. My kids were in school, and my wife was working. I had nothing to do, and I was getting really bored. My whole identity was tied to my performance. I had to perform to be worth something, and God was trying to change that in me. I didn't understand it, though, at the time. After a couple of weeks with nothing to do, I decided to start reading the Bible since I had a Bible plan for school I had to finish. I start doing this every day after school, and once I was in, I couldn't stop. I was reading and reading, and I was starting to see my life in a different way.

In December 2018, I got invited to a conference called Jesus Image in Florida. We arrive there and were in a room full of six thousand people. These people were experiencing the power and presence of God, and half the people were lying on the floor. It looked like a bulldozer went through there. I was new to this and had no idea what was going on. My friend Arthur said, "Let's go to the front and get prayed for." I followed him, and on the way up he was like, "Yo, Joshua, no courtesy falls." I was completely new to this kind of stuff, so I had no idea what he was talking about. I went to the front and got prayed for, and nothing happened. I didn't feel anything, and I was salty. I was looking at what was going on around me, and my conclusion was this was fake.

We were there at the conference for a couple of days. Near the end of the conference, this man named Brian Guerin was speaking, and he started losing it, laughing uncontrollably. It was Holy Spirit laughter, but I had never seen or experienced this. The next thing I knew, I was laughing too. Then people started running to the front, and I ran to the front as well. As soon as I was there, I felt what I know knew to be the glory of the Lord. It was so heavy I couldn't even stand up. I hit the ground, and my laughing turned to weeping. I was there for two hours, and I had a crazy encounter with God. I got delivered on that floor 100 hundred percent. At that moment, I gave up doing business my way. The way I saw myself completely changed, and it went from a businessman to a son. Not just any son, but the son of a King. That means I'm an heir to a Kingdom, which makes me royalty. It was a turning point for me. I came back from that conference, and my quiet times looked different. I was not just reading the word; I was on my knees. I was worshiping. I was having this close intimate relationship with the Lord, and I was falling in love with Him.

For Christmas that year, I decided to give all my friends wallets. A wallet, to me, symbolizes prosperity, so me gifting wallets was my way of letting them know I wanted this to be a prosperous year for them. I spent a while shopping online for wallets and also purchased one for myself. At this time, I had no idea or intention of starting a wallet company, but this was the seed for something that was about to grow.

A couple months later, I went on a getaway trip with my family to Breckenridge, Colorado. During my quiet time here, I was journaling to the Lord. I was expressing all of my gratitude because my life had completely changed. My family, my marriage, and my heart had been restored. I was no longer depressed, and I was just thanking God. At the end of this time, God told me, "Son, I'm going to give you a billion-dollar business." I was like, "Whoa, wait, what'd you just say?" I was really new to hearing the Lord at this time, so I was not 100 percent sure I was hearing Him correctly. I have a friend, Jeffrey, I met from Bible college who was really prophetic, and I reached out to him and joined his course on how to hear the Lord's voice. It was six weeks long and really in-depth. At the end of this course, I get off my last call, and I heard the Lord say, "Pick up a pen and grab a piece of paper." So I did. The Lord said, "Do you remember when I told you I was going to give you a billion-dollar business?" I was like, "Yes, I do." He was like, "Okay, good. Now later today, your friend Arthur is going to come over. He's going to sow into your marriage. Let him know that everything he gives you will come back a hundredfold."

It was really specific. I wrote this down, dated the paper, and left it in my room. Two hours later, my friend Arthur came over, and he was acting all weird walking around my kitchen. Then all of a sudden, boom, he slapped some cash on the counter and told me, "Hey, man, I'm getting married, and I want to sow into your marriage." I looked at him like a deer in headlights. I told him, "Man, you're not going to believe this. Come with me." We went to my room, and I grabbed the piece of paper from earlier and handed it to him. It was like a receipt. He started crying, and I started crying. This was confirmation for me that I was hearing God's voice clearly.

Shortly after that, I was looking at the wallet I had purchased back in December, and I started to think that I could do this better, I could make a better, more functional wallet. I was sitting in class and I started getting all of these ideas for a wallet. It was just being downloaded to me, and I started drawing this out on paper, and I was so stinking excited. I took this design and made it with paper, and I was showing it to everybody. People were looking at it, and they weren't impressed, but I was looking at it, and I was not seeing what it was; I was seeing what it could be. I decided to go to Hobby Lobby, and I bought a sewing machine and some leather. I set this all up in my kitchen, and I was determined to make this thing. My wife was laughing at me. She was like, "You don't even iron your own clothes. How are you going to sew?" But I was like, "Baby, I'm going to figure this out." I turned on YouTube and started watching videos on how to sew. I stitched this wallet together, and it was hideous. I was clearly not a craftsman, but I had a vision. I realized I needed a manufacturer and started searching for one. The first one that got back to me was the same one I am still working with today. It was a God thing. I sent him my design, and a month later he sent me a prototype. I got a notification on my phone that the package was delivered, so I went to the post office with a little knife. I got the package, went back to my truck, and opened it up. I pulled the wallet out of the box, and I saw it for the first time. I started crying. This vision that was in my head was now in my hands. It was the greatest feeling in the world.

I had a product now, but I knew nothing about e-commerce. God was showing me, though, that business His way was partnering with the Holy Spirit. I was making breakfast one morning, and the Lord spoke to me. He was like, "Hey, Joshua, I'm going to give you a marketing plan. I'm going to teach you how to market and help you sell this product." I was like, "Okay." Then I had a vision of this ad that I had seen two years prior. It was a drunk guy, and it was an ad for a book called *DotCom Secrets* by Russell Brunson. I was thinking, "Why is the Lord giving me a vision of a drunk guy saying to go buy this book? Is this my flesh?" Despite my doubts, I went to Barnes and Noble, and there is one book left. I bought the book, started reading, and realized this was a crash course on digital marketing. I was learning all about copy, hooks, stories, and funnels. While reading this book, I also learned about the Two Comma Club Award, which was awarded to a business that reached seven-figures within the first year of a ClickFunnels funnel. Immediately upon reading about it, I knew that would be my goal.

Through this book, my world is opened, and I got connected to all these other entrepreneurs. I ended up going to a conference called 100x, and I heard this girl, Jamie Cross, speaking on stage. She was sharing how she started her billion-dollar business with soap and that she went to farmer's markets and trade shows. So that's what I decided I would do. I got back from the conference and went on Amazon and bought a tent and display shelves. On September 28, 2019, my buddies and I went to a trade show in Boulder, Colorado, and that was the day I sold my first wallet. We sold fifteen wallets that day, and it was a huge win for me. I started doing trade shows every weekend, and things were going well. Then March 2020, Covid-19 hit.

I had invested all the money I had into Kings Loot. I had paid entry in advance for all these trade shows that couldn't be refunded, and I had bought lots of inventory. My savings were completely wiped out. I was $40,000 in debt and in the worst financial situation I had ever been in. My wife was still working, but her income wasn't enough to cover our expenses, so we were going negative $2,000 every month. I knew God wasn't surprised by what was going on in the world, and I knew I had a word from Him.

I met this woman named Stephanie Blake through one of the Facebook groups I was in called 100x. She had a coaching group to help businesses build online. I was willing to do whatever it took. Our credit cards at the time were maxed out, but I got a $2,000 extension, which was enough to cover one month of coaching. On our first call I told her, "I'm going to be a miracle story for you because I really need this right now."

Stephanie helped me to build my very first funnel. I launched it and it flopped. I rebuilt it and launched it a second time, and it flopped again. I was getting discouraged, but I kept hearing the Lord tell me, "You are going to build a successful funnel."

One night, my wife and I were in bed, and she just started crying. She was so discouraged by our finances. She was telling me that we couldn't stay in Colorado and this wasn't going to work. I told her,

"Just have faith. It's going to be okay." She went to bed, and I got up to pray, and I was like, "God, please, please, I need you. My wife is losing hope. I'm losing hope. I know what you've told me. I know what your Word says, and I believe it's true, but I'm not experiencing your truth, and I want to experience it, Father." I got a vision of the floodgates opening, and I heard God tell me, "Joshua, just hold on a little longer. The floodgates are opening." I turned on that song from The Greatest Showman called "A Million Dreams" and listened to it over and over. In my spirit, I just knew this was going to happen. It was going to work.

A month later, I built another funnel, and it finally hit. When it hit, it really hit. At this point, I had only done $4,000 in sales online, which was less than what I had been making at trade shows. We went from $4,000 to making $28,000 in revenue in one month. My goal at the time in the coaching program was just to make $10,000 a month, and I'd just doubled it. It kept going up. I started to see crazy multiplication. The floodgates literally opened up. It was growing so fast now that I needed to hire people, so I added two people to my team. In October 2020, we hit our first million, and a month later we hit our second million. By the end of 2020, we did almost three million in sales.

That year, in 2020, I was awarded the Two Comma Club Award that I had read about in *DotCom Secrets*. It was a dream come true. After winning that award, I had dinner with other Comma Club Award winners, hosted by Russell Brunson, and through that I was invited into the Inner Circle. Joining this group has been one of the coolest experiences. It's changed the way I think about things. You are in a room with some of the most elite entrepreneurs in the world, and I quickly realized I'm a small fish in a big pond. It's helped me to focus on why I do what I do and what I want to be remembered for. Beyond that, I've met amazing people who have become good friends for life.

All the success I've experienced, though, came from an identity shift in me. Before Kings Loot, I had experienced some success in business, but it was all worthless because I went about it the wrong way. Miles Monroe once said, "The one thing that is keeping you away from your greatest success is your past success." When my identity shifted to a Son, I no longer wanted to do business my way; I wanted to partner with God and do it His way. I had to forget everything I had learned about business before because the way the world does things is upside down, but the Kingdom is right side up. Everything in the world is pursued, but in the Kingdom, it is attracted. When I made God the CEO, things became easier. My wife was able to quit her job, and I am able to have the freedom to spend time with my family and be there for my three daughters. Our third one was born here in Colorado in 2021.

Right now, wherever you are, I want you to take a moment and ask yourself, "What is the lie that I am believing that is holding me back from all I am meant to have?" When you get the answer, replace this lie with the truth.

For me, the lies were: I'm not good enough, the success others have isn't real, and I'm only valuable when I perform well. The truth that replaced those lies was: I am good enough, the success others experience is real, and it can be real for me, too, and I am valuable not based on my performance but because I am a Son. I changed the way I saw myself, and in the process changed the life I have.

For every belief you have, there is a story you tell yourself. When you change the story, you change your belief. When your belief changes, so does your outcome.

JOHN GOLAT

Who Is John Golat?

John Golat is an incredible example of success. He hails from Austin, Texas and has the special power to help entrepreneurs use Mind Hacking to take control of their lives. Through his company ClickMind.com AI, John can make sure that aspiring business people get a head start on achieving greatness! His hard work has earned him not only personal achievements but awards as well - three prestigious ClickFunnels 2CCs! But what makes John truly remarkable is how he uses these successes for good: always striving to give back in whatever way possible so others may enjoy similar benefits.

Who is John Golat?

I'm an entrepreneur, just like you. And I know what it's like to feel scared, alone, and lost, even when you're surrounded by people who love and support you. Welcome to the inside of my brain. So sit back, relax, and enjoy the ride!

Let's be honest . . . Most entrepreneurs only show the good stuff on social media—the fancy cars, the successes and millions made.

The reality is that most of us are working long hours and late nights, struggling to make ends meet financially, and never having enough free time to do things that you want to do because we're always too busy growing our business instead.

But before we go further, let me make something abundantly clear:

I am NOT your typical entrepreneur "lemonade stand" story . . .

I was the first in my family born in the United States. I grew up with my mom and sister. I watched as she struggled to make money every day on a waitress's salary, living only on tips. I still remember my mom coming home late at night, smelling the sweat from her work clothes. She would bring home leftovers from the restaurant so she would have enough left to pay rent.

My entrepreneurial journey started as a young kid; I've always been fascinated by money and how it works. When I was eight years old, I started reading books about investing in stocks and learning how to win and influence people.

On Saturdays, I would help my grandma go through dumpsters located in the back alleys of section 8 housing in the worst part of Chicago. Watching her do this every day showed me how hard she worked and how much she cared.

I learned the system of survival at a young age. No matter who you are or where you are in life, we all have to hustle and learn how to survive.

My freshman year of high school, I did really well academically and even made the honor roll. However, I started hanging out with some kids who were a bad influence, which led me to start experimenting with drugs and alcohol. It got to the point where it became a real problem—I was doing heavy drugs and getting arrested frequently. My life became an agonizing cycle: wake up, get money for drugs, repeat.

I went through years of professional rehabilitation, but nothing seemed to work. I always went back to my old ways.

One morning, something clicked. I told myself that I was done with this life and that I wanted something better for myself. I changed my life and never looked back.

It all starts with **YOU AND YOUR MIND**.

I started at the bottom and, against great odds, have worked my way up step by step. I've always stayed true to my core belief that three elements are essential to success: brains, courage, and persistence.

I used these principles to navigate the ups and downs of being an entrepreneur, ultimately leading my first software as a service (SaaS) company, HostedDialer. As one of the first predictive dialers on the cloud, I advertised that our solution required no technical knowledge and within weeks had fifty call centers signing up. Our business made over a million dollars in revenue our first year.

Years later . . . I was tired of the business I was in. Most importantly, I was not aligned with my business partner. I wanted to give up since I felt more like an employee than an entrepreneur.

I had been feeling stuck in my business for a while and was looking for some direction. This boot camp promised to give me the tools I needed to take my business to the next level. I bought the offer and got sold on two upsells totaling around $550. I sat there in awe at how I had just spent all that money without even thinking twice about it.

I was curious how this one person could make so much money online, so I decided to study their methods by "hacking" their sales funnel. At the time, I didn't know what "funnel hacking" was, but I figured if it worked for them, maybe it would work for me in another industry. After struggling for two to three months testing copy, images, and headlines, I almost gave up on the idea.

I was looking for a new marketing software and came across ClickFunnels. Russell Brunson sold me on the idea, and I'm so glad I switched! The business has exploded since relaunching on ClickFunnels. It's much easier to use than other software out there.

I made a small change to my advertising budget, and it had a big impact on my sales. I went from $200 per day to $2,000 and saw an increase in business right away. My sales reached $100,000 within the first month, and by the third month I was up to $240,000.

We were on top of the world when we started our family and bought our six thousand-square-foot dream home. We had unlimited credit and no financial worries during the recession. Sometimes things change and life doesn't always go as planned.

Within two years, we made many careless mistakes as business owners and failed to pivot the business with new market trends. We struggled financially, and whatever method or marketing technique we tried wasn't effective. We kept trying other ideas, but they all failed, and as more time went on, we had more bills and less money in our accounts.

We thought for sure this was the end. We were standing outside watching as everything we ever worked so hard for went up in flames before our eyes. But little did we know that God had different plans for us.

He showed us that even when it feels like everything is crumbling down around us, He will always be there to pick us back up again.

When we ran out of money and had to reset our lives, I knew what I had to do—sell our home and everything we had, including my son's toys. It was the most devastating experience of my life, but I did what I had to do to provide for my family.

We sold our home and moved to Austin, Texas, to start our new chapter as entrepreneurs. When we failed, we didn't give up. We saw the opportunity in front of us and took it, which led to an even bigger success than before.

Heavenly Father blessed us with new friends, family members who stepped in to help where they could, and complete strangers who offered words of encouragement when we needed them most. He gave us a second chance and taught us how to start over from scratch—but this time relying on Him instead of ourselves.

New Chapter of Our Lives

No one ever said that becoming successful was easy . . . In fact, it's quite the opposite.

More often than not, success comes after lots of failures. I also know what it feels like to have a big dream and watch it crumble before your eyes, to put everything you have into something—only to see it fail miserably. It happened to me more than once, but I never gave up on my dreams. Eventually, those failures led me to my biggest success yet —a company that generates millions in revenue every year.

You have the power to change your life for the better, no matter what obstacles may be in your way. This great power is within you, and it is up to you to harness it and direct it toward whatever goals you want to achieve. With this power, you can overcome poverty, lack of education, fear, and all other negative forces that might hold you back from success. Use these powerful hacks wisely and with determination, and there is nothing stopping you from achieving anything you desire in life.

Most of us are creatures of habit who find it difficult to break out of our comfort zones, even when we know that making a change could improve our lives. If the discomfort caused by staying where you are becomes greater than the fear of taking a leap into the unknown, then you'll finally summon the courage to make a positive change.

The Inner Circle

In order to be accepted into Russell Brunson's Inner Circle, you must make $1 million through a funnel. This creates a high caliber of people in Russell's Inner Circle that are some of the best marketers I have ever seen.

The people inside Russell's Inner Circle are some of the sharpest minds in marketing. If you want to be successful in business, it's important to associate with people who think like you do and are on a similar wavelength. This is because they challenge and push you to be better and inspire you to reach new levels in your business.

Napoleon Hill's mastermind principle states that two heads are better than one, and three heads are even better. When you have a group of people working together on a problem or challenge, it becomes much easier to find solutions. This is because the increased energy created by the alliance between like minds makes it available to every individual brain in the group. So if you want to achieve something big, surround yourself with other smart and ambitious people.

The information and resources that I received in the Inner Circle have been invaluable. Not only did I get clarity on what I needed to do to grow my business, but also I found my calling and purpose in life while making new friendships with other entrepreneurs who are on a similar journey.

Being a part of Russell Brunson's Inner Circle, I have gone through more growth in one year than in the last decade.

I will be forever grateful to Russell Brunson and everyone who has expanded my knowledge and growth exponentially and helped me become the person I was meant to be.

My New Story

My mission is to help entrepreneurs create abundance in their lives and return time to themselves and their families.

I want to help you create abundance in your life so you can have more time for the things that matter most to you. The MindHacking.com

Community helps entrepreneurs overcome mindset blocks and achieve their goals. If you're ready to create lasting change in your life, I invite you to join us on this journey.

The HubMind.AI platform is the perfect way to make your company more efficient and productive. We are constantly working on new ways to utilize artificial intelligence so you can automate tasks, keep track of important data points, and improve communication among employees.

If you're an entrepreneur, then you know that writing can be a time-consuming process. But what if there was a way to reduce the amount of time it takes to create content? Enter Blogly.com, an AI created specifically for entrepreneurs. With Blogly's assistance, you'll be able to churn out blog posts and books in no time! Everything you've read in this chapter today was written and coauthored with Blogly.com.

I help people just like you who feel overwhelmed by the growth in their businesses. You're not alone, and I'm here to help in any way I can.

Also, I'd like to give you a FREE GIFT. Just shoot me an email at John@mindhacking.com.

What's Your Story?

Everybody has one, and yours is worth sharing. It doesn't matter if you think it's boring or not—chances are someone out there will find it interesting. Don't discount your experiences just because you think they're mundane. To someone else, they could be fascinating. So sit down and really think about what makes you unique and share your story with the world.

We all have to face change at some point in our lives, but that doesn't mean it's easy. It can be tough to watch the ones we love go through difficult times, especially when we feel helpless. But remember, even though things may be hard now, they will eventually get better. And you never know . . . maybe your story will inspire others to follow their dreams too.

If there's one thing I want you to take away from my story, it's this: "Don't give up on your dreams no matter how many times they seem out of reach or unattainable."

I'm so grateful for my wife, Kari Golat, who has always been my business partner. I can't imagine going through this journey without her by my side. She's helped me navigate some of the toughest challenges we've faced, and she's always been there to support me, no matter what. I'm also incredibly grateful for my son, Grayson Golat, who has the entrepreneurial spirit inside him. Watching him grow and learn is such a joy, and I know he'll go on to do great things in his life. Lastly, I'm grateful for my daughter, Kaylee Golat, who is growing faster than I know. It's amazing to watch her develop and change every day.

And remember . . . Life happens for you, not to you. You can choose how to react to the events in your life—try and see them as opportunities instead of problems!

MIKE SCHMIDT & AJ RIVERA

How Russell Brunson & Inner Circle Helped Us
Revolutionize Digital Marketing with FunnelHub

Mike Schmidt founded website design and digital marketing agency Anchor Wave in 2003. In 2018, the same year Russell Brunson killed the website, Mike and co-owner Anthony "AJ" Rivera had an epiphany. What people needed was a FunnelHub; a strategically built hub which takes advantage of all the most cutting edge marketing strategies, paired with the innovative strategies taught in Russell's Expert Secrets.

In 2015, AJ and I attended the Traffic and Conversion Summit in San Diego, California, and heard some guy talking about how we could hack his funnel doing $17K/day.

We'd never heard of a funnel, but we were eager to know more because . . . at that time, our agency was twelve years old and we were beginning to feel like we had slayed all the dragons. We were ready and searching for our next quest.

So we joined ClickFunnels. And then we went to the first Funnel Hacking Live in Las Vegas. Having just invested in another program, AJ and I convinced ourselves to leave our credit cards in the hotel room because we knew after seeing Russel speak in San Diego that it would be hard to resist jumping in on whatever he had to offer.

At FHL Las Vegas, our lives were transformed. It was the first time we saw the perfect webinar performed live on stage. The crowd running to the back to enroll in the ClickFunnels certification—it was insane.

We weren't holdouts for long. Six months later we joined Russell Brunson's Inner Circle, where we remain to this day.

The Inner Circle is one of the most amazing places you can be. We were surrounded by success. We just knew it was a matter of time before we would be the ones walking across the stage to accept our Two Comma Club Award.

But our success never came. We built funnel after funnel, launched ad after ad. We attended mastermind after mastermind. We fought and came up short and couldn't figure out why. We amassed $200,000 in debt and were on the verge of putting ourselves and our agency out of business.

On our last legs, Russell's words finally cut through. "You've already achieved so much in your agency, and you wouldn't have done that without passion. There are so many people on this earth who want exactly what you have. Teach that."

Mind blown! The successful people in the Inner Circle didn't get there by their tactics or their strategies or their funnels. They were successful because of their passion for helping people.

Here we were trying to take over the orthodontics, real estate, or mortgage industry because we saw dollar signs. But when the going got tough, we didn't have the fire inside of us that came from the passion or genuine interest in helping those people.

We found our passion. We launched Agency Coach and our flagship product, ReviewPro Launchpad, a course to teach agencies how to help businesses get more 5-star reviews. Our agency was already using this strategy, and we knew other agencies could use it too.

Now, we were not only operating our own agency but also teaching other agencies how to really OWN their agency so they can OWN their lives.

Russell always said, "If you want a million dollars, do your webinar every week for a year." He was mostly right. Every week we ran our ReviewPro webinar. Fourteen months later, we achieved our Two Comma Club Award.

As we basked in the glow of this major accomplishment, the world changed.

March 2020—lockdown. Businesses shuttered, and our agency's clients and our students were rightfully scared. Projects stalled or canceled. Leads dried up overnight.

We didn't know what to do, but we knew it wasn't sit and wait. We asked our agency's top salesmen to start dialing businesses to test the waters. He called a list of local pool building companies.

The first business to pick up the phone cussed him out, saying, "Don't you know what's going on in the world? How dare you call at a time like this!"

Fortunately, Tom is used to hearing no and continued dialing. Then he heard, "Oh man! I'm so glad you called. We were just talking about how we need help with our digital marketing right now, considering what is going on."

WOW.

Two businesses in the same industry, in the same town—maybe even down the street from one another—saw the world in a totally different light. People needed help. We had to send out the bat signal to find them.

Our instincts kicked in. A few days later, our agency launched a new webinar titled: "How to Attract and Activate Clients and Customers that STILL Need Your Products and Services, Even in an Unpredictable Market."

We went from zero leads and being afraid to thirty-eight local and incredibly hopeful businesses asking for OUR help.

Once again, we had a strategy for our students in Agency Coach.

That webinar and the sales training around it have gone on to make an unimaginable impact on the lives of our students in every corner of the world. The ripple effect impacted their families, their clients, and the communities those businesses exist in. ClickFunnels played a major role during this critical time.

Our agency and our coaching continue to grow every day. The icing on the cake is our recent induction of one of our students, Jason Burrows, into our *own* million-dollar agency award for reaching $1M in annual revenue.

In addition to all this, ClickFunnels has allowed us to discover a strategy called FunnelHub. It plays a key role in maximizing the impact of other funnel-driven and local businesses. Russell calls this the "biggest digital marketing opportunity of the next ten years" and has gone on to build this feature into ClickFunnels 2.0.

We couldn't have done any of this without ClickFunnels or our friends in the Inner Circle. We never imagined the impact we'd have on our own agency or the agencies of our students. It would have been hard to imagine not only walking on stage to collect our Two Comma Club Awards but also to be featured as speakers at FunnelHacking Live. ClickFunnels and Inner Circle have made all of this possible and more. We're so grateful for this community. We've made friends that will last a lifetime.

THE INSURANCE DUDES - JASON FELTMAN AND CRAIG PRETZINGER

The Secret to Success with Insurance Internet Leads:
Unleashing the Power of the TeleFunnel

Being a business owner shouldn't be painfully agonizing. It shouldn't be a contest to see who can handle the most pain or tread water the longest. We've come to understand that our businesses can be the vehicles to making impact in the world and to positively affect the lives of everyone we cross paths with. We're here to tell you, our thinking wasn't always this way.

Thinking back to where we started our journey with this community, we're reminded of the story of the circus elephant, Barry, being chained down since he was young enough to walk. When he was young, he didn't have the strength to break the chains that kept him confined to his lonely circus tent. He tried and tried, and through failure after failure, he finally gave up and accepted his condition. As he grew into an adult, weighing as much as a car, Barry could have easily broken the chain clamped around his leg, as his strength far exceeded that of the chain which held him captive. Sadly, the indoctrinated belief that he wasn't strong enough to break the chain, because of his past failures kept him pinned down in his tent, even though his freedom was one "heave-ho" away. His confinement was an illusion!

Like Barry the elephant, we started our careers with self-limiting beliefs in what we could achieve and how we could do it. We were chained to the traditional methods of selling insurance, believing that these were the only way to generate leads and grow our businesses. We were told to write a list of our friends and family, cross-sell our book, join networking groups, meet loan officers, or many other time-consuming, inefficient, non-measurable, inconsistent strategies.

We saw the top 1% of insurance agents at the top of all the lists, winning awards, and selling millions a year in auto and home insurance. We wanted to model what these top agents were doing, but we didn't even know where to start–the secrets to their success seemed guarded and kept secret. If we were going to break the chain that tied us down, we needed access to the players so we could pick their brains to understand how they were outperforming the herd.

We kept hearing they were buying internet leads[1] from the big online lead vendors like Everquote and Quotewizard, which confused us even more: we'd bought leads from both of these companies many different times in the past and *never* gotten results. Any of the normal agents we'd spoken to or interacted with on Facebook, meetings, or agent

---

[1] Insurance internet leads are leads generated by media buyers who publish ads, websites, and advertorials all over the internet in order to generate

events, shared that they too hated internet leads and for the same reason: no results and waste of money.

We had to crack the code of *how* a very select group of agents were using these internet leads and getting astronomical results while everyone else (ourselves included) had failed with the very same thing! Our solution to learning how was to start a podcast and leverage it to interview the top agents from around the country to learn their secrets. We saw this as the perfect "stack" because we'd be learning how to get the results we wanted and at the same time we'd be helping our insurance-agent podcast listeners learn and aggregate the pieces of the puzzle they also needed to free themselves!

Embracing our discomfort, we pulled on the chain that tied us down by going for it. We knew nothing about podcasting—we just went for it! We bought microphones, turned on Zoom, and started recording. The early episodes were cringy, but we managed to improve over time, even doing our own editing and marketing. It was a hot-mess at times, but we were determined to get good at it.

To secure guests, we created a cute blurb about our mission to serve insurance agents and sent it to the top agents, online marketers, and interesting personalities on Facebook and Instagram messenger. Just like a funnel, we ended up snaring a certain number of the people we'd reached out to. We acquired guests who were the top-agents we were trying to learn from as well as top-online marketers such as Garret White, Christa Mashore, Patrick Bet-David, Robin Sharma, Trey Lewellen, and many more. Even if they weren't insurance industry-related, we'd figure out a way to tie it back and make it relevant to our audience. With each successive episode, we improved our skills of podcasting, while gaining the insight and skills to move us closer to developing the processes we needed in our agencies to unlock consistent, predictable results.

After about 100 episodes or so, we felt like we had the pieces we needed to develop a framework within our own insurance agencies. We began testing our concept in our own agencies through 2019, and after many ups and downs, and plenty of resources spent, we began to gain traction: the process we developed from what we learned from podcast interviews was actually working! In the first quarter of 2020, right as Covid was announced, we both had record months skyrocketing us to the top of the results-lists with our insurance company. With Covid starting to shut down the world, people were panicking and cutting their marketing investment, but we followed the advice of Warren Buffet and did the opposite of the herd. We ran into the fray while everyone else was running for cover.

Prior to launching the podcast, we'd bought Click Funnels and didn't even use it for the first year. After we'd gained some listeners, and had some traction, we finally dove into Click Funnels and started learning the software and what it could do for us. Even though we didn't have a product or service to offer yet, we figured we could use it to help us grow the podcast and build a list. We kept getting emails from Russell and one of the things he kept talking about was the value of your mailing list, we felt like we were on the right track.

We consumed a ton of content that's hosted inside the Click Funnels platform, from Russell's potato gun story to deeper concepts like the attractive character and creating a movement. We realized we had so much to learn and that we'd stumbled upon a gold mine that was replete with the resources we needed so that we could best serve the audience we'd been speaking to through our podcast – insurance agency owners who wanted to scale their agencies, but hadn't quite cracked the code. We were looking for the 3 year older versions of ourselves.

We kept getting emails, texts, boxes with books, t-shirts, and other swag from Russell—he was relentless and we both loved it! We identified with him and his passion to serve his followers. Without realizing what was happening, we were being indoctrinated into the Funnel Hacker community. We'd been hooked by Russell's promise to help us serve the insurance agency owners properly. We were certain they needed the same tools we'd learned to unlock wealth and freedom. Russell's frameworks would map how we would acquire the agents and then how we would build out and deliver what they needed from us. The question was still, what was it?

Russell's passion, supported by incredible stories, drove us to a place of belief. We went from being agents who were struggling making less than $100k a year to believing we could be successful with our own insurance agencies. Russell's confidence in his process shifted us from not having a product or service to *knowing* that we could take the knowledge and frameworks we'd develop and offer those to other agents so that they too could model our results (and the awesome part was we could offer them all the resources they'd need to be successful like lead callers, leads, scripts, and a CRM!

We placed our faith in the process, knowing that God, the universe, or whoever you fancy, would provide what we needed to help insurance agency owners become successful if we kept our focus on the mission to serve them. And serve we did: even though we had developed our frameworks and achieved great results for our own agencies, we continued to publish a minimum of three episodes per week, still with a mission to help insurance agency owners get awesome results for themselves. We could have ended the podcast at that point and focused solely on growing our agencies (we had the ingredients), but we continued to see so many agents struggling and were receiving so many emails and messages about how the concepts we talked about on the podcast and the guests we interviewed were making an impact to their agencies.

In March of 2020 as Covid took over the world, agents started reaching out to us asking us to teach what we were doing and to help provide the services we were using. Our overall framework combines knowledge and actions needed to be most successful with lead acquisition, activation of these leads with the right tools and actions, tactical sales conversion methods, and sales optimization to ensure improving results based on the feedback received from tracking and measuring specific activities. We packaged all of our frameworks into lessons in a Click Funnels membership site, added weekly coaching, a CRM dialer, and a lead calling specialist as our initial offer.

Our first client, who is now a friend and a partner in a separate company (yes, you guessed it, it's a lead company), reached out to us one day in early March because he was a newer agency owner, associated with the same big insurance company we are with. He'd heard about our results from the company lists, and he'd been listening to our podcast: he wanted the same results we were getting, was bought in, and willing to go big, fast, but he wanted some more details about how it worked. He believed, he was bought in, his mind just needed some understanding of some of the logistics.

We explained to him that it was a process of buying a certain quantity of internet leads per day, using a special CRM that could instantly receive delivery of the leads and then automatically assign those leads to a human, outsourced lead calling expert who would make the dials needed to make contact, and then a means to transfer those contacted leads over to our licensed insurance sales closers. Finally, we told him, there was a whole back-end set up in the CRM/dialer that would follow up with the people we'd quoted but not sold. It took the *prospecting* out of the hands of the sales agents, and put the necessary activity (dials and contacts) on the leads to ensure results.

Over the last year, we'd spend thousands of hours and a couple hundred thousand dollars on leads to nail process down. We were tracking and measuring the same analytics as major call center and doing sizeable volume just with our own agencies. Our dataset of analytics over our first year of building and testing gave us *real* insights from millions of dials on hundreds of thousands of leads. We had the real math and were able to reliably predict future results based on various variables. It was a gamechanger.

He told us he'd never had results with internet leads in his first year as an agent, which we understood: before understanding the TeleFunnel, we'd also struck out with internet leads. We told him that we'd previously blamed the lead companies, just like everyone else—they were the easy patsy (it was either us or them). We shared with him that without the framework we'd built, leads were a bust, no matter where they came from.

In absence of this framework, we told him, you forced your high-cost and highly trained sales agents to make the needed dials (and then you experience high staff turnover) or you just didn't make enough contacts at top of funnel to get enough opportunities at the bottom of funnel: the math didn't work without a very quantifiable level of activity. The *real* activity needed, we continued to tell him, was far beyond what a licensed sales agent could handle day after day and also be expected to close people. He understood what we were saying and then asked how he could get started.

Since we didn't yet have one, we created an offer, secured the additional lead callers and helped him get leads, and TeleDudes was born. We grew very rapidly after that.

In early 2021, we joined 2CCX and really got focused. Later in 2021, we went to *Funnel Hacking Live,* and because of our success with our first two funnels, we got to go onstage to receive two, 2-Comma Club Awards. Robbie from Click Funnels reached out and offered us an opportunity to join *Inner Circle*. We were on the fence, thinking that the investment was an insane amount of money! Remembering back just a couple years prior, we'd both been earning less than 100k a year, working *in* our agencies at an unsustainable pace on what seemed like a never-ending hamster wheel, and here this dude was asking us for $50k!

We remembered Barry the elephant and how his early conditioning had limited his ability to go beyond what he'd already known. We spoke in depth about the ideas and concepts that we'd learned from 2CCX, about the explosion to over $4 million in revenue between March 2020 and attending our first FHL event in late 2021. Even the days prior to flying out to Orlando for FHL, we were unsure about making the jump to Inner Circle.

At FHL in 2021, we experienced a shift that helped us make our decision: we weren't going to be like Barry any longer. We'd broken though the self-limiting beliefs that we had shouldered for so long. We had been able to build our TeleFunnels and achieve life-changing results in our agencies. In just around a year and a half, we'd also been able to grow TeleDudes from 0 to over $4 million in revenue and agreed that if we were going to get to $10 million in revenue and beyond, it would take a different level of thinking, operating, and *doing*.

At FHL, as Russell went through the details of the program, we realized that most of the speakers who'd been on the big stage at FHL were also *Inner Circle Coaching* members. They had all been so passionate, so informative, so willing to help, and as a result, so extremely successful. They were living their dream and helping others achieve theirs, which was precisely the path we wanted to take, we were incredibly inspired.

At lunch, for the 2-CC award winners, Russell explained *Inner Circle,* told the story of reopening it, and delivered his stack of all the things we were going to get, for some reason, the BIG price tag didn't seem to be of an issue as we'd believed before. We thought about how we'd be interacting with and have access to some of the most successful entrepreneurs in the world several in-person masterminds over the next year. We imagined these top-entrepreneurs were in the top 1% of the entrepreneur pool in the same way that, in our own world, the top-producing agents were in the top 1% of the insurance world.

For the insurance-world-side-of-things, we had been successful because we'd spent immeasurable hours meeting and interviewing the best insurance agents and then designing our frameworks (a la *Expert Secrets)* and spending a vast amount of capital to test and optimize. As we reflected on that journey, and related it to *Inner Circle Coaching,* we had the epiphany that to invest in this program would be a lot like investing in speed: with access to entrepreneurs executing the frameworks that we'd been learning we could compress time from years down into months for our next milestone of ten million in revenue.

We took the plunge right there at lunch on that Friday of FHL 2021. We ran to the back of the room after Russell made his offer because we wanted to be part of *the Inner Circle* Community and gain access to amazing entrepreneurs who we believed could help us achieve our desired results much faster than if went after it through trial and error. Over course of the last year, we'd shared an increased amount of our time between more and more projects and as our time became more scarce, the value of our time increased considerably.

You may already have a sense of the impact that joining *Inner Circle* has had on us as entrepreneurs, creators, business leaders, and as humans. In sharing our two journeys: the first journey of growing our own insurance agencies and then the second journey of packaging our successful process to help other insurance agents achieve the same results. In the next couple pages, we'll articulate the biggest impacts we've noticed.

Steve Jobs said, "the ones who are crazy enough to believe they can change the world are the ones who do." The community that embodies

Inner Circle is filled with a dynamic group of entrepreneurs sharing ideas and resources to make quantum leaps in their businesses and make a positive impact on the world. Steve was right, and he'd also probably agree, it's a lot easier if you have people supporting you throughout your journey versus having to swim against the current the whole time. The *Inner circle* community provides the support we all need to push us through the difficult times, and the peers to celebrate with us when we win.

The community affords access to the right people, processes, and products because the tools needed to get results in business, at this level are very similar, regardless of industry. Additionally, the obstacles that we all run into are also very similar. We've found the community to be even more supporting than friends and family at times.

Even after joining, we suffered our own "imposter syndrome" or "not good enough" thinking. It was (and still is) challenging to be a small fish amongst the whales. Embracing and pushing through that fear has been part of the experience, and that has helped lead us both into a place of incredible business and self-growth, evidenced by having the honor to be part of this book project

The second greatest impact on our businesses from *Inner Circle,* are the relationships we've developed. John Lee Dumas from *Entrepreneurs On Fire* (also a prior guest on our podcast) says you're the sum of the five people you spend the most time with. This applies to your business-self too. We've made dozens of key relationships, who have helped us shape our business and help us accelerate towards greater and greater impact and results. As this is being written, we're on a plane to *Category Kings* member (and prior *Inner Circle* member) Bill Allen's office, in Nashville, to take part in a 2-day event for his 7-Figure Flipping program if we were still struggling to make our agencies work, we likely wouldn't be exploring other business opportunities and continuing to create other sources of revenue, such as this excursion to Tennessee.

With the help of another OG *Inner Circle* member, Rob Kosberg and his company *Best Seller Publisher,* we're releasing a 200-page book called *The Wealthy Insurance Agent,* that lays out our entire TeleFunnel framework to help insurance agency owners grow quickly with predictable results. We're told it will be a New York Times bestseller and help establish further credibility so that we can help an even larger group of insurance agents transform their agencies like we did ours.

Through other members, we were introduced to the *Entrepreneurial Operating System* (EOS) which helped us tear down our entire operation and restructure it so that it can grow into a much larger business, and in turn help more agency owners achieve their dreams. We're even hosting a live event to help insurance agency owners install our TeleFunnels process in their own agencies. Prior to being members of *Inner Circle,* this wouldn't have even been something we'd have been able to conceive, let alone pull off.

Each additional relationship we've made, has shed more light and additional clarity what we do, why we do it, and how to get it done. The other members, along with Russell's team are here to support and help everyone to improve their business' impact on their clients, their industry, and their world. Without *Inner Circle* none of these relationships would exist for us, and we would have lost our steam after a couple mistakes only to returning to the old way of thinking that permeates everyday life. Without *Inner Circle,* we would be wearing old Barry's leg chain again.

The third major impact to our business is the knowledge we've gained from *Inner Circle* through an incredible amount of evergreen content and Russell's *Inner Circle Only* presentations (live and recorded). As a result of the vault of information at our fingertips, we've implemented shifts and enhancements in our businesses, from minor funnel tweaks to overall content delivery upgrades and everything in between. As an example, with some of the YouTube strategies we have implemented, our subscriber count has grown from less than 1000 back in 2021 at the time we joined, to over 6000, only a year and a half later.

Inner Circle has cracked open the limitations and freed the 200 octane versions of ourselves, helping us develop an architecture for our businesses to increase the liklihood of more wins and less losses, based on the lessons others have already suffered through. Earlier we spoke to the importance of speed—we are all working with a finite set of years, days, hours, minutes, and seconds left to make our impact on the world. From one mastermind session in Boise, the concept of *Thinking Bigger* was a major theme, and has been a major theme in our own company meetings, as well as the meetings we have with our clients, our teams in our insurance agencies, and even in our personal lives.

We've learned and implemented so many concepts from the *Inner Circle* collective body of knowledge which are now critical components of our business. We have been able to elevate the results of our funnels by having a much deeper knowledge of the very specific nuances that can make big impacts on your funnel results. Some of these insights took other people years of trial and error to discover and then perfect. Access to the knowledge contained within the confines of the *Inner Circle* takes us from a place of trial and error into a place of momentum and results much, much faster. This shortcut to the path of faster, better results, for us, was worth the price of admission!

We're grateful to be members of the *Inner Circle Coaching* program and excited to welcome you to the group if you make the decision to join. If you're on the fence, or worried about whether you'll benefit from being in this group, you may seek comfort in knowing that this program could be what breaks the chain that may be holding you back from realizing your full potential. As a group, we're able to share ideas, create shortcuts, and save time from painful lessons. *Inner Circle* could carve out your path to discovery and unlock the massive results you're looking for in your business, but first, you must break the chain.

BART & SUNNY MILLER

The Secret Sauce of Entrepreneurial Growth: Discover How One Couple from a Tiny, Two-Stoplight Town in Idaho Went from Dial-Up to 10 Million

Bart and Sunny Miller are an entrepreneurial couple from a tiny little two-stoplight town in Idaho. They have been married 28 years and have four kids, one son-in-law, four horses, and two dogs. They have been in the digital marketing space for almost 20 years, meaning they were eBay when eBay was the hottest thing online. They were also early adopters of course creation, subscription websites, website development, video production, YouTube channel specialists, and Amazon.

Together they have a silver YouTube Play Button award, as well as two Two Comma Club awards and one 10x Award through ClickFunnels.

*Today they can be found hosting **EpicDay**, a powerful high-performance networking + accountability + personal growth program,*

*as well as **I Do Epic Masterminds** (quarterly live mastermind events),*
I Do Epic Accelerator ($0 100k group coaching and accountability),
*and **I Do Epic ELITE** (individual coaching for high-achieving*
entrepreneurs who are above $100k levels). They are also the hosts of
the Bart and Sunny "We Play Full Out" Podcast.

You can find them online at www.bartandsunny.com.

We hate to start our introduction this way, but first and foremost we have to admit we are technically Old-Timers in the digital marketing space. We were introduced to digital marketing when 'online' was still the Wild, Wild West and no one quite knew what to do with it. It was new, it was thrilling… and it was dial-up. For those of you too young to remember dial-up, we encourage you stop reading right now and look up 'The Sound of Dial-Up Internet' on YouTube on your smartphone. Make sure you have the volume turned all the way up. Hit play, listen, and pretend like you are trying to get online in the time it takes now. Notice how the nails-on-chalkboard sound-bite lasts a full thirty seconds of excruciating impatience. Of course, in those days it only lasted thirty seconds if it actually connected the first time. If you got a busy signal you had to keep trying over and over again. Feel free to play it again and again for a minute or two if you want to experience the full effect.

That's our version of "walking a mile to school in the snow, uphill, both ways."

But seriously.

We didn't have Internet capabilities at home until after we were married, sometime around 1997. We were both young -18 and 21- and were really quite sheltered in our bubble of a tiny little town in Idaho, which, fun fact: to this very day, still only has two stoplights. So how did we end up with two "Two Comma Club" Awards (two one-million-dollar awards) and a "10x Award," (a ten-million-dollar award) as well as being members of Russell Brunson's Inner Circle for the past five years? While still living in that same tiny little town? It all started on one fateful day about twenty years ago when Bart was introduced to the fact that there was MARKETING on the Internet (say, what?!) by a super affiliate named Jeremy Johnson. If you don't know Bart, it's important to take note here that he has a very strong background in networking, marketing and sales and he is the action takers of all action takers. He is old-school when old-school is needed and isn't afraid of the Zig Ziglar approach of knocking doors if he has to in order to make things happen.

When Jeremy Johnson literally opened up a whole new world to Bart, we were currently into International Business Sales in the reformulating fuel and lubrication business. We were brick and mortar and didn't know or dream of anything different. It was high ticket, high volume, but a tough, tough sale. Sunny was also working full time at the Post Office, which gave us incredible health benefits and was great pay for an entry level position.

When Bart saw the blindingly bright vision of Jeremy's brilliant model, it was over. He knew this was something much bigger than anything he could ever dream of. Bart called Sunny up, painted her a picture of the vision, and basically said "We are burning all the boats to become digital marketers. This is it!" Sunny agreed, and we were off to the races!

At this point it might be tempting to think that if you had been able to tap into the Internet when practically no one was selling anything online you would absolutely crush it! But remember: the Internet was still brand new. We didn't know anything about it other than how to turn it on. And, on top of that, nothing online was "easy". There was no ClickFunnels to build drag-and-drop landing pages for us. Everything had to be hard-coded, and we mean everything. If we wanted a fully designed, functioning landing page with even ONE upsell it was a minimum of $20k and 6 weeks. Payment gateways like Stripe and PayPal didn't exist. If we wanted something changed, we were at the mercy of our programmer to code for us and our graphic designer to design for us.

Nothing was changed quickly or easily, and it always came at a high cost.

The benefit of high cost is that you most likely aren't going to be crazy or fickle enough to start something "just to see if it will work." No side hustle here. You are either all in or you are all out. You are going to do your research and exhaust every resource you have in order to make absolute certain it's going to work before you make that kind of investment.

We started doing our research together and discovered women never gave up their makeup during World War II. Women bought and wore makeup, even through tough, tragic and depressing times because it would help them retain a feeling of humanity, femininity and dignity.

It also helped boost their morale and allowed them to have a little bit of fun, even if it was only for a little while.

We felt like this was the space we wanted to be in online. We only had three super minor issues (*cough, cough*) to work through at this point: we didn't know how to do anything on the Internet, we didn't know anything about makeup, and we didn't have any connections into the makeup world.

Easy, right?

To make a really long and actually pretty entertaining story super short, Bart worked his huge network and found Robert Jones, a mutual friend of one of our close friends (who also happens to be a celebrity Japanese comedian with a name as big as Oprah's in Japan). Robert Jones is a celebrity makeup artist (Cindy Crawford, Selena Gomez), who also works on supermodels andedits for huge companies like Nieman Marcus, Saks Fifth Avenue, Vogue, Glamour, and so on.

He is also a best-selling beauty author and is known for timeless, classic, fresh, clean, beautiful makeup looks. We loved that he was more about bringing out the unique beauty of each of his clients versus trying to cover them up and turn them into someone or something different. On topof all of that, Robert was an amazing makeup application teacher with exact formulas to follow.

Robert was a huge blessing in disguise and together we developed the Robert Jones Beauty Academy. Our Robert Jones Beauty Academy was the first online makeup school of its kind, and as such we started to grow.

As we grew, we started to have an abundance of people reaching out asking us how to do what we did. They wanted to know if we had a formula or method for building online schools. We told them we did, and if they followed our specific criteria, they could build an online school that would pay for itself within six months to a year.

They would reply, "If you can do that, we'll come to you and start shooting video as soon as possible!"

So… what could we do? We opened a video production company.

We started shooting, editing, and building online schools (aka membership sites), and that was our start in the online, done-with-you agency space.

Our time consumption for our businesses was minimal at this point. Our beauty schools were built and running so the majority of putting astronomical start-up time in was over for us. Our automated systems still take the brunt of most of the work for us. Our video production company didn't take much of our time because we hired an editor to shoot and edit for us. As a result, we decided to start dabbling in eCommerce. eCommerce quickly became one of our passions, and ultimately led us to our $10 million dollar award with ClickFunnels and Russell Brunson.

To get there, it would take us being willing to invest in ourselves at a higher level than we had ever considered or done before. We just didn't realize it quite yet.

We are both advocates of attending events because we know the network and information gained is priceless. Bart attended most of the events by himself at the time because we had three small children at home and Sunny stayed home to take care of them. Bart is incredible at networking and his network has benefited us greatly over the years, so it wasn't even a question of who should go and who should stay home.

Bart attended an event in California and the person putting on the event did an outstanding job of emphasizing the need for a mentor. The messaging was on point and the need for a mentor became glaringly apparent to Bart if we wanted to go faster and further, while at the same time at a higher rate of cost-effectiveness and time efficiency. The purpose of the event was, of course, to sell us into hiring him as our mentor.

As stated, our businesses were doing quite well and were running almost on autopilot. Our eCommerce was taking off, but we knew we could do even better than where we were currently at. We recognized we were becoming simply "content" and maybe even getting a little "lazy" in our ambitions. After attending the event, Bart knew we could go to the next level with the help of the "right" mentor and we were both on board and ready to do it.

Que Russell Brunson.

At the time, ClickFunnels had recently launched and we started having more and more videos of Russell slowly seeping into our online awareness. How in the world was this Russell guy in our heads? It was almost freaky. He knew inward and outward exactly what we were going through in our entrepreneurial journey and, magically enough, he had all the exact solutions we needed right down to a T.

He had what he called an "Inner Circle" where he would work with us and get our businesses to the next level; however, being the overachievers we are, we decided we would go through a process of selecting the "right" mentor for us and not just pick the first one that popped up. We researched everyone we could think of and would hire them for an hour of their time. Bart would literally call them up and say, "What does it cost for an hour of your time? I want to meet with you." We did that so we could fly to wherever they were and interview them in person.

Another superpower of Bart's is the ability to quickly understand the type of person you are by having a face-to-face conversation with you. We would sit down and meet with some of these business mentors and pay them $3k or more for an hour of their time. They would say all the right things to get us excited, but Bart always caught the red flags. He knew immediately they were not the right fit, more especially when we ended up teaching them more in the hour then they taught us. Sometimes they were incredibly smart, but they just weren't great at coaching.

We knew we needed the perfect combination of both, but it also had to be someone who had already accomplished what we were trying to do. That was the one non-negotiable for us.

We came back to Russell again and again, but the time didn't seem right. Sunny finally brought him up again and said, "Hey, what do you think about Russell Brunson? I really, really like what he says." Bart said, "Well, let me find out."

Bart went to work within his network. He found a good friend of his who knew Russell personally and actually had his personal cell phone number. Yep, you read that right: his personal cell phone number. Bart called Russell, left messages, and never got an answer or a call back. Bart sent Russell text messages, and Russell finally texted back and said, "You need to go through the process."

For someone with Bart's personality, that does not go over well. He was livid. Bart is all about personal networking and personal communication, and right then and there he was done with Russell Brunson.

However, Sunny, being the calming influence of the two of us said, "Hey. If you had a system set up, you'd want people to follow it, too."

Bart reluctantly agreed, although he was still a little bent out of shape over the whole fiasco. On a funny side note, we didn't know Russell's personality. He was an introvert around people he didn't know and didn't want to talk to anyone one-on-one, especially about his programs. He avoided it like the plague. He hired salespeople to do the talking specifically so he wouldn't have to.

To make another long but mildly entertaining story short, we were driving down the road one day, and Sunny said, "I'm just going to fill out Russell's Inner Circle Application Form, and we're just going to see what it does."

She filled it out and got a call on the calendar with the Closer. At that point we were really ready to just hire Russell and get on with it. We got on the phone, and the Closer asked us all the golden questions, such as "How do you know about Russell?" and "Why do you think you'd be a good fit for his program?" We were like, "Can we stop this conversation right now and you just take our money?"

He said he would have to call us back.

Call us back?!

He did call us back, took our credit card information over the phone, and we were in! We joined right before FHL in San Diego, California. We met Russell for the first time in person at the event, and as soon as we talked to him, we were validated. We knew right off he knew how to get us where we wanted to be and he knew how to teach it.

The interesting thing about leaders is the fact that they attract people who have the same characteristics they have. Russell's Inner Circle is filled with people who are givers. They have kind hearts but they also operate at a high business level. They want to make an impact as well as a profit. They want to be game changers, and they want to change the world for better with their messages.

We were really excited to attend our first Inner Circle meeting, and it did not disappoint. The network we gained of not just business associates, but close personal friends was worth every penny. Our initial groups included people like Myron Golden, Alex Hormozi, Rachel Pedersen, Annie Grace, Alison Prince, Dave Lindenbaum, Brandon and Kaelin Poulin, and so many, many more.

If you're on the outside looking in, you may wonder what the Secret Sauce is to this whole concept of Inner Circle and if it's worth it or not. We remember wondering the same thing. Is it all just a bunch of hype? If that's you, we would love to offer you a quick glimpse of the top benefits we've gained, and continue to gain, by being in Inner Circle:

-We were taught marketing strategies and key concepts that allowed us to accelerate our growth to a million, to multi-million, and then to the ten-million-dollar levels. Some of these were taught by Russell at Inner Circle, and some were shared by those (at Inner Circle) who had already implemented exactly what we needed and could help us through it. The combination of network plus Russell is powerful.

-We can reach out to anyone in Inner Circle with questions and they will bend over backward to help. And we will do the same.

-We've got an entire 100-person strong network of high-achieving entrepreneurs who understand us and have our back.

-We've got a leader who is running several multi-million-dollar companies, teaching us the same exact concepts he used to get them there. He also isn't afraid to share with us what isn't working.

-We've got full access to a mindset coach to help us through the tough times

-We've got a whole network of business coaches and staff that are cheering us on

-We've got regularly scheduled events we all attend together that feel more like family reunions than business events. We all truly just want to help each other succeed.

If that's not a recipe for success, we're not sure what is.

Where are we at now?

We are still in Inner Circle, and guess what? We followed, and continue to follow, Russell's model. We have built out our full I Do Epic brand based on what Russell teaches and does with his own value ladders.

It looks like this:

EpicDay (low-ticket high-performance networking + accountability + personal growth program) Mastermind (I Do Epic Mastermind in-person event) à Accelerator ($0-$100k program) à I Do Epic ELITE (high-ticket one-on-one coaching program for those making over $100k).

We are thankful for the knowledge and network we have gained in Russell's Inner Circle and can't wait to continue to be a part of this extraordinary community for years to come.

If you would like to jump right into our world and get inside our heads, sign up for our free "We Play Full Out 5-Shot Friday" newsletter at friday.weplayfullout.com. Gain access every Friday to the top five things we have been reading, exploring, trying or discussing: books, podcasts, gadgets, supplements, hacks (and more) each week!

We would also love to have you come on over and have an EpicDay on us! Try out the world's #1 unfair advantage for high-achieving entrepreneurs for seven full days…for free! Gain momentum add seven figure entrepreneurs to your personal network and achieve your potential faster. Visit www.idoepicday.com to start your free trial.

The next few excerpts are stories we get asked about quite often and thought would be fun to include here so you can get an even further taste of the fun culture surrounding Inner Circle. We hope you enjoy them! They are "The Story of Bart Becoming Russell's Personal Stylist" and "The Bart Doll: How Demanding Excellence from Russell Went Viral and Then Weird."

The Story of Bart Becoming Russell's Personal Stylist

As stated previously, Bart understands networking like no other, and he knows if he dresses a certain way, people will seek him out and want to talk to him. As a result, he used to dress in high-end suits when we attended Inner Circle because he knew it would get people talking.

At one Inner Circle event, it was our turn on stage and we were discussing style. Sunny asked how many people googled Bart before they met him simply because of how he was dressed. It was a high percentage - probably ¾ of the room. Russell was planning his next Funnel Hacking Live and didn't want to have to figure out what he was going to wear – he already had too much going on in his head that he had to deal. He looked at Bart and in true Russell fashion said, "Hey,what would it take to get you to style me for FHL?"

Bart simply said, "Why don't you show up, and I'll style you for free." Russell said "No, I want to pay you for it."

Russell had just finished giving us a big, long speech about how we don't charge enough and don't know our value. He looked at Bart again and said, "What's it going to take? What does it look like?"

Bart decided to go all in on the "not charging enough" speech and threw a substantial number back at Russell. Russell didn't even bat an eye. He simply said, "Okay, wire Bart the money."

We were shocked, and when the shock wore off Bart entered panic attack mode. Bart takes what he does very seriously and does not want to be "that guy" that made Russell look ridiculous.

When it comes to fashion, there's no hiding behind it because it's there for all to see! On top of that, style is a personal thing, and it also requires you to be in someone's very personal space.

That being said, Bart is also exceptionally good at it. There is much more to style (especially at an event and on camera) than making people look good, but it's too much to cover all the logistics of event style here.

Bart started styling Russell and things mostly went well. Russell was adamant that he would not wear shirts that had to be tucked in or suit coats. That meant that Bart really had to focus on watches and shoes.

In this particular instance, we got to catch a glimpse of Russell's character when the shoe was on the other foot – literally!

There was one specific pair of shoes that Bart absolutely loved. Bart knew what the stage looked like, and he knew beyond anything that those were THE shoes of all shoes; however, Russell disagreed. He didn't love them and felt like he would be super uncomfortable in them because they were quite literally out of his comfort zone.

Bart looked at him and said, "Russell. You keep telling me if I follow what you say I'll be successful. You get frustrated when people don't follow your model. I'm telling you, from an expert standpoint, that these are the shoes you need to wear. Do you trust me and will you follow my model?"

Russell said yes. He wore the shoes and got more compliments on them than anything else he wore for the entire event. People went crazy over them and were trying to google them to see where they could get them.

That is a tremendous leader. Russell was as coachable as he expected others to be. He was willing to listen and step outside himself to trust the process.

The kind of leader Russell is was again apparent to us in an extremely uncomfortable experience that happened three days before Funnel Hacking Live. All of the outfits Bart had picked out for Russell specifically for Funnel Hacking Live showed up – ALL OF THEM – 100% tailored incorrectly. Nothing fit. It was all wrong. Again, this was three days before Funnel Hacking Live and Russell lives in Boise, Idaho where there is basically zero shopping.

And Bart didn't have a Plan B.

Instead of freaking out, looking at Bart and placing all the blame on him for an epic fail, he simply said, "Hey, let's roll with this. What can we do?"

That put Bart in an empowered position to make something work. Bart was able to step in, put everything together with some other clothes he had shopped for with Russell, and it turned out better than ever. It could have easily gone in an uncomfortable direction if Russell had chosen to react differently.

But he stayed true to the leader he is.

The Bart Doll: How Demanding Excellence from Russell Went Viral and Then Weird Bart competed in a bodybuilding competition and was in the best shape of his life. Weeks before his competition we attended an Inner Circle meeting and while on stage for our business presentation, Russell may or may not have started heckling Bart to take his shirt off and do a little posing. Hilarity ensued as dollar bills were thrown onto the stage by the likes of Dave "Golden Showers" Lindenbaum.

Shortly after the Inner Circle Shirt Stripping Incident, Russell asked Bart to work with him and help get him in better shape for wrestling. Bart was shocked at being asked by Russell to do this because we all know Russell has just about anyone at his fingertips that he could call. When Bart asked him, "Why me?" he basically said Bart was one of the few people who wasn't afraid to tell Russell like he saw it, and he knew he would hold him accountable.

Bart put a program together for Russell and they lifted together a few times. Russell was checking in with Bart regularly, and then the unthinkable happened: Russell skipped a leg day and did upper body instead. His legs were super sore from a previous workout and he thought it would be fine to do something different.

Bart was feeling his oats that day and was not going to settle for even one tiny little variation from his program. He expected Russell to hold him accountable to what he said he was going to do, so he was not willing to do anything less back for Russell. He got on Voxer and started a rant that even Sunny was tongue tied at ("Did you really just say that to Russell?!") The Voxer said something to the effect of: "Russell, you're the toughest guy I know. You're a next level wrestler, which means you know what it's like to dig deep, feel massive pain, and do it anyway. I don't want to hear any more excuses from you because I know what you are capable of and I won't settle for anything less. I demand excellence from you Russell Brunson!"

Little did Bart know Russell would get that Voxer and it would immediately go viral around the ClickFunnels office from everyone getting a massive laugh from it. Someone had just told Russell they demanded excellence from him! Epic! ClickFunnels staff started shouting at each other that they "demanded excellence!" from each other. It became a highly popular catch phrase that Bart knew nothing about...

Until the day Bart received a group Voxer from none other than both Russell and James P. Friel.

Uh-oh. If you know those two, you know something sinister (aka probably howling funny) is up, and it will most likely be at your expense. James is the ultimate, next level prankster.

The Voxer was a video of Russell opening a gift from James on his birthday. They were dying of laughter. Inside the gift was a "Bart Doll" that was dressed exactly like Bart. And when we say exact, we mean James P. Friel had found an old profile photo of Bart on Facebook that he had the doll fashioned after. The doll had his exact outfit on, right down to the glasses he was wearing.

But it doesn't stop there.

James is also a master impersonator. When you press a button on the doll's hand it says, "I demand excellence from you Russell Brunson! Now... let's go shopping!" It sounds just like Bart!

That doll was our "surprise guest" at the next Inner Circle meeting and the Bart doll has a tendency to pop up every now and again when we all need a good laugh.

If you would like to jump right into our world and get inside our heads, sign up for our free "We Play Full Out 5-Shot Friday" newsletter at friday.weplayfullout.com. Gain access every Friday to the top five things we have been reading, exploring, trying or discussing: books, podcasts, gadgets, supplements, hacks (and more) each week!

We would also love to have you come on over and have an EpicDay on us! Try out the world's #1 unfair advantage for high-achieving entrepreneurs for seven full days...for free! Gain momentum, add seven figure entrepreneurs to your personal network, and achieve your potential faster. Visit www.idoepicday.com to start your free trial.

Made in the USA
Monee, IL
08 March 2023

29416120R00201